To Michael
with best wishes
Jim

D1615616

One Europe or Several?

Series Editor: **Helen Wallace**

The One Europe or Several? series examines contemporary processes of political, security, economic, social and cultural change across the European continent, as well as issues of convergence/divergence and prospects for integration and fragmentation. Many of the books in the series are cross-country comparisons; others evaluate the European institutions, in particular the European Union and NATO, in the context of eastern enlargement.

Titles include:

Sarah Birch
ELECTORAL SYSTEMS AND POLITICAL TRANSFORMATION IN POST-COMMUNIST EUROPE

Sarah Birch, Frances Millard, Marina Popescu and Kieran Williams
EMBODYING DEMOCRACY
Electoral System Design in Post-Communist Europe

Andrew Cottey, Timothy Edmunds and Anthony Forster (*editors*)
DEMOCRATIC CONTROL OF THE MILITARY IN POSTCOMMUNIST EUROPE
Guarding the Guards

Anthony Forster, Timothy Edmunds and Andrew Cottey (*editors*)
THE CHALLENGE OF MILITARY REFORM IN POSTCOMMUNIST EUROPE
Building Professional Armed Forces

Anthony Forster, Timothy Edmunds and Andrew Cottey (*editors*)
SOLDIERS AND SOCIETIES IN POSTCOMMUNIST EUROPE
Legitimacy and Change

James Hughes, Gwendolyn Sasse and Claire Gordon
EUROPEANIZATION AND REGIONALIZATION IN THE EU'S ENLARGEMENT TO CENTRAL AND EASTERN EUROPE
The Myth of Conditionality

Andrew Jordan
THE EUROPEANIZATION OF BRITISH ENVIRONMENTAL POLICY
A Departmental Perspective

Christopher Lord
A DEMOCRACTIC AUDIT OF THE EUROPEAN UNION

Valsamis Mitsilegas, Jorg Monar and Wyn Rees
THE EUROPEAN UNION AND INTERNAL SECURITY
Guardian of the People?

Helen Wallace (*editor*)
INTERLOCKING DIMENSIONS OF EUROPEAN INTEGRATION

One Europe or Several?
Series Standing Order ISBN 0–333–94630–8
(*outside North America only*)

You can receive future titles in this series as they are published by placing a standing order. Please contact your bookseller or, in case of difficulty, write to us at the address below with your name and address, the title of the series and the ISBN quoted above.

Customer Services Department, Macmillan Distribution Ltd, Houndmills, Basingstoke, Hampshire RG21 6XS, England

Europeanization and Regionalization in the EU's Enlargement to Central and Eastern Europe

The Myth of Conditionality

James Hughes
Reader in Comparative Politics
London School of Economics and Political Science

Gwendolyn Sasse
Lecturer in Comparative East European Politics
London School of Economics and Political Science

and

Claire Gordon
Visiting Lecturer
London School of Economics and Political Science

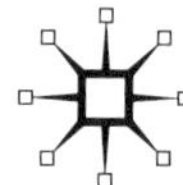

© James Hughes, Gwendolyn Sasse and Claire Gordon 2004

All rights reserved. No reproduction, copy or transmission of this publication may be made without written permission.

No paragraph of this publication may be reproduced, copied or transmitted save with written permission or in accordance with the provisions of the Copyright, Designs and Patents Act 1988, or under the terms of any licence permitting limited copying issued by the Copyright Licensing Agency, 90 Tottenham Court Road, London W1T 4LP.

Any person who does any unauthorised act in relation to this publication may be liable to criminal prosecution and civil claims for damages.

The authors have asserted their rights to be identified as the authors of this work in accordance with the Copyright, Designs and Patents Act 1988.

First published 2004 by
PALGRAVE MACMILLAN
Houndmills, Basingstoke, Hampshire RG21 6XS and
175 Fifth Avenue, New York, N. Y. 10010
Companies and representatives throughout the world

PALGRAVE MACMILLAN is the global academic imprint of the Palgrave Macmillan division of St. Martin's Press, LLC and of Palgrave Macmillan Ltd. Macmillan® is a registered trademark in the United States, United Kingdom and other countries. Palgrave is a registered trademark in the European Union and other countries.

ISBN 1–4039–3987–X

This book is printed on paper suitable for recycling and made from fully managed and sustained forest sources.

A catalogue record for this book is available from the British Library.

Library of Congress Cataloging-in-Publication Data

Hughes, James, 1959-
Europeanization and regionalization in the EU's enlargement to Central and Eastern Europe: the myth of conditionality / James Hughes, Gwendolyn Sasse, and Claire Gordon.
p. cm. – (One Europe or several?)
Includes bibliographical references and index.
ISBN 1-4039-3987-X (cloth: alk. paper)
1. European Union–Europe, Eastern. 2. European Union–Europe, Central. 3. Regional planning–Europe, Eastern. 4. Regional planning–Europe, Central. I. Sasse, Gwendolyn, 1972–II. Gordon, Claire E., 1963–III. Title. IV. Series.

HC240.25.E852H84 2004
341.242'2'0943–dc22

2004051673

10 9 8 7 6 5 4 3 2 1
13 12 11 10 09 08 07 06 05 04

Printed and bound in Great Britain by
Antony Rowe Ltd, Chippenham and Eastbourne

Contents

List of Tables

List of Figures

List of Boxes

List of Maps

Preface

This book is based on research conducted within the framework of the Economic and Social Research Council project 'Elites and Institutions in Regional and Local Governance in Central and Eastern Europe' (Award no. L213252030) which formed part of the ESRC Programme 'One Europe or Several?' (OEOS). In over four years of research, including large-scale fieldwork in several EU accession countries, we have benefited from the support, encouragement and criticism of many colleagues and friends. The initial research project was devised by James Hughes in 1998. Peter John (Birkbeck College) and Gwendolyn Sasse made valuable input into the initial research design, and helped to refine the methodology and interview schedules. The project was transformed after some months of initial research into one that focused more specifically on the impact of EU enlargement. Gwendolyn Sasse joined as a main researcher and Claire Gordon was appointed as Research Officer. Our project has, thus, been a real team effort from the outset and, thankfully, has remained so through to its end.

The original aim of the project was to explore economic and political transition through a comparative study of the role of elites in the institutional design and practice of governance at the sub-national level across six Eastern European post-communist states. The research focused on 'second' cities. After a preliminary analysis the research team recognized that one of the most critical dimensions of regional policy and sub-national institution-building in the CEECs was the relationship between the European Union, enlargement conditionality, central governments and local and regional elites, and consequently we shifted our research efforts increasingly to exploring this nexus. The project involved an extensive programme of interviews in five CEEC candidate countries (Estonia, Hungary, Poland, Romania, Slovenia), and in two 'outsiders' (Ukraine and Russia). Only the 287 interviews completed in those four CEEC states that were among the group that joined the EU on 1 May 2004 have been used in this book.

The fieldwork was critically dependent on the assistance of several academics and researchers from the candidate countries who assisted us with the interviews between 1999–2002: Dr Jüri Ruus of the University of Tartu in Tartu (Estonia), Katalin Sule of the Transdnubian Research Centre, Centre for Regional Studies, Hungarian Academy of

Sciences in Pécs (Hungary), Dr Tanja Majcherkiewicz of the London School of Economics in Katowice (Poland), Professor Igor Lukšič of the University of Ljubljana in Maribor (Slovenia). We express our profound thanks to these colleagues and to all of the interviewees who gave their time freely and generously to assist us with the research. As we agreed with the interviewees, we have preserved their anonymity. Similarly, we would like to thank the officials from the European Commission, in particular from DG Enlargement and DG Regio, and the various Country Delegations in Brussels who met with us to discuss our research and helped to illuminate the complexities of enlargement.

We have also drawn ideas and inspiration from the workshops organized within the framework of the OEOS ESRC programme and a range of conferences at which we presented our findings. The most important of these were: the European Consortium for Political Research Joint Sessions in Grenoble (April 2001) and Turin (April 2002); the conference co-organized by James Hughes and Michael Keating on 'EU Enlargement and the Regions' funded by the Robert Schuman Centre and held at the European University Institute in Florence (May 2002); the Central and East European International Studies Association conference in Moscow (July 2002); the OEOS conference on 'Convergence and Divergence in the New Europe' held at the University of Sussex (July 2002); the workshop on 'States of Transition in Europe: Linking the Internal and International Dynamics of Change' organized by Gwendolyn Sasse at the LSE (June 2001); the 'Opposing Europe' seminar co-organized by Claire Gordon at the LSE (December 2002) as part of the series of ESRC research seminars on 'The Comparative Party Politics of Euroscepticism in Contemporary Europe' (ESRC no. R451265110); and the end of project OEOS policy dissemination seminar titled 'Institutional Reform, Citizenship and Civil Society in the Enlarged Europe' co-organized by James Hughes and Dario Castiglione (University of Exeter) and held at the LSE (March 2003).

We are also grateful for the moral support from several colleagues within and outside the LSE. Dominic Lieven has been a considerate and inspiring head of department during the last two years of the project, which in no short measure helped us to draw the book to a conclusion. In particular we appreciate immensely the time and effort taken by our colleagues and friends Waltraud Schelkle, Eiko Thielemann, Margot Light, Klaus Goetz, Heather Grabbe, Frank Schimmelfennig and Uli Sedelmeier, and Jan Zielonka, all of whom offered comments, insights and encouragement of the work at the various stages of its progress. The ESRC project funded three periods of sabbatical leave (for James Hughes, Gwendolyn Sasse and Peter John) which allowed us to fully concentrate our attention on the research and were vitally important for the completion of the research and data analysis. James Hughes also thanks the Robert Schuman Centre for Advanced Studies of the European University Institute in Florence for awarding him a Jean Monnet Fellowship in the European Forum for the academic year 2001–02.

Parts of chapters 3 and 6 draw on our previously published articles and chapters 'Conditionality and Compliance in the EU's Eastward Enlargement: Regional Policy and the Reform of Sub-national Governance', *Journal of Common Market Studies*, Vol. 42, No. 3 (September 2004); 'Saying "Maybe" to the "Return to Europe", Elites and the Political Space for Euroscepticism in Central and Eastern Europe', *European Union Politics*, Vol. 3, No. 3 (September 2002); 'EU Enlargement, Europeanisation and the Dynamics of Regionalisation in the CEECs', in Michael Keating and James Hughes (eds), *The Regional Challenge in Central and Eastern Europe: Territorial Restructuring and European Integration* (2003); and the working papers published as part of the One Europe or Several series (http://www.one-europe.ac.uk/). Full details of the outputs from the project are available on the ESRC's Regard database (http://www.regard.ac.uk/).

Above all, we would like to thank Helen Wallace, the first Director of the OEOS programme, and currently Director of the Robert Schuman Centre, for commissioning the project and for her patience and understanding in allowing the project to be reshaped so soon after its inception. She has been a generous mentor of our project and her encouragement has been important for us in completing the fieldwork, disseminating our findings and delivering the book long after her official involvement in the ESRC programme had ended.

James Hughes
Gwendolyn Sasse
Claire Gordon

List of Abbreviations

ACP/EC	Africa, the Caribbean and the Pacific Countries/European Community
AWS-UW	Solidarity Electoral Alliance-Freedom Union
CAP	Common Agricultural Policy
CEECs	Central and Eastern European (Candidate) Countries
CEORG	Central European Opinion Research Group Foundation
CFSP	Common Foreign and Security Policy
CMR	Comprehensive Monitoring Report
CSCE	Conference on Security and Cooperation in Europe
DG	Directorate-General of the EU
EBRD	European Bank for Reconstruction and Development
ECU/ecu	European currency unit
FRY	Federal Republic of Yugoslavia
FSU/CIS	Former Soviet Union/Commonwealth of Independent States
FYROM	Former Yugoslav Republic of Macedonia
HDF	Hungarian Democratic Forum
IMF	International Monetary Fund
ISPA	Instrument for Structural Policies for Pre-Accession
NATO	North Atlantic Treaty Organization
NDP	National Development Plan
NPAA	National Programme for the Adoption of the *Acquis*
NUTS	*Nomenclature des unités territoriales statistiques*
OECD	Organization for Economic Cooperation and Development
OEOS	One Europe or Several? ESRC Research Programme
PAO	Public Administration Office (Hungary)
PHARE	*Pologne-Hongrie: aide à la reconstruction économique*
PSL	Polish Peasant Party
RDA	Regional Development Agency
RDC	Regional Development Council
SAPARD	Special Accession Programme for Agriculture and Rural Development
Tacis	Technical Assistance CIS
TEU	Treaty on European Union
USAID	US Agency for International Development

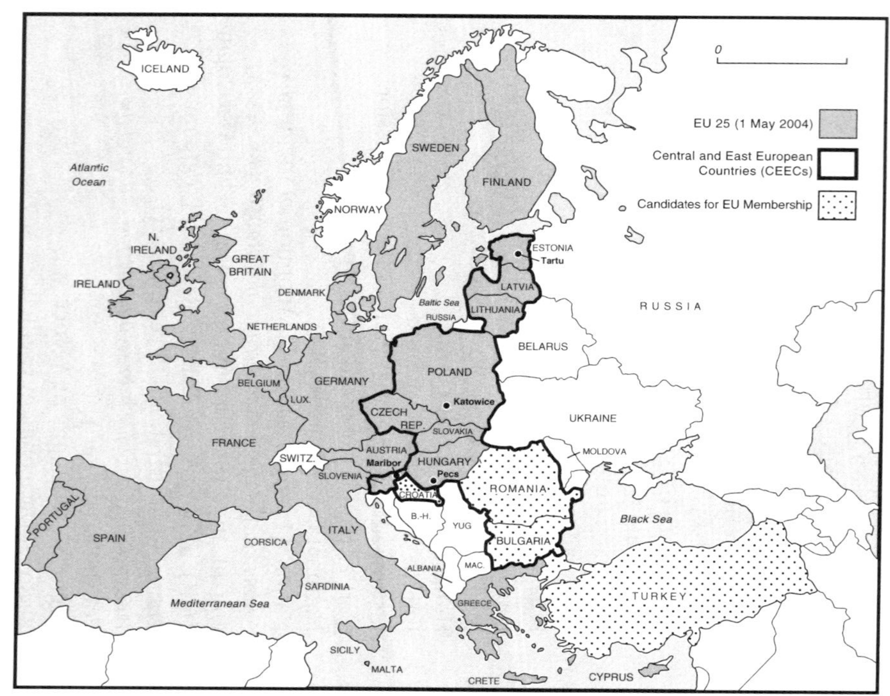

Map 1 EU-25 2004

Introduction

> The EU's accession strategy has proved a success. It has supported the candidates in their drive to reach precisely defined goals at a number of staging posts. The most powerful motivation for achieving the necessary reforms was the clear and credible prospect of joining the EU.
>
> Günter Verheugen, Commissioner DG Enlargement[1]

> The key question on the EU side was not whether enlargement should take place, but how and when. But the 'when' and 'how' were difficult problems with a continuing fear in many quarters that the applicant countries had not made sufficient progress or preparation to apply the EU rules and policies. Most important, the key factor in ensuring a good preparation was the conditionality of the accession process.
>
> Graham Avery, Chief Adviser DG Enlargement[2]

> We were like mice in laboratories.
>
> From authors' interview with an Estonian official in Brussels[3]

> This is the end of World War Two.
>
> Prime Minister Vladimir Spidla on the result of the Czech referendum on EU accession[4]

The absence of alternative ideological or systemic paradigms for the Central and East European Candidate Countries (CEECs), other than the appeal of a vaguely defined 'return to Europe' encapsulated by EU membership, has underpinned the study of enlargement. There is a widespread assumption of power asymmetry derived from the supposedly unprecedented scope for EU conditionality to both shape the policy and structural outcomes in the new member states, and to promote the normative assimilation of their elites. In recent studies of conditionality and enlargement there is an evident tendency to mythologize the positive relationship between the two especially where, as can be seen above, authors have been closely involved in the process itself. This conventional understanding of conditionality emphasizes the asymmetric power relationship between the actor applying the conditionality and encouraging 'socialization' and the complying and 'socialized' actor on the receiving end. The EU's conditionality for the accession of new members is thus seen as constituting a powerful incentive and disciplining structure for the CEECs. In principle EU conditionality should give the Commission a sanctioning mechanism to impose compliance with the Copenhagen criteria and the adoption of the *acquis communautaire* (hereafter *acquis*) on the CEECs as a precondition of their joining the Union. If this logic of conditionality works in practice then we should be able to track clear causal relationships between the Commission's use of conditionality and the compliance of the candidate countries through policy, or institutional adjustments and normative change. In the absence of direct causal linkages, has EU conditionality been a myth?

We depart from the conventional approaches to the study of conditionality, which tend to take its causative effects as a given, and then proceed to examine its outcomes. This book argues that the phenomenon of conditionality is insufficiently understood within a narrowly positivist framework whereby EU conditionality is seen as a formal instrument for the transposition of the EU's rules, norms and institutional templates to the CEECs.[5] It is a study of the phenomenon of EU conditionality as well as an empirical investigation of the process of its operation. It asks whether we can attribute any 'Europeanizing' effects from EU conditionality in institution-building, norm construction (including attitudinal impacts) and convergence with regard to enlargement. We aim to demonstrate that our wider process-based definition of EU conditionality, which includes not only the formal technical requirements on candidates but also the informal pressures arising from the behaviour and perceptions of actors engaged in the political process, offers a deeper understanding of the enlargement process as a dynamic interaction between international incentives and rules and domestic transition factors.

The phenomenon of conditionality as an ideal type has certain essential characteristics. It should involve a consensus on its substance between the actor(s) applying it and the actor(s) who must fulfil it. It should be defined by clear criteria which are verifiable. The fulfilment of conditionality should be readily subjected to testable benchmarks. The power flows in the process of employing conditionality should be readily transmitted and understood by all concerned, and should lead to outcomes (whether rewards or sanctions) that have been explicitly predetermined (Figure I.1).

Figure I.1 Conventional model of conditionality

Our analysis focuses on three key issues arising from the use of conditionality and the role of the Commission as the EU's institutional motor for enlargement. Firstly, we examine the nature of EU conditionality. What were its main elements and were they consistent over time? Moreover we locate EU conditionality within a historical context of Western conditionality. Secondly, we focus specifically on the role of the Commission as the key EU agency with the chief responsibility for monitoring and reporting on the candidates' progress in meeting the conditions for membership. Did it act as a unified actor with a clear understanding of conditionality and with a coherent and consistent approach to compliance and implementation in the CEECs? Moreover, did the Commission communicate the requirements of conditionality clearly and consistently to the candidate states over time? How important was conditionality for strengthening the Commission's capacity to ensure compliance and 'systemic convergence' between the EU and the candidates? Thirdly, we explore how effective conditionality was by examining the actual policy and institutional outcomes in the CEECs, and by testing how resilient the domestic institutions were in resisting conditionality, instrumentalizing it and preferring endogenous policies and structures over EU 'models'. Thus our definition of conditionality is one that defines it by the process of its application rather than by an ideal-type assumed power relationship (see Figure I.2). It is the interaction between multi-level actors, perceptions, interests, different rewards and sanctions, temporal factors, institutional and policy compliance, that characterizes conditionality.

Figure I.2 Process-based model of conditionality

To analyse the impact of conditionality this book takes a policy tracking approach to evaluate CEEC compliance in one key policy area that was generally regarded as being of critical importance for enlargement: regional policy. In particular, we analyse how the candidates configured regional institutional architectures in the context of the requirements of EU regional policy. This process of regionalization is understood in this book as the territorial and administrative configuration of regional governance, both in the form of elected regional governments and administrative-statistical units. This broad definition is applied because both forms of regionalization were undertaken in the CEECs and because the process was increasingly shaped from 1996 by the need to conform with the EU's NUTS classifications which are the basis for allocations of the EU's primary redistributive instrument, the Structural and Cohesion Funds. This is not to say that regionalization did not impinge upon the sub-national arena of regional and local politics but it should not be confused with regionalism, for whereas the former is concerned with the territorial and administrative configuration of the state the latter involves the political mobilization of regional identities and interests.[6] Moreover, the sub-national arena of regional and local politics is critical for the interrelated processes of post-communist political and economic transition as well as EU eastward enlargement. For transition to be consolidated, political and economic changes must be embedded at all levels of governance. Similarly, EU membership will have an immense impact on how sub-national actors and institutions would operate. Thus, this empirically grounded book aims to facilitate a better understanding of the linkages between the processes of transition and enlargement.

Four conditions frame the analysis of the trends of regionalization presented in this chapter. First, regional policy should have been one of the most significant elements in the incentive structure for enlargement given its financial implications for both the Union and the new members. Along with agricultural subsidies, regional policy will be a main conduit for financial aid flows from the EU to the new members. The CEECs stand to benefit substantially from the EU's structural funds and regional and cohesion policy upon accession to the Union on 1 May 2004. The financial package agreed at the Copenhagen Council in December 2003 committed €40.8 billion to the ten new members in 2004–06, over half of which (€24.45 billion) is to be spent on 'structural actions' (see Table I.1).[7] The new member states are also expected to be the main beneficiaries of regional funds in the next budgetary cycle, from 2007–13, irrespective of how the budget is reformed. This incentive structure, underpinned by the power asymmetry characterizing the relationship between the EU and the CEECs, left considerable scope for EU conditions, rules and norms to shape institution-building, perceptions and practices in the transition countries. The institutional configurations, capacities, norms and attitudes at the regional and local levels in the CEECs will have a direct impact on the future expenditure of significant EU funds. One could therefore expect a significant and detectable impact of the EU on sub-national governance in the CEECs as well as a degree of convergence in the institutional outcomes across these states. In fact, regional policy was one of the most protracted issues in the negotiations between the EU and the CEECs. Previous analyses of eastward enlargement have described the formal architecture of regional institutional changes in the context of administrative and economic reforms during the 1990s.[8] Our analysis specifically aims to explain the extent to which this architecture was designed and evolved in relation to enlargement conditionality.[9]

Secondly, despite the prominent role of regional policy within the EU, the institutional environment at this level of governance is flexibly arranged. Regional governance is a sovereignty issue of the member states, and the EU's emphasis in regional policy is on process and outcome rather than on particular institutional models. Accordingly, the *acquis* is very 'thin' on regional policy. The divergent models inside the EU and the poverty of legal requisites in the *acquis* counterbalance the potential leverage of EU conditionality on the candidate countries. We can therefore hypothesize that the impact of EU enlargement on the CEECs has been constrained by the lack of institutional detail tied to conditionality in this policy domain.

Thirdly, the apparent thinness of the *acquis* in the field of regional policy contrasts with the centrality of this domain in EU policy-making and its budgetary implications. The lack of a complex set of explicit and codified institutional rules in the *acquis* and even the Structural Funds Regulations suggest a wider scope for informal or 'soft'

Table I.1 EC aid to the ten accession countries, 2004–06 (as finalized in December 2003) (million euros)

Country	Objective 1	Objective 2	Objective 3	Interreg	Equal	Cohesion fund*	Total
Czech Rep	1,454.27	71.30	58.79	68.68	32.10	936.05	2,621.19
Estonia	371.36	0.00	0.00	10.60	4.07	309.03	695.06
Cyprus**	0.00	28.02	21.95	4.30	1.81	53.94	113.44
Latvia	625.57	0.00	0.00	15.26	8.03	515.43	1,164.29
Lithuania	895.17	0.00	0.00	22.49	11.87	608.17	1,537.70
Hungary	1,995.72	0.00	0.00	68.68	30.29	1,112.67	3,207.36
Malta	63.19	0.00	0.00	2.37	1.24	21.94	88.74
Poland	8,275.81	0.00	0.00	221.36	133.93	4,178.60	12,809.70
Slovakia	1,041.04	37.17	44.94	41.47	22.27	570.50	1,757.39
Slovenia	237.51	0.00	0.00	23.65	6.44	188.71	456.31
Total	**14,959.64**	**136.49**	**125.68**	**478.86**	**252.05**	**8,495.04**	**24,451.18**

Notes

* Average; ** Including the Financial Instrument for Fisheries Guidance (FIFG).

Of the Objective 1 funds 61 per cent will be from the European Regional Development Fund (ERDF), 25 per cent from the European Social Fund (ESF), 12 per cent from the European Agricultural Guidance and Guarantee Fund (EAGGF)-Guidance Section and about 2 per cent from the FIFG.

Source: *inforegio news*, Newsletter, No. 118, January 2004.

conditions as well as individually tailored guidelines and pressure from the Commission during the enlargement process. Informal conditionality increases the likelihood of inconsistency in the message communicated by Commission officials over time. Depending on the power of domestic actors, the impact of the EU could still be significant, though it could also be ambiguous or even contradictory. An inconsistent Commission policy would contribute to confused, incomplete or weak institutional outcomes in the CEECs. By tracing the developments in the Commission's approach to regional policy before and during the accession process, the domestic policy responses of the CEECs, and the interaction between the two, this book attempts to shed light on these dynamics.[10]

Fourthly, the pre-accession negotiations have exhibited a 'regional deficit' in that they have been confined to the Commission on the EU side and national elites from the executive structures in the CEECs. The lack of involvement of sub-national actors in the preparation for EU regional policy suggests a cross-national preference for minimalist and formal rule adoption, including a bias against politically empowered regions. Moreover, one could expect disengaged sub-national elites to be more Eurosceptic than the acculturated 'Europeanized' national elites. The role of elites at the regional and local levels tends to be overlooked by theorists and practitioners whose focus is on the power and bargaining strategies of national elites and the nation-state level as the critical units of analysis in studies of transition and enlargement.[11] Too little attention has been paid to the hierarchy of elite power within states, not only as regards the power and networks of different sectors of the elite, but also to the ways in which power may be institutionalized at different territorial levels of governance.

Sub-national elites are important policy gatekeepers in two key respects: firstly, they are critical for coherent rule compliance and the implementation of whatever new rules of the game are devised; and secondly, they act as a key mechanism for embedding commitment to the rules by the filtering of norms into society. Our research into the engagement and perceptions of sub-national elites aims to demonstrate empirically how deeply embedded these norms are and where there are different intensities of elite assimilation into EU norms. Existing differences in the normative commitment of elites in the candidate countries to EU norms is a useful predictor of future commitment and compliance strategies and problems.

Our policy study is comparative across institutions, countries and temporally. Chapter 1 of this book sets out the conceptual framework, drawing on the literature on Europeanization, conditionality and transition. We offer a critical exploration of the relationship between conditionality and Europeanization. Chapter 2 presents an overview of the historical-structural legacies of sub-national government informing the initial starting conditions and choices faced by the CEECs at the outset of transition, and charts the broader policy trends in regionalization across all the CEEC states. Chapter 3 traces the evolution of the Commission's approach to regional policy and regionalization. We analyse interviews conducted with officials in the Commission and the CEEC delegations in Brussels to illustrate the perceptions of the key actors during the negotiation process and the interactions between the Commission and the CEECs. Chapter 4 presents a systematic analysis of the EU's main monitoring and enforcement mechanisms during the enlargement process, in particular the Commission's annual Regular Reports and their emphasis on the need for regional 'administrative capacity'. Chapter 5 offers a comparative case study of regional policy and regionalization by analysing the two main trends of regionalization in the CEECs: administrative-statistical regionalization (Hungary) versus democratized regionalization (Poland). The interaction between domestic politics and external incentives and pressures regarding regional reforms is compared. Based on large-scale elite interviews in four key regional cities in the CEECs, Chapter 6 examines the extent of normative and attitudinal 'Europeanization' among the sub-national elites.

As we shall see, the conclusion to this book emphasizes the fluid nature of conditionality, the inconsistencies in its application by the Commission over time, and the weakness of a clear-cut causal relationship between conditionality and policy or institutional outcomes in the CEECs. The domestic institutional changes in the CEECs in the context of EU adaptational pressures have varied significantly across countries, with considerable room for manoeuvre for domestic actors. These findings are in line with the tentative conclusions drawn from some of the more empirically grounded studies of Europeanization which have detected lower levels of Europeanization and convergence with regard to political structures than in specific policy areas. While real or perceived external pressures have interacted with domestic transition politics to shape the institutional design during the latter stages of regional reform in the CEECs, on balance, domestic institutional choices made during the early transition period outweigh and actually constrain the importance of external factors during enlargement. Moreover, sub-national elites have by and large been disengaged from the accession process. Their decisional calculus has been dominated by immediate problems related to the transition process. While they are not actively Eurosceptic, these elites still exhibit a relatively low level of connectedness with the EU as an institutional actor and framework for policy-making, and thereby pose a major challenge to the effective implementation of EU policy in the short to medium term.

The analysis draws on two main bodies of evidence. Firstly, we conducted a large-scale programme of structured elite interviews with a total of 287 sub-national elites from key regional cities in four candidate countries: Tartu in Estonia, Pécs in Hungary, Katowice in Poland and Maribor in Slovenia. These interviews were supplemented by 35 interviews conducted with middle to high-level officials in the EU Commission and CEEC delegations in Brussels. The interviews were carried out over a three-year period (1999–2002). Secondly, we provide a systematic study of the EU's own documentary record of the enlargement process, primarily through its Opinions and Regular Reports on the CEECs. Consequently, our study investigates enlargement at three levels – the European, the national and the sub-national.

1 The Logic of Enlargement Conditionality and Europeanization

Despite the importance of conditionality during the current EU enlargement, there are few theoretical or empirical studies of the concept. The study of EU enlargement conditionality is characterized by a concentration on the analysis of its correlation with macro-level democratization and marketization, rather than empirically tracking clear causal relationships in policies and institution-building. Most studies tend to focus on two cumulative levels of conditionality. Firstly, they attach great salience to the broad 'principled' or normative conditionality established by the Copenhagen European Council in December 1993, the so-called 'Copenhagen criteria', which was subsequently elaborated in the Accession Partnerships for individual candidate countries from 1997. Secondly, they emphasize the 'technical' preconditions for the CEECs to accelerate the adoption of and adaptation to the *acquis* in order to fulfil all the responsibilities of membership. The speedy adoption of the *acquis* was the benchmark for measuring CEEC progress on accession – a condition that only Austria, Finland and Sweden, all advanced industrial countries, had previously met prior to membership. There is a wide spectrum of opinions as to whether EU conditionality has had positive or negative effects on the CEECs. Grabbe views the way that conditionality has operated as a factor that has potential to frustrate moves toward greater European integration in the medium term because conditionality involves costs to the CEECs in the implementation of what is essentially a 'moving target' within an 'evolving process that is highly politicized, especially on the EU side'.[1] Smith, in contrast, stresses that conditionality performs the vital task of enforcement of the 'admission' rules to the Union 'club'.[2] There is a consensus among these studies that the conditionality for the adoption of the *acquis* has strong causal effects in the steering of policy and institutional change in the CEECs. Grabbe describes the levers of conditionality available to the Union as 'powerful tools to shape institutions in CEE' which made policy-makers 'choose EU models because of the incentives and constraints imposed by the EU accession process'.[3] She has also argued that the 'readiness' of the CEECs to join is a 'political question on the EU side'.[4] Schimmelfennig et al. have qualified these assumptions by treating the EU's normative democratic conditionality as a 'reinforcement strategy' rather than a strong causal mechanism in its own right.[5] The emphasis in these studies tends to be on the salience of conditionality at the macro-political level, rather than tracking specific impacts on policy-making in the CEECs. In general, EU conditionality has been viewed as an important lever for 'democracy promotion', and is seen as having made a significant contribution to 'foreign made democracy' in the CEECs.[6]

While existing studies have assessed how the EU has constructed conditionality and described the mechanisms by which the EU has attempted to implement it in the CEECS, the fundamental problem with the use of the concept of conditionality remains that it is underpinned by positivist assumptions. Positivist assumptions that conditionality generates compliance and or adaptation are tautological and, thus, are not analytically meaningful since they tell us nothing about the substantive nature of conditionality or the nature of the compliance and the relationships between the two. These relationships can only be analysed by observation of how they work together in the real world. Two key problems remain very weakly analysed and explained. Firstly, there is the question of the scale of commitment and effectiveness of compliance of the CEECs in their policy implementation in response to conditionality. We need to distinguish better between the transposition of the *acquis* into domestic law, which the EU's own Regular Reports tend to equate with a successful outcome of conditionality, and the actual implementation of policy. The latter can only be demonstrated empirically by tracking policy changes over time, and this is precisely where there is a gap in the existing study of EU enlargement.[7] In studying conditionality and compliance it is important to distinguish between the effective implementation of policy derived from EU conditionality, which is generally weak, and rhetorical or formal conditionality and compliance, which is strong.

Secondly, the analysis of conditionality tends to be too one-dimensional, in the sense that it does not sufficiently contextualize the EU conditionality of the 1990s' enlargement process by comparing it with previous, parallel, and sometimes overlapping models and applications of international conditionality, or locate it within the evolution of internal EU debates and developments that have shaped its application. EU enlargement conditionality is in fact more comprehensible if it is seen as part of a broad pattern of 'Western' international conditionality. Conditionality involves the exercise of power. It involves, according to Schmitter, 'the deliberate use of coercion – by attaching specific conditions to the distribution of benefits to recipient countries – on the part of multilateral institutions'.[8] This kind of implicitly coercive conditionality reached new levels of intensity in the EU's enlargement process to the CEECs. In the case of EU conditionality three categories of power are inherent in the conditionality for enlargement: economic power, bureaucratic power and normative power. The Commission's motivations and actions in driving enlargement have not been systematically explored. Nevertheless, the growing power of the Commission and the EU's own drive for integration and supranational governance is strongly correlated temporally with the process of enlargement in the 1990s. Having been tasked by the Copenhagen Council of June 1993 to manage the enlargement process the Commission has instrumentally employed its enhanced role as one of the levers to justify the further expansion of its competences through the new constitution and to engage in budget maximization.[9]

Conditionality toward the CEECs was strongly shaped by the transfer of development aid models, policies, personnel and institutional culture, and consultants from the bilateral aid programmes of member states, and from the EU's existing development aid programmes to the Developing World.[10] The EU was engaged in the provision of aid or 'development assistance' to the CEECs from 1989, that is to say several years prior to the beginning of the enlargement process. The EU's main instrument for delivering aid to the CEECs was PHARE, created in 1989 and run by the EC Commission as a conventional developmental aid programme modelled on those provided to the Third World.[11] Consequently, within the Commission an institutional culture that viewed assistance to the CEECs in terms of an asymmetric power relationship between 'donors' and 'recipients' was strengthened. It was only in 1997 that a review of PHARE's mission reoriented it and tied it exclusively to the goals of 'accession', primarily, the preparation of the CEECs for the obligations of membership and, in particular, assistance with the speedy transposition of the *acquis*. The 'eastward enlargement' of the EU became a gargantuan extension of the EU's external developmental strategy, the key difference being that the prospective members would be steadily connected to and ultimately included within the EU's internal economic developmental strategy for its own poorer regions through its regional policy and structural and cohesion funds. EU conditionality also reflects a shift in the economic interest of dominant EU member states away from their long-standing 'historic' ties with former colonies in the ACP (encapsulated by the defunct Lomé Convention) to a focus on the 'Europeanization' of the CEECs and the potential vast new markets in the region.

The argument has been made that opposition from existing member states to eastward enlargement was outflanked by 'rhetorical entrapment' resulting from the process by which the EU defined the rationale for enlargement and its conditionality. Since the project of European integration was legitimated around a collective identity based on liberal norms of capitalist democracy, and as enlargement conditionality was steadily infused with these norms, the EU became politically obligated to open membership to those European states which complied with these norms.[12] The plausible counter-argument to this view traces the logic of enlargement back to national interests and realpolitik.[13] The rhetoric surrounding enlargement and EU conditionality was strongly embued by a *mission civilisatrice* approach of 'Europeanization'. The perception was promoted whereby the political and economic models in core member states were seen as normatively 'superior' and readily transferable to displace 'inferior' models in candidate countries, and where a speedy substitution of values by candidates and their compliance with EU norms was equated with the quality of their commitment and 'Europeanness'. However, intergovernmentalism in EU policy-making also means that in many policy areas there are different traditions, norms and models competing with each other. Consequently, there is no single EU policy template in many policy fields and its norms are generally so nebulously stated and erratically enforced that they lend themselves to wide interpretation. Aid dispersion is a case in point, as the models of aid and conditionality pursued by member states varied widely, from the paternalistic and interest-based models of former colonial powers such as the UK and France, who have strong records of post-colonial tied aid, to the more normatively driven and humanitarian oriented aid strategies of the Scandinavian countries.

International conditionality

International conditionality is embedded in the delivery of foreign aid and development assistance, whether bilateral or multilateral. Studies of this kind of conditionality are generally focused on Western aid to the Developing World. This kind of aid conditionality is typically seen as involving 'donors' in pursuit of their own self-interest, and 'recipients' who are subject to donor conditionality and, consequently, are in a position of dependency.[14] In principle, aid conditionality in the Developing World provides a reservoir of debates about policy practices and ideas that can inform our understanding of EU economic assistance to the post-communist states of Eastern Europe and the process of EU enlargement. While there is no commonly agreed definition of international conditionality, the literature tends to agree on three main aspects. Firstly, as Stokke explains: 'conditionality is not an aim in itself but an instrument by which other objectives are pursued'.[15] Secondly, there has been a steady evolution and expansion of conditionality since the end of the Second World War, with an increasing linkage between aid disbursement and conditions imposed by donors, and a greater complexity in the nature of the conditionality. Two main categories of conditions are employed: positive conditionality takes the form of rewards for compliance, and negative conditionality involves punitive actions and sanctions to secure compliance. Thirdly, while superficially one might differentiate between altruistic and interest-based motivations in the giving of aid, studies generally accept that donor interests are paramount and the developmental interests of the recipient are secondary. This suggests that one of the key defining characteristics of the concept of conditionality is that it operates in an environment of power asymmetry between dominant and subordinate actor(s). Furthermore, the domestication of donor norms through aid conditionality has tended to override and marginalize local knowledge and supplant rival models as they are necessarily presented as 'inferior'.

The early Cold War period in the late 1940s and early 1950s saw a congruence of complementary changes in the management of aid that embedded two key notions of the aid conditionality of the European colonial era: the transference of superior norms, and the tying of aid to donor security and economic interests. The first was evident in the way that the development needs of the emerging post-colonial states were managed. The new institutions of global governance (the UN, the IMF and World Bank) became the key international agencies for the management of aid, and new channels for the post-colonial transfer of norms, expertise and technology from the advanced Western states to the Developing World.[16] Concurrently, the US protected its security, economic and sectional interests in Europe through the Marshall Plan, which was conditional on recipient states having an 'open market economy' and agreeing to the procurement tying of aid.[17] The latter was an attempt to promote and induce systemic change and is a direct antecedent of system-transforming aid conditionality that became stronger in the late 1970s. A serious side effect of these aid practices was, in effect, a 'double whammy' for the recipients to the extent that they not only were subject to economic conditionality and procurement tying, but also these instruments meant that the value of the aid was often significantly eroded by higher costs and reverse flows of funds to donors through the purchase of 'expertise' from private sector consultants.

International conditionality has evolved from 'first generation' economic conditionality to a 'second generation' of combined economic and political conditionality. The 'first generation' conditionality was that of IMF/World Bank structural adjustment programmes following on from the development of IMF formal guidelines on conditionality in 1968. During the 1970s IMF conditionality for credits to debt-plagued states in the Developing World was increasingly targeted at promoting a global trend for neo-liberal macroeconomic reorganization. A policy orthodoxy developed around the adoption of 'Chicago School' neo-liberal economic policies of market liberalization, budgetary austerity and financial administrative reform. Historically, the aims of international aid are concerned with the promotion of 'systemic and private sector interests – economic, cultural, ideological, strategic and/or political – of the donor country'. In sum, then, aid is 'an instrument to pursue foreign policy objectives'.[18] The result was 'a world economy more closely integrated and more intrusive in the domestic policy affairs of developing countries', while social unrest and protest grew.[19]

There was a paradigm shift in 'Western' aid conditionality in the early 1990s to take advantage of the political opportunities created by the fall of communism. To supplement neo-liberal economic policies and administrative reform, policy-makers placed a much greater emphasis on the export of 'Western' political norms, in what is often referred to as 'democracy promotion' or 'democracy-building'.[20] The new conditionality involved a much greater intrusiveness by international organizations for systemic change in particular states. The substantively new character of 'second generation' conditionality is that it is based on a notion that gained sway among Western governing elites around 1989–90 which held that there was a 'symbiosis between democracy and development'.[21] In fact, the idea that there is a correlation between democracy and development, in the basic sense that 'economic abundance' provides ideal conditions for democracy, had been made by Lipset and other modernization theorists thirty years earlier, and debated at length in the 1960s.[22]

There is a clear temporal relationship between 'second generation' conditionality and the fall of communism, but the latter was not a trigger. The shift to a more overt coupling of economic and political conditionality developed over time during the 1980s. There are strong reasons why neo-liberal ideology favours such a linkage in principle. Markets prefer non-interventionist or weak but stable states. Liberal Democracy is the preferred means of delivery because it dilutes state power and allows a greater latitude for the free play of markets.[23] The fall of communism and the removal of Soviet hegemony in Eastern Europe created new security and economic national interests for the USA and the member states of the EU, and opened new opportunities for them to advance and protect these interests. It also created new dilemmas for the application of international conditionality, for as Stone's study of IMF lending to post-communist states demonstrates, where US foreign policy interests were paramount the credibility of conditionality generally was undermined.[24]

The EU and conditionality

The question of the leading role of the EU in systemic transformation in Eastern Europe falls within what has been referred to as a 'Western project' to encourage democracy in Eastern Europe.[25] In fact, there is a clear and logical progression between the traditional agenda of international aid conditionality and the new role of EC and EU conditionality. Following the collapse of communism in 1989, aid conditionality was one of the main instruments employed by the EC/EU to expand its influence in Eastern Europe and to promote systemic change. Initially, the primary mechanism was direct tied aid through the PHARE technical assistance programme created in 1989 along with the G24 Poland and Hungary aid programme (though the Commission coordinated both). Subsequently, once the enlargement process became a serious near-term prospect from 1996–97, PHARE aid incentives and other pre-accession instruments like SAPARD and ISPA were supplemented by the even greater potential benefits of massive developmental assistance from EU structural funds. Consequently, one of the principal benefits for the CEEC candidates to comply with enlargement conditionality is the coffers of developmental aid that will be open to them once they are members of the EU.

The new European agenda of coupling economic and political conditionality in its policy towards the post-communist states of Eastern Europe originated with an OECD Development Assistance Committee report at the time of the revolutions in Eastern Europe in 1989.[26] The EBRD, established in May 1990, was the first multilateral organization to entrench a link between economic and political conditionality in its founding charter, though this has proven to be a formal rather than an actual policy.[27] The rhetorical pace in European politics was set by the UK when in a speech at the Overseas Development Institute in London in June 1990 British Foreign Secretary Douglas Hurd specifically related the new policy agenda of tying aid in Africa and elsewhere with 'good government'. Economic success, Hurd argued, 'depends to a large degree on effective and honest government, political pluralism, and observance of the rule of law, as well as freer, more open economies', and that henceforth aid disbursement would be influenced by a recipient country's record on 'pluralism, public accountability, respect for the rule of law, human rights and market principles'. Furthermore, the post-communist transition in Eastern Europe, according to Hurd, offered 'ample evidence that economic and political liberalization are inseparable'. Rather enigmatically, he stated that 'aid must go where it will do good'.[28] For Hurd there was a clear link between the capacity of the 'West' to promote Liberal Democracy and its aid disbursement policies, whether in Africa or Eastern Europe. The British position was followed by a cascade of similar policy statements from other European and Western governments during 1990 and 1991 which transformed the concept into a new Western orthodoxy.[29] In November 1990, USAID made 'progress towards democracy' a condition for its aid.

Following Hurd's speech, several significant landmarks paved the way for political conditionality to become rapidly embedded in EC norms. The European Council took up the political conditionality agenda and the June 1990 Dublin Summit issued a Declaration on the importance of human rights and good governance in Africa.[30] The CSCE's Paris Charter for a New Europe of November 1990 embodied the new rhetoric about democracy, and at the Rome Summit in December 1990 democracy promotion and human rights protection was extended to become a normative principle of the EC's external relations in general.

When the EC, contemporaneously with the collapse of communism, forged a policy consensus on the broad mission and principles of conditionality in its external relations, and in particular towards the states undergoing post-communist transition in Eastern Europe, it developed a uniquely comprehensive compound conditionality of the old 'first generation' IMF/World Bank economic conditionality of market liberalization and administrative reform embodied in the 'Washington consensus', and the 'second generation' political conditionality of democracy promotion, rule of law and respect for human rights. It is this totality of economic and political elements, and the attempt to operationalize them simultaneously across a whole region of states, that makes EU conditionality exceptional in its scope and intent. It informed the Europe Agreements between the EC and the Central and East European states in 1990–91 which gave most preferential economic status on the basis of the new marketizing, democratizing and human rights criteria. Two key decisions followed which further embedded the linkage between economic and political conditionality in EC policy. Firstly, the Luxembourg Summit of June 1991 resulted in the 'Declaration on Human Rights' which proclaimed respect for universal human rights as one of the 'cornerstones' of the EC, stressed the attachment of the European Council to 'the principles of parliamentary democracy and the primacy of law', including the protection of members of minorities, and declared these to be the basis for 'equitable development'.[31] Secondly, the Council and the representatives of member states meeting of 28 November 1991 passed a resolution on EC strategy for development which instituted a 'common approach' on linking 'good governance' with development aid and included punitive sanctions for non-compliance.[32]

These declarations formed the framework for the human rights and democracy clauses of the Maastricht Treaty of European Union agreed in February 1992 and effective from November 1993. Title 1, Article F (2) of the treaty made respect for human rights as guaranteed by the European Convention a general principle of EC law, ipso facto informing 'all of its activities'. Title 5, Article J. 1 (2), creating the CFSP Second Pillar, made the 'development and consolidation of democracy and the rule of law' as well as 'human rights and fundamental freedoms' principle objectives of the EU's external relations.[33] Title XX Article 177 (2) of the Treaty of Amsterdam of 1997 restated the policy commitment to linking development aid to a 'general objective of developing and consolidating democracy and the rule of law and to that of respect for human rights and fundamental freedoms'.[34]

In fact, the new declared conditionality policy was saturated with inconsistency in its implementation, the details of which are well documented.[35] There have been numerous cases demonstrating the inconsistency with which the EC, Western governments and multilateral organizations applied conditionality and their backsliding from sanctions when their own selfish economic and security interests were considered to be paramount to normative political conditionality. The clearest cases include: China (after 1989), Indonesia (1991), Algeria (1992), Nigeria (1993), Turkey (1995), Colombia, Egypt and Israel.[36] There have also been many examples from the Former Soviet Union post-1991 where Western economic and security interests have largely negated the link between political conditionality and economic assistance, in particular with regard to Russia and the other resource-rich states such as Azerbaijan, Kazakhstan, Turkmenistan and Uzbekistan. Consequently, the post-communist experience of aid conditionality offers many additional cases to validate Stokke's assessment that Western aid conditionality 'has been confined to a very large extent to declaratory policy'.[37]

There was also much incoherence from the EU itself, with 'each country touting its own model'.[38] One suspects that an additional complication was the clash of political cultures over how to manage conditionality within the Commission itself, whose functionaries are recruited from across the member states and therefore are acculturated by very different political, economic and social models of governance and development. Such differences do not co-exist easily in a bureaucratic setting, and certainly do not make for consistency in administrative action. There is, moreover, the underlying dynamic of any aid conditionality employed by a multilateral organization, namely, the conflicts of interests among the donors. In the case of enlargement to Eastern Europe the conflicting interests and divisions among existing member states are well established.[39]

When the European Council at Copenhagen in June 1993 issued a declaration of the broad norms that new members would be required to meet, thereafter known as the 'Copenhagen criteria', it drew directly from the norms previously established by the CSCE Paris Charter and the EU's own Europe Agreements with the East European states, which were being drafted at the time. The Copenhagen declaration of conditionality was simply a succinct restatement of the, by then, well established norms in the EU's external relations (with the exception of the reference to minority rights protection), but it now became the foundation for EU enlargement to proceed (see Box 1.1).[40] If the conclusion drawn by studies of 'second generation' international conditionality is that it is a 'declaratory policy', which is not meaningfully or consistently applied when it conflicts with Western self-interest, then what is the implication for EU conditionality? Does it fit within this trend?

Box 1.1 Three stages in the normative development of EC/EU conditionality

Europe Agreement

'REAFFIRMING their commitment to pluralist democracy based on the rule of law, human rights and fundamental freedoms, a multiparty system involving free and democratic elections, to the principles of a market economy and to social justice, which constitute the basis for the association;

'RECALLING the firm commitment of the Community and its Member States and of Hungary to the process of the Conference on Security and Cooperation in Europe (CSCE), including the full implementation of all provisions and principles therein, particular the Helsinki Final Act, the concluding documents of the Madrid and Vienna follow-up meetings and the Charter of Paris for a new Europe.'

Source: Excerpt from the *Europe Agreement with Hungary* (1993), L 348 (31/12/93).

Copenhagen Criteria

'The European Council today agreed that the associated countries in Central and Eastern Europe that so desire shall become members of the European Union. Accession will take place as soon as an associated country is able to assume the obligations of membership by satisfying the economic and political conditions required.

'Membership requires that the candidate country has achieved stability of institutions guaranteeing democracy, the rule of law, human rights and respect for and protection of minorities, the existence of a functioning market economy as well as the capacity to cope with competitive pressure and market forces within the Union. Membership presupposes the candidate's ability to take on the obligations of membership including adherence to the aims of political, economic and monetary union.

'The Union's capacity to absorb new members, while maintaining the momentum of European integration, is also an important consideration in the general interest of both the Union and the candidate countries.'

Source: European Council (1993), *Presidency Conclusions* para. 7 A (iii), Copenhagen European Council, 21–22 June.

Treaty of European Union 1997

Article 6 (ex Article F)

'1. The Union is founded on the principles of liberty, democracy, respect for human rights and fundamental freedoms, and the rule of law, principles which are common to the Member States.'

Article 49 (ex Article O)
'Any European State which respects the principles set out in Article 6 (1) may apply to become a member of the Union.'

Source: Excerpts from the *Consolidated Version of the Treaty of European Union* (1997).

EU 'democracy promotion'

A multilateral strategic vision and consensus on broad principles inevitably runs into difficulties when tested against state-specific interests and objectives. In the realm of post-communist economic transition there was a consensus among the advanced democracies around the need for a 'shock therapy' application of neo-liberal policies known as the 'Washington consensus'. There was no such consensus, however, about the 'Western project' for consolidating democracy. The tenets of Western economic orthodoxy had no equivalent in the political sphere as there were radically different views as to what were the most appropriate institutional models for Eastern European countries. Consequently, the EU and the US competed by promoting rival models through their aid delivery programmes.[41]

The political environment in which conditional economic aid is delivered is critical for determining the credibility of the conditionality and the results of the aid. Western aid to post-communist states, and US aid in particular, was often targeted at supporting corrupt leaders or elites committed to a 'pro-Western' foreign policy and the neo-liberal economic agenda, to the detriment of democratic institutional development and political accountability. This tendency took an extreme form in Western policy toward Russia and the Former Soviet Union, but was also a policy trend that was evident in some Eastern European states.[42] While Western support is widely seen as having been critical for the democratic consolidation of many states in Eastern Europe, and significant progress toward democracy in others, there is a widespread failure to sufficiently distinguish either between periods of conditionality or the different forms of conditionality applied to Eastern Europe.

The EU's economic interests and developmental objectives had caused it to re-divide post-communist Europe into three main zones of influence in the early 1990s. The first zone was the EU's 'near abroad' of states in Central and Eastern Europe, which as the most likely candidates for EU membership were designated the 'CEECs'.[43]

Geographically contiguous to the EU this zone offered an immense new market for the EU, where states as a whole were viewed as more subject to and willing to comply with EU conditionality, and where 'democracy promotion' was, in any event, progressing apace irrespective of the EU. Secondly, the FSU/CIS zone, which was of vital economic and security importance to the EU, but where the prospect of EU membership was remote, if not inconceivable.[44] Thirdly, the Balkans zone of the FRY, which was a paramount security concern for the external relations of the EU but where membership was seen as a more distant prospect.

Enlargement conditionality required new EU commitments in terms of the establishment of new financial instruments, institutional structures and expertise. Although PHARE was created in 1989, budget lines to support democracy promotion and human rights were only created in late 1991, that is to say after the first democratic elections in most Central and East European states. During the 1990s, aid budgets for the CEECs expanded dramatically, as did the competences of the Commission to manage the disbursement of aid. One of the interesting features of the set-up of PHARE within the Treaty on European Union is the rather unusual, and from an EU law viewpoint anachronistic, division of competences between the First and Second Pillars regarding policy towards Eastern Europe. PHARE is funded from the Commission's budget, and the Commission administers it, but it is legally in the Second Pillar, that is, it is subject to the control of the European Council. The explanation for this highly unusual arrangement is the desire by member states to control external relations with Eastern Europe and to constrain the development of the Commission's competences or the European Parliament's interference in this respect. This situation contrasts with Development Aid, which is funded by member states separately. In the critical transition period of 1991–96, the EU provided 57 per cent of the total cumulative G24 PHARE assistance amounting to over 6.6 billion ecus.[45]

The bulk of the EU's efforts and aid disbursements were channelled to the support of economic transition and the building of viable market economies as opposed to support for political transition, institution-building and democratic consolidation. Paradoxically, this imbalance in aid was most significant during the early transition phase in 1989–95, prior to the initiation of the enlargement drive. An indication of the priority attached to 'democracy-building' is that PHARE's activity heading 'civil society and democratization' accounted for just approximately 1 per cent of the total PHARE funds distributed in the CEECs (see Table 1.1). Furthermore, there is an inherent tension, if not in practice a contradiction, between the EU's accession objectives for PHARE from 1997 of building institutional capacity in arenas necessary for the market and improving the 'absorption' capacity (that is, the capacity to apply for and spend EU funds appropriately) of states, and the consolidation of democratic accountability over state decision-making in these nascent democracies. The fact that the overwhelming bulk of EU economic assistance channelled through PHARE was targeted on the priorities of the economic, rather than the political, dimensions of transition suggests that the EU was intentionally seeking to influence the sequencing of transition in this direction. Moreover, the EU prioritized aid delivery to those countries that were considered to be most economically important for the EU, as about one-third of PHARE funding allocated in 1990–96 went to just two countries: Poland (20.9 per cent) and Hungary (10.3 per cent).[46]

Consequently, although the EU's rhetoric stressed that the political Copenhagen criteria must be fulfilled *before* the accession process could begin, in practice EU aid has been overwhelmingly targeted on improving the market economies of the CEECs. This prioritization in

Table 1.1 Total PHARE commitments, contracts and payments (inc cross-border cooperation) by country and sector, 1990–98 (in million euros)

Country

Partner country	**Commitments**	**Contracts**	**Payments**
Albania	493.13	347.82	315.88
Bosnia & Herzegovina	282.33	206.98	152.11
Bulgaria	746.94	518.13	479.44
Czech Republic	389.73	246.12	196.46
Estonia	162.83	116.76	95.48
FYROM	167.33	127.68	93.57
Hungary	864.04	586.59	566.92
Latvia	206.57	149.56	115.07
Lithuania	272.03	197.33	146.46
Poland	1,731.51	1,386.04	1,251.30
Romania	971.85	675.75	598.13
Slovakia	253.23	149.45	132.95
Slovenia	131.29	95.65	77.67
Ex-Czechoslovakia	232.71	228.85	229.17
Multi-country	880.69	701.07	544.67
Horizontal programmes	1,104.68	963.51	593.81
Total	**8,890.88**	**6,697.3**	**5,589.10**

Table 1.1 Total PHARE commitments *continued*

Sector

Sector	**Commitments**	**Contracts**	**Payments**
Administration & public institutions	761.23	395.35	291.58
Agricultural restructuring	562.60	459.01	438.57
Civil society and democratization	104.84	79.79	64.95
Education, training and research	1,012.09	959.93	867.51
Environment and nuclear safety	753.12	544.62	447.19
Financial sector	268.68	257.82	248.76
Humanitarian, food and critical aid	533.02	521.07	501.52
Infrastructure (energy, transport and telecoms)	2,145.59	1,298.24	958.04
Approximation of legislation	84.07	73.81	19.66
Consumer protection	12.91	12.63	8.97
Private sector, privatization & restructuring, SMEs	1,156.02	924.98	815.81
Integrated regional measures	340.15	124.91	83.34
Social development and employment	272.84	233.64	202.37
Public health	105.57	98.92	88.46
Other (multidisciplinary, general TA. etc.)	778.15	712.59	552.39
Total	**8,890.88**	**6,697.3**	**5,589.10**

Source: PHARE 1998 annual report; http://www.europa.eu.int/ comm/enlargement/pas/phare/statistics/index.htm.

aid disbursement for economic development and the administrative and institution-building and capacity-building required by advanced market economies has been strengthened by the accession process.[47] The pattern of aid suggests that the EU focus on economic development, while expecting the CEECs to meet political conditionality more or less independent of aid, is driven by the EU's overriding concern with markets rather than democracy or human rights.

Conditionality dilemmas in the *acquis*

The widespread use of the term 'conditionality' both in EU and academic sources suggests that there is a perceived consensus over its meaning. In principle, conditionality should be based on a catalogue of succinct criteria, as well as clear enforcement and reward mechanisms to ensure the credibility and predictability of its application. The Copenhagen criteria, however, do not define the benchmarks or the process by which EU conditionality could be enforced and verified. The perception that there is clarity is sustained by the ubiquitous use of the metaphor of the 'club rules' in describing EU conditionality. Thus, conditionality is seen as a gatekeeping mechanism embodying clearly identifiable and generally understood norms, rules and institutional configurations that are applied consistently and with some continuity over time to regulate the entry of new members. Even if we accept that conditionality is an implicitly coercive instrument wielded by the Commission to secure certain desired policy or institutional outcomes, we must also recognize that the features of EU conditionality, in particular its prescriptive essence, are far from being well defined. The ambivalence and ambiguity is evident in the way that the 'Copenhagen criteria' were highly politicized and operationalized in a selective manner. By the time enlargement negotiations accelerated from 1997 it is doubtful that the political conditionality as laid out in the Copenhagen criteria was a significant factor in the process at all, as the democratization of the CEECs was generally accepted as a reality and a starting-point for the other three Copenhagen conditions. Nevertheless, the creation of a 'queuing' system for enlargement in December 1997 ostensibly strengthened EU conditionality as a significant lever for prioritizing economic conditions and regulation through the Council's 'Accession Partnerships' with each candidate country. The priority was to secure the transposition of the *acquis* rather than to promote the consolidation of democratic society. The Opinions, Accession Partnerships and the Regular Reports on each candidate country, as we shall discuss in Chapter 4, created a new vocabulary of loyalty and new means of auditing convergence and compliance.[48]

The weight of conditionality, consequently, fell on the CEECs through the 'technical' requirements to adopt the 80,000 odd pages of the *acquis*. The conditionality of the *acquis* itself, however, was flawed by its inherent structural characteristics, and especially its unevenness. In fact, an *acquis* consisting of some 80,000 pages of law and regulations, and divided into thirty-one chapters for ease of adoption during enlargement, could not be uniformly conditional across policy areas. Fundamentally, the *acquis* reflects the evolution in the power balance in the EU between the competences of member states and the EU-level institutions. The *acquis* is supposed to dress states with the technical accoutrements of laws and regulations that build their capacity to operate effectively as new members of the Union, but the pattern of technical detail in the *acquis* is not uniform but is in fact highly uneven both across and within policy areas. Thus, where the detail in the *acquis* is 'thick' on a particular policy issue we can plausibly expect it to provide strong leverage for the Commission to achieve particular outcomes in its interactions with the CEECs, but where the *acquis* is 'thin' we should expect the explicit leverage, and thus the formal conditionality, to be weak. Consequently, a useful initial hypothesis would be that the EU conditionality does not have a uniform logic, but rather has a wispish nature that shifts and transforms depending on the content of the *acquis*, the policy area, the country concerned, and the political context.

This ambivalence and vagueness of the *acquis* across policy areas, we argue, has significantly weakened the impact of conditionality. We follow Olsen's observation that the EU's effectiveness at institution-building and policy change even within the Union has varied across institutional spheres such as competition policy, monetary affairs, external and internal security, culture and so on, and thus there is need for greater sensitivity to the 'dynamics of various institutional spheres and policy sectors'.[49] Moreover, Olsen also notes that clear causal relationships between the EU and changes at domestic policy levels are difficult to trace since causation operates in both directions. Such processes are, he believes, best studied as 'an ecology of mutual adaptation'.[50] This kind of flexible method of case study, we believe, is the most appropriate method for analysing the application of EU conditionality during enlargement. We distinguish between two main categories of conditionality: between *formal conditionality*, on the one hand, which embodies the publicly stated preconditions as set out in the broad principles of the 'Copenhagen criteria' and the legal framework of the *acquis*, and *informal conditionality*, on the other hand, which includes the operational pressures and recommendations applied by actors within the Commission to achieve particular outcomes during their interactions with CEEC counterparts in the course of enlargement. These two forms of conditionality are not always easily distinguishable since often they operate in tandem. Similarly, we distinguish between the adoption of the *acquis*, a largely formal process of legislative engineering, and adaptation to the *acquis*, a largely informal process, by which mainly legal and institutional norms and practices are adjusted to the new ecology of enlargement.

The analysis which follows in subsequent chapters demonstrates how the unevenness of the *acquis* was reflected in a great deal of variation in the leverage of conditionality, and gave the Commission and the CEEC governments a wide degree of flexibility. Thus, while thinness and ambiguity in the *acquis* reduced the formal conditionality of enlargement, paradoxically it increased the space for the use of informal conditionality, giving the Commission greater scope for ambiguity and imprecision in its policy recommendations to the CEECs. Similarly, while thinness of the *acquis* may have reinforced the power of the Commission to make politically determined assessments as to whether a particular candidate country had complied with the conditionality for membership, it also gave candidate countries more leeway over selecting from the menu of the *acquis* in an *à la carte* fashion.[51]

Conditionality and Europeanization

As with the term conditionality, the term 'Europeanization' has become a part of the common currency of academic debates about the nature of the EU and the project of European integration, and yet it remains a rather nebulous notion. There is still no coherent explanatory framework for the concept though there is a general emphasis on how domestic adaptation to European norms, structures and policies is facilitating greater systemic convergence and advancing European integration. The significance of specific domestic 'context conditions' in the study of Europeanization has only been emphasized fairly recently.[52] Similarly, the 'Europeanizing' effect of EU conditionality for eastward enlargement to the CEECs has so far been generally assumed rather than empirically investigated. As with the term 'conditionality', 'Europeanization' implies a consensus on rules and their transmission mechanisms within the EU, with clear-cut benchmarks, and consistency and continuity in rule adoption over time.

Per definitionem 'Europeanization' suggests a 'top-down' diffusion of common political rules, norms and practices in Europe, but there are significant differences of opinion as to the substantive content of the concept and whether it has meaningful effects within national political systems.[53] When defined broadly, Europeanization is most often associated with 'domestic adaptation to the pressures emanating directly or indirectly from EU membership'.[54] It is also seen as a process that involves 'the penetration of national and sub-national systems of governance by a European political centre and European-wide norms'.[55] With specific reference to EU regional policy Europeanization has been described as 'a positive external shock for promoting institution-building, learning and policy-making innovation at regional and local levels'.[56] At its most fundamental, Europeanization is viewed as 'ways of doing things' which are first defined and consolidated in the making of EU decisions and then incorporated into 'the logic of domestic discourse, identities, political structures and public policies'.[57] A key assumption in this regard is the existence of a mis-fit between state-level and EU-level rules and norms, which pushes the former to converge with the latter. Studies by political scientists of 'Europeanization' tend to emphasize one or more of three key dimensions: its source at the EU level (though there is a lack of precision as to which EU institutions are responsible or have the most effect), its impact on advancing the convergence of institutions and policies, and its role in the norm diffusion essential for 'European' identity construction.[58] By linking institution-building and identity-formation at the European level with domestic change in member states, 'Europeanization' has come to be widely regarded as a main transmission belt for the project of European integration.[59]

A fundamental problem for the concept, however, is that macro-level and policy-level studies are inconclusive about the causal effects of 'Europeanization' and demonstrate the persistence of deep structural divergences across national and policy contexts. Macro-analyses of political structures detect lower levels of Europeanization and convergence than policy-level studies.[60] Studies have suggested that variation of outcomes is inherent in the process of 'Europeanization'. For some the variation is 'incremental, irregular, uneven over time and between locations', suggesting a kind of determinism or developmental inevitability to 'Europeanization'.[61] For others the variation in impacts and outcomes is more deeply structural and indeterminate because the 'domestic impact of Europe varies with the level of European adaptation pressure on domestic institutions and the extent to which the domestic context ... facilitates or prohibits actual adjustments'.[62] Such weaknesses of 'Europeanization' as an analytical tool in the study of EU governance have led Goetz to question whether it is 'a cause in search of an effect'.[63]

Nevertheless, it is generally assumed that the enlargement of the EU has confirmed the successful operation of 'Europeanization', where conditionality has been employed by the EU as a 'reinforcement strategy' to secure compliance with its norms.[64] In principle, there were incentives for CEEC elites to engage in a kind of competitive 'European emulation' and to cooperate with the Commission. The ideocratic and institutional debilitation arising from the exit from communism and the subsequent political and economic transitions, potentially made the key actors and elites in the CEECs weak protagonists in the accession negotiations. The EU's capacity to pressure for policy and institutional change was further enhanced by the fact that the CEECs were transitioning countries that were engaged contemporaneously in fundamental systemic reform that required good relations with the EU. The adjustment to be made by the CEECs, moreover, often involved satisfying conditionality in 'new' policy areas that had had no clear equivalents under the previous communist regime. The process involved wholesale changes in rule of law and regulation, policy-making, institution-building and normative adaptation.

As we shall discuss in the following chapters, however, the detailed analysis of the application of EU conditionality in practice does not substantiate positivist assumptions about norm transfer and 'Europeanization', but rather demonstrates the ambiguities, inconsistencies and contradictions of the process of enlargement.

2
Communist Legacies and Regionalization

Studies of transition generally focus more on the immediate events and processes and less on the historical background which shapes it. Nevertheless, historical legacies and the extent to which a transition state has a 'usable past' are generally recognized as having an important bearing on the transition outcome.[1] The term 'historical legacy' and the issue of 'usability' are, however, not systematically researched in the study of transition. Paradoxically, the more routinely employed concepts of 'path dependency' and 'initial starting conditions' tend to focus on the predetermining effects of decisions taken at the outset of the transition process rather than exploring the influence of historically rooted factors which may be equally important.[2] Moreover, it is also important to take into account not only whether a 'usable past' is present in a particular case but also whether the elites that drive the transition process are willing to draw on it. The decisional calculus of elites is of central importance in transition studies as successful reforms are viewed as being largely dependent on the attitudes and behaviour of elites and how differences between elite segments are negotiated in the 'games' of transition.[3] This kind of emphasis on the role of elites in implementing universalizable progressive change tends to overlook how the context in which transition occurs can have significant constraining effects on the outcome. Transition states are not a *tabula rasa*. Schmitter's definition of transition as an 'interlude' between regimes is much too passive in this regard as it suggests a *pause* and thus fails to capture the essential dynamic attributes of transition, which involve the transformation of one type of regime into another. Consequently, the legacy of the old regime will continue to loom large over the transition process itself. Transitions involve the dismantling of the old regime, generally by the transformation of old elite power networks and the institutional structures which they colonize. It generally involves significant change to the institutional architecture of the state organization. This is not to say that such structures and institutions must be completely displaced, as this would not be a transition but a revolution. Logically, then, transition is the bridging period between regimes which links the old and new structures and elites in a dynamic interplay of change, which is mainly characterized by new forms of 'institution-building'.

One of the most underestimated aspects of post-communist transitions in Eastern Europe is the extent to which they are influenced by the legacies of the communist regimes.[4] While we do not wish to argue that historical legacies overly determine post-communist transition outcomes, the communist-era institutions were the starting-point for domestic political struggles and the interaction with EU conditionality. A specific institutional legacy, including in some cases politicized and regional-level governing structures, meant that post-communist political choices and EU conditionality did not evolve in a vacuum. Moreover, historical legacies also underpinned the resurgence of national and regional identities in the context of transition and Europeanization.[5] As Wolczuk has pointed out: 'Democratization, administrative efficiency, fiscal considerations, EU accession requirements and so forth were cited as the compelling reasons for regionalization, rather than the accommodation of diversity.'[6]

On coming to power after the Second World War communist leaderships rode roughshod over pre-existing regional and local identities and territorial organization, and imposed changes to the territorial organization of power based on two main logics; firstly a power logic, to ensure that state organization was adjusted to secure the power and control of communist parties; and secondly, a functional logic, to configure state organization in a way that maximized the efficiency gains expected from the centrally planned economy. This chapter explores the communist legacy in the organization of sub-national governance structures in Eastern Europe to highlight the complexities of reform faced by post-communist leaderships as they grappled with reform during transition. It demonstrates how one of the key legacies inherited from communism was a systematic weakness of effective institutions of governance at the regional and local levels. The reason for this legacy is straightforward. Communist systems were highly centralized authoritarian systems that were institutionally engineered to secure compliance with communist rule. Communist systems were organized around the Leninist principles of 'democratic centralism', the key element of which was the subordination of nominally independent state structures to the will of the party organization, which itself was highly centralized.

The second part of this chapter explores the different approaches taken by the newly established post-communist governments after 1989 to the reform of sub-national government. In their search for alternatives to the communist model, the post-communist regimes have often looked back to their pre-communist pasts, and to the countries of Western Europe. Equally, they have been faced with a dilemma of adapting structures that were inherited from communism and which have an economic functional logic, for example the communist era statistical-planning units. One of the first democratizing reforms implemented by the new post-communist governments was the reintroduction of local and municipal self-government. In contrast, the establishment of meso-level or regional structures of government has been a highly contentious arena of reform, and as we shall discuss later, in many states it was stalled by party political struggles and crowded reform agendas, thus leading to a somewhat anachronistic situation where power was strongly centralized. In the latter part of the 1990s, the regional reform issue was given a new urgency by the EU enlargement process and in particular by a framing of the debate and negotiations over regional policy in a way which created pressure to accelerate regionalization in order to adapt the institutional environment to the EU's regional policy requirements.

The communist model of sub-national governance

Though governing systems in the countries of Eastern Europe were characterized by a considerable degree of authoritarian uniformity throughout the communist period, this was in stark contrast to the varied history and evolution of sub-national government arrangements in the region up until 1945. Prior to the communist takeover, there was a diversity of local government systems in the countries of Central and Eastern Europe. In those countries and regions which had been part of the Habsburg empire, such as Hungary, Bohemia and Moravia (the Czech lands), and Galicia, a relatively strong system of local self-government had been established. This system remained in place with certain alterations until 1945.[7] The Polish lands had been divided among the three neighbouring imperial powers until 1918 and as a consequence were governed according to three different systems of sub-national administration – the Prussian, Russian and Habsburg –

with differing degrees of centralization and decentralization over time. In the immediate aftermath of the Second World War a number of Eastern European countries initiated decentralizing local government reforms. In the case of the Baltic republics, newly absorbed into the Soviet Union, the highly centralized, hierarchical system of soviets subject to party control was quickly introduced. Likewise, following the communist takeover in Central and Eastern Europe, the countries of the region proceeded to established systems of government based on the soviet model, which allowed no room for genuine democratic accountability in local or regional self-government.[8]

Under the communist one-party-state system, the role of local government was viewed radically differently from the principles espoused by the liberal democratic systems. In the post-war Western European democracies, issues of local democracy and the search for the most efficient mechanisms for service provision predominated.[9] The essential role of local government structures was closely tied to two overriding priorities of the communist system of power: firstly, the maintenance of political control by the party and, secondly, the efficient management of the centrally administered economic system (primarily the implementation of central planning decisions in the localities). These two goals influenced the shape and functioning of sub-national government arrangements as well as the organizational and territorial reforms that were introduced at different times during the communist period. Broadly, the prioritization of the power logic took precedence in the early period of communist rule, while the prioritization of the functional logic came to predominate in the later years of communist rule as the economic system increasingly failed to deliver growth and communist parties found themselves overwhelmed by managerialism in the shift from an extensive to a more intensive pattern of economic production.[10] For the communist party leaderships both of these objectives necessitated a highly centralized, hierarchical system of sub-national governance embodied in the organizational principle of 'democratic centralism'. This principle had two main elements: that the decisions of higher party bodies were binding on lower party bodies, and that party-state organs and party secretaries at every level were formally selected by the party membership, either directly or indirectly (although in practice the selection was made by the higher echelons of the party apparatus).[11]

Given that 'democratic centralism' was a common underlying organizational principle the actual configuration of local government structures was relatively homogeneous across Eastern Europe during the communist period. A vertical pyramidal system of 'elected soviets' (councils) extended down from the national structures at the centre to the regional, district and local levels. In the case of federal systems such as the Soviet Union, Yugoslavia and Czechoslovakia there was also a constituent republic level. These organizational structures provided a façade of popular legitimacy for the regimes while real power was highly centralized to communist party structures. While local councils were supposedly democratically elected, the elections were a sham as candidates were vetted by the communist party apparatus, and in most cases electorates were offered no choice of candidates. Local councils and their executive apparatuses were subject to multiple levels of oversight by parallel and generally overlapping hierarchies, by vertically superior bodies in the soviet administrative hierarchy, and by horizontally superior bodies in the territorial equivalent communist party apparatus and its higher bodies. A key mechanism of control employed by the communist party was the *nomenklatura* system of appointments, which allowed it to approve all important positions in political, economic and social life, and saturate the elite structures with its members. The key personnel at each level generally held equivalent posts in party and soviet bodies, and the key power-holder at the regional and local levels was the party secretary. In this so-called 'command-administrative' system the lines of control and communication moved along the vertical hierarchies, top-down, and there was a lack of horizontal interaction, and accountability in general, across different levels of government and between local and regional governments.

Under the soviet system there was no authoritative separation between representative bodies of local government (in generic terms the 'soviet') and the public administration (the executive council of the soviet). In addition, in line with the emphasis in Soviet Marxist-Leninist ideology on social unity, conflicts of interests between the national, regional and local level were mediated in secret by the communist party. In other words there was no need for the representation of local interests, because either these were synonymous with the interests of the party, and therefore the country as a whole, or alternatively these were manifestations of the phenomenon of 'localism', which was assumed to be in opposition to the party and thus constituted a threat. In principle then, the role of sub-national government structures was to act as a 'transmission belt' for party control from the central government level down through the structures of the state. In reality as socialist countries modernized and became more complex, regional and local leaders (both in the state and party structures) had to be power-brokers, balancing and mediating between the centre and the local interest.[12] The economic means at their disposal, however, were limited as local government competences were characterized by a 'gulf between the fairly wide and unspecified functions to be fulfilled, and the lack of financial and other resources available for their fulfilment'.[13]

As the institutions of sub-national government were an appendage of the communist party in the localities, they became an important mechanism for implementing the 'leading and guiding role' of the party in the country. Organized in a dual but parallel and intersecting hierarchy of party and state institutions, the state administrative units were charged with the implementation of party policy decisions taken at the centre, while the party organs at each level were responsible for exercising 'control' over the implementation process. Not surprisingly, there was a considerable divergence between the principles behind the organization of the system and the way it actually functioned. In practice the roles of party and state organs were often blurred; party officials were under pressure 'from above' to meet plan targets and thus ended up having to interfere in day-to-day management decisions in order to circumvent bottlenecks and other problems arising from the inherent structural defects of central planning. This intensified authority leakage from the state structures to the party apparatus, and led to an actual hollowing out and supplanting of the state by the party.

The particular form of organization of the soviet-type centrally planned economy with all the important (and many minor) economic decisions being taken by the planning agencies and sectoral (branch) ministries at the centre, created an additional chain of control of sub-national government – the ministerial structure. Similar to the state and party vertical line structures described above, the ministerial system was structured in vertical hierarchies from the branch ministries in the centre down to the economic enterprises in the localities, in some cases with the presence of intermediary managing units at the regional level. The branch ministries operationalized the central plans through their enterprises in the localities. The centrality of the plan to communist society meant that economic enterprises also often supplanted local government by performing important service provision locally (building roads, running schools and hospitals, providing welfare services and so forth). The functional importance of the managers was often translated into political dominance of the party apparatus in many areas, thus further undermining the authority of local government structures.

Moreover, the fact that the ministerial system was based on the sectoral organization of the economy whereas the party-state apparatuses were structured along territorial lines was a major source of tension in the communist system and posed a perennial problem of coordination of local government. This tension between sectoral and territorial management was one of the main contributing factors to the intermittent waves of economic and administrative reform that were introduced throughout the communist period in the countries of Eastern Europe.[14] The territorial–sectoral problematic was exacerbated by the fact that the economic organization of each country into planning regions (for the convenience of the sectoral planning and administrative authorities) did not necessarily coincide with the political territorial organization of the party-state.[15] These functional problems with the one-party state and the command economy provided the main impetus for perestroika under Gorbachev.[16]

During the communist era most states in the region made attempts at local government reform. Given the weakness of political accountability and the coercive power of the communist state, territorial boundaries were changed according to shifting political and economic exigencies with little or no concern for the historical and socio-cultural identities attached to particular regions and areas. Public administration, as Surazska et al. have argued, was considered to be 'a short-term organizational task rather than a long-term institutional one'.[17] The nature of territorial organization and reorganization varied depending on the orientation of different leaderships and the goals behind the particular reforms. Notwithstanding intermittent efforts to maximize the efficiency of territorial organizational arrangements for the operation of central planning (for example by changing the number of territorial units, re-weighting the relationship between sectoral and territorial units, and shifts in the balance of competences between central, regional and local governance units), there was a pattern of continuity in the basic institutions of sub-national political and economic governance in Central and Eastern Europe. In fact, the basic institutional architecture in the late 1980s was more or less unchanged from that which had been established in the post-1945 period when communist parties came to power across the region. The reforms (with the exception of the federal reforms in Yugoslavia in 1974, and Czechoslovakia in 1968) did not fundamentally alter the highly centralized nature of the communist system of governance and the largely impotent structures of local government.

The relatively stable continuity that characterized the communist organization and operation of sub-national governance systems in Eastern Europe is diametrically opposed to the trend towards decentralization and deconcentration which emerged to varying degrees in the countries of Western Europe in the post-war period. Devolving responsibilities to the regions (or at the very least establishing deconcentrated state organs at the sub-national level) was not only seen as a conduit for providing improvements in the delivery of services but also was viewed as an important mechanism for raising low levels of public participation and empowering citizens at the local level, and thus exerting a check on central government. The idea that competences should be rooted at the levels which were most appropriate for delivering good governance is a rather ambivalent one, but it is embodied in the principle of 'subsidiarity' in the EU, first formally adopted as an integral part of the EC's regional policy in 1988 and later entrenched by the Treaty of Maastricht (1992).[18]

The trend for the rationalization of smaller local government units into larger entities was common to both Eastern and Western Europe, though the rationale was different. Since the 1970s, states in Western Europe have undergone major reforms of regional and local government that have reduced the number of territorial authorities, in many cases endowing them with new competences and in some cases devolving new powers. This process was partly driven by strategies for modernizing service provision and, from the early 1980s, by 'New Right' ideology that favoured 'shrinking the state' through privatization and the use of private sector agencies to deliver public goods at the local level. In contrast, the system of economic management in communist countries meant that the party-state organs were responsible for the entire formal economy and not just key services. Though economic policy-makers and planners in Eastern Europe, especially in the late communist period, were also motivated by the need to improve service provision and were seeking ways of improving economic performance in the economy as a whole, the notion of 'shrinking the state' or 'reining in the state' was anathema in the context of the soviet-style communist system. For much of the period communist leaderships failed to recognize that the economic problems that dogged their economies were derived from structural flaws in the centrally planned economy itself. Even those reforms which introduced some element of decentralization, such as Kadar's 'new economic mechanism' were driven more by a goal of technocratic and managerial improvements to central planning rather than fundamentally changing its modus operandi or ideological foundations.[19] Furthermore, the use of territorial reorganization to create larger regional structures and to rationalize the distribution of communes and villages into larger intermediary structures was often directed at breaking up the power bases of regional leaders who were seen as acting too independently of the control of the communist party in the centre.[20]

The communist-era legacy described above directly impinged upon the post-communist transition debates about the reform of sub-national government. The communist legacy involved tiers of local and regional state institutions which had little financial or planning responsibility, and performed the function of a systemic transmission belt for 'top-down' party directives. Moreover, these tiers of state administration were designed to control participation and act as a check on spontaneous political mobilization 'from below'.

Transition and the reform of sub-national governance

Following the collapse of the communist regimes in Eastern Europe, the newly installed democratic governments moved quickly to reform their systems of local government. In a reaction against the over-centralization of the communist era all the countries in the region passed legislation in the early 1990s granting broad rights of autonomy to local self-governing units and abolishing or significantly curtailing governance structures at the regional level, which was the level most associated with the former communist party apparatus through the regional party secretaries.[21] The reforms of the early transition period established a firm legal basis for the jurisdictional separation of central and local governments, with the system of self-government at the lowest level enjoying the most autonomy, while central governments retained a strategic role of supervising the legality of local government activities and controlling the funding arrangements.[22] In the absence of provisions for the regional tier, central government ran the administration at the county level and above. Thus the centralized management of many governance functions persisted, largely through the proliferation of deconcentrated units of state administration, that is, state administrative bodies that were located locally but controlled and funded centrally. An exception to this rule was Hungary, where the HDF passed a 1990 Law on Self-Government which instituted a prefect-like system of Commissioners of the Republic who oversaw local government operations and the activities of local branches of state administration in seven regions and the capital. This system was abolished by the socialist government through amendments to the law in 1994 (see Chapter 5).[23]

Having taken this major step towards democratization at the local level, the new national governments opted to delay decisions over the organization and functions of the regional or meso-levels of government. The reasons varied from country to country but generally included: first, a reluctance to decentralize further fearing a loss of government control of political and economic transition; second, the limited resources at the disposal of central government; third, the deep hostility among pro-democracy parties towards the perceived 'conservative' regional tier of government due to the pivotal role of regional party secretaries under communism; fourth, a lack of consensus among the main political parties about how to reorganize the meso-tiers, including how to reconfigure the state territorially, the number of regions, and the extent of devolution of competences; fifth, a political–ideological cleavage between more reformist and neo-liberal national ruling elites and more conservative regional and local elites, where old communist elites remained influential; and sixth, an unwillingness among the newly empowered local-level elites to relinquish powers upwards to a regional level.

The immense rent-seeking opportunities inherent in administrative power during transition provided a sub-text for this struggle over reform. In addition, electoral sequencing also had a damaging effect on centre–regional–local relations and the potential for institutional reform. In many cases the different sequencing of national and local elections, combined with political cycles, led to situations of confrontation between ideologically opposed central and local governments as was the case in Hungary from 1990 to 1994, Poland from 1993 to 1998, and Romania from 1992 to 1996. Such territorialized political conflicts slowed down the process of decentralization, and indeed, in some cases resulted in recentralization.[24]

The organization of sub-national government in the countries of Eastern Europe in the first half of the 1990s shared a number of common characteristics and contradictory trends. With the passage of local self-government legislation across the region, the number of self-governing units at the local level mushroomed in a direct riposte to the communist-era practices of extreme centralization, disenfranchisement and forced amalgamation of local government units. Thus, contrary to the processes of rationalization and reduction in the number of local authority units that have characterized the development of local government in Western Europe in recent decades, the post-1989 trend in most of the CEECs has been for multiplication and consequently greater fragmentation. The extremely small size of many of these local self-government units made for a high degree of dysfunctionality as they lacked a sufficient tax base to fund service-provision. This not only greatly complicated the politics of resource allocation by the central governments, but also increased public disenchantment with the decline of service provision and the transition process in general.

The problems arising from the dysfunctional fragmentary nature of local government provided an additional disincentive for further decentralization, if not offering a rationale for recentralization tendencies at the national level. Attempts to voluntarily amalgamate or promote cooperation among local government units, however, have had minimal success. Legislation in Hungary, for example, to regularize the procedures for amalgamations both on a voluntary and compulsory basis has proved to be unenforceable.[25] In Estonia, there has been a similar apprehension towards mergers among local self-governing units despite generous incentives offered by the central government. The failure to establish appropriate financing arrangements at the local level to enable the newly empowered local governments to carry out their competences also fostered this trend to frame reform in terms of recentralization. The elimination of the former regional level organs without regard to consideration of alternative structures contributed to a 'democratic deficit' at the meso-level of governance.[26] In the majority of countries of the region then, the immediate post-communist period saw the establishment of a single tier of self-governing structures at the local level and deconcentrated units of central government at the meso-level. In the short run at least, this framework inspired a trend towards greater centralization of resources and responsibilities. Thus, we see two opposing trends: a push for self-government at the local level but without providing the necessary administrative and financial resources required to make it effective; and the continued centralization of governmental tasks relating to the regional level.

The question of regionalization was not altogether absent from the policy agenda, although the situation varied across the region. In a number of countries provision was made in the new constitutions for the establishment of a regional tier of government as was the case in the 1993 constitution of the Czech Republic, although a moratorium was imposed on its implementation. In Poland, the post-communist Solidarity government of Tadeusz Mazowiecki had even drawn up the necessary legislation for the establishment of a self-governing tier at the regional level in 1992, but following the fall of the Solidarity coalition government in 1993 and the election of the first post-communist socialist government formed by the SLD in coalition with the PSL, the regionalization process was blocked due to political opposition on the part of the PSL and disagreements over the shape and number of regions to be established.[27] The debates and development of regionalization in Poland and Hungary is further analysed in Chapter 5.

Regionalization and enlargement pressures

The prospect of EU enlargement from 1993 onwards was slow to concentrate the minds of the CEEC elites on how best to comply with the details and implications of EU conditionality on regional policy beyond the general democracy criterion. The design of sub-national government structures has involved policy choices about appropriate organizational models (number of self-governing tiers, role and location of deconcentrated state offices (if any), relation of executive and legislative structures, financing arrangements) as well as the regional territorial breakdowns particularly in terms of establishing a regional development framework (see Table 2.1). The problem of design has been compounded by the weakness or absence of legal provisions concerning the activities of local government. Following the decentralization of power to the local level in the early 1990s, local units of government have not only inherited a whole range of new competences that were previously performed by the central government or sectoral ministries, but they have also been given inadequate financial, administrative and personnel resources to perform the new functions.[28] Paradoxically, the blurring of the separation between party and state structures that was so characteristic of the communist period has carried over into the post-communist period as the roles of local state administrative bodies and of local self-governments are poorly demarcated and are suffused with party political clientelism. In addition, neo-liberal tight fiscal policies, whether driven by pressures from international lenders or ideological rectitude on the part of governments, has meant that there have been scant resources and questionable will on the part of central governments to fully fund the local level.[29]

During the period of communist rule, territorial organization was regarded as an instrument to further the goals of the party at the centre, which meant that governments regularly resorted to manipulating territorial arrangements and to introducing administrative changes in the search for short-term solutions to particular institutional or economic problems. This practice of manipulating levels of territorial

Table 2.1 Sub-national government in the CEECs

Form of governance	Czech Republic	Estonia	Hungary	Poland	Slovenia
Regional	14 regions with elected assemblies based on a party list system (2000)	No regional level of government	No regional level of government	16 regions (*województwa*) with some self-governing powers (1999), with quasi-prefects (*wojewoda*) appointed by PM. Elected regional assembly elects a Marshall	No regional level of government
RDA/ROC[a]	1 'Regional Coordination Group' in each NUTS II region as a basis for RDCs	National RDA set up in 1997	8 RDAs based on 7 NUTS II regions confirmed in 1999	16 RDAs under Polish Agency for Regional Development	12 functional planning regions corresponding to NUTS III statistical units created in 1999, with provision for RDAs
County	77 districts with assemblies composed of delegates from local self-government authorities	15 counties. No county self-government. Govemor appointed by central government for 5 years	19 counties with elected assemblies	373 districts (*powiaty*) including 65 urban municipalities with elected councils	No district level

Table 2.1 Sub-national government in the CEECs *continued*

Form of governance	**Czech Republic**	**Estonia**	**Hungary**	**Poland**	**Slovenia**
State Offices	Powerful and extensive system of state district offices were abolished in late 2002	State administrative offices at county level to supervise legality of local government acts	State officials at local level appointed by central government and have specific powers in key policy areas	State administrative offices are integrated into administration	58 deconcentrated state administrative units largely carried over from the communist system
Local government	Approx. 6200 local governments. Mayors elected by local councils, both have a 4-year term	254 municipalities with considerable autonomy over local services. Largely dependent on national budget. Local councils elected for 3-year term. Mayors elected by local councils	3126 local self-governments with extensive powers over local affairs. Mayors directly elected	2489 self-government authorities (*gminy*) with elected councils. Mayor elected by the local council	193 municipalities (11 urban) of varying sizes and with responsibility for local service
NUTS II regions	8 NUTS II regions created in 1998	The whole country is classified as a NUTS I and NUTS II region	7 NUTS II regions created in 1999	*Województwa* correspond to 16 NUTS II regions	The whole country is classified as a NUTS I and NUTS II region until 2006

Table 2.1 Sub-national government in the CEECs *continued*

Form of governance	Czech Republic	Estonia	Hungary	Poland	Slovenia
Current state of reform	Still not clear how far state offices will withdraw from previous roles	Process of voluntary merger of local governments underway	Powerful county-based interests obstruct stronger regional government	Consolidation of *województwa* level continues	Further regional governance reform unlikely

Table 2.1 Sub-national government in the CEECs *continued*

Form of governance	Slovakia	Romania	Bulgaria	Latvia	Lithuania
Regional	8 regions with elected assemblies	No regional governance tier	9 regions headed by governors appointed by the central government	No regional governance tier	No regional governance tier
RDA/RDC[a]	Regional Coordinating and Monitoring Committees established at the NUTS II level and regional development agencies at the NUTS III level	8 Regional Development Agencies created in 1998 under the National Agency for Regional Development. Subordinated to Ministry of Development and Prognosis in 2000	No RDAs. A number of 'experts' are appointed by regions and government to the Ministry of Regional Development	No RDAs. The Regional Development Law of 2002 established a National Regional Development Council	No RDAs
County	79 districts	41 counties (*judets*) plus Bucharest, with directly elected councils headed by presidents. Prefects appointed by the government	273 municipalities, with councils and most mayors being directly elected	Two-tier system of 26 districts and seven cities with the combined functions of districts and municipalities	10 districts headed by governors appointed by the PM

Table 2.1 Sub-national government in the CEECs *continued*

Form of governance	Slovakia	Romania	Bulgaria	Latvia	Lithuania
State offices	22 branches of state administration	N/A	N/A	5 ministries are deconcentrated partly to local offices.	N/A
Local government	2675 local self-governments, dependent on central government for funding	2688 communes, and 263 town governments, of which 84 have municipality status. Directly elected councils and mayors. Legally have similar status and powers as *judets* level	Almost 4000 urban and rural councils with minimal powers	69 towns, 1 regional, and 483 rural municipalities, responsible for basic services	56 municipalities, with elected councils and indirectly elected boards headed by mayors, Some financial independence based on local income taxes
NUTS II regions	4 NUTS II regions	8 NUTS II regions	6 NUTS II regions	The whole country is classified as a NUTS I and NUTS II region.	The whole country is classified as a NUTS I and NUTS II region
Current state of reform	Regional boundaries are highly ethnified and controversial	Strong political focus on centralized government	Further decentralization of powers likely	Further regional governance reform unlikely	A new law on regional development is in preparation

Note: [a] Regional Development Agency/Council.

organization to achieve particular political and economic ends continues to have a strong influence in the post-communist period. Thus, another factor explaining why the process of regionalization has been heavily politicized during the transition is that regional and local government is an important mechanism of political control and patronage dispersal for governments and opposition alike, and the parties have jockeyed for position to maximize their advantage from any institutional outcome.[30] Once countries opened negotiations with the European Commission on their accession in 1998 and began the lengthy process of fulfilling the political and technical criteria for membership the focus of party political struggles over regional issues shifted to include the question of how to configure the regions to match the NUTS II criteria and thus maximize the benefits from EU structural funds, thereby reinforcing the political instrumentalization of regional issues. Discussions about regionalization became an integral part of the accession negotiations. At the same time, the Commission was attempting to shape the regionalization process by employing PHARE to provide technical advice on regionalization strategies to meet the requirements of Chapter 21 of the *acquis*. What influence the Commission had on the shape of the reforms is discussed in Chapter 3.

Hungary was regarded as an 'icebreaker' in this regard, and cooperated quickly and closely with PHARE officials in designating statistical-planning regions that matched NUTS II criteria in 1995–96.[31] Other large CEEC states, such as Poland, the Czech Republic, Slovakia, and Bulgaria lagged some two years behind and, as we shall discuss below, did not accelerate their regionalization plans until 1998, after the first Regular Reports had criticized their weaknesses in this area. The smaller candidate states such as Slovenia, Estonia, Latvia and Lithuania have settled on a two-tier structure with deconcentrated administrative offices at the regional or county level. Romania has also followed this path with self-governing units at the local level and a system of centrally appointed prefects at the county level.

Case studies

Czech Republic

Prior to the formation of Czechoslovakia in 1918, administrative and territorial organization differed considerably in the Czech lands and Slovakia. Under the Habsburg empire's dual monarchy, Slovakia was subject to centralized, hierarchical rule from Budapest as part of the

Hungarian kingdom, whereas the Czech lands, which belonged to the Austrian part of the empire, enjoyed a considerable degree of autonomy with three tiers of local government (municipalities, districts and regions) each with its own elected body.[32] Despite initial intentions to adopt a prefect type administrative system at the time of the establishment of Czechoslovakia, in the event the land system with limited self-government was introduced enabling the central authorities to better 'manage' the substantial German and Hungarian minorities in the country. After the Second World War and in the wake of the communist revolution in 1948 the 'land' system in Czechoslovakia was replaced with 20 new sub-national territories (*kraje*) (including Prague). The *kraje* resembled the small prefect type units that the pre-war government had contemplated but never implemented.[33] The country was divided into a hierarchy of national committees at the local, district and regional levels which, as in all communist systems, were responsible to the party rather than to their local constituents. The constitutional and administrative reforms of 1960 halved the number of regions and concentrated more power to the regional party secretaries. The latter process was consolidated further by the post-Prague Spring reforms of October 1968, when the unitary state was replaced by a federal system.[34]

With the collapse of the communist regime, Czechoslovakia, like its neighbours throughout the East European region, moved quickly to pass new legislation to reform local self-government, granting both political and economic powers to municipalities. Further constitutional-administrative reforms in 1971 had consolidated the role of the National Committees as a key link between the centre–regional–local command chain of the communist party, and thus during the transition they were viewed as an obstacle to democratization. There was widespread agreement on their abolition but the question of what kind of regional-level government should replace them was left unresolved. The neo-liberal governments of Klaus preferred to keep strong central control in order to push through reforms with the minimum of institutional challenges from 'below'.[35] The provisions of the legislation on local self-government contributed to the proliferation of local municipalities (with elected assemblies and local administrations) creating serious problems of fragmentation and deterring further decentralization. Between 1990 and late 1993 the number of municipalities increased by 50.9 per cent reaching a total of 6196.[36] This was in part a democratic reaction to the extreme centralization of the communist period, and in part the result of the financial incentives contained in the legislation.

Thus, despite the democratic euphoria of the early post-communist period, the Czech Republic in fact remained a highly centralized state. The absence of county-level government structures left an institutional void that was filled by sectoral ministries and other national agencies which proceeded to establish deconcentrated offices with overlapping territorial responsibilities.[37] In effect the deconcentrated offices of state administration, established at the district level to carry out the functions delegated by the central government, were the most powerful institutions in local governance.[38] The seventy-seven district offices were headed by nominees of the central government and were supposed to act as a check on the indirectly elected district assemblies (composed of the delegates of local self-governments). These assemblies enjoyed the critical function of approving the budget of the district office. This system was, in essence, a return to the Habsburg administrative model of central supervision of local self-government.[39]

While Articles 99 and 100 of the 1993 Czech constitution provide for the establishment of regional self-government (what is termed a tier of 'higher territorial self-governing bodies'), the delay in establishing a regional tier was largely due to the opposition of the main governing party, Vaclav Klaus's Civic Democratic Party (ODS) (1992–97) which favoured turning the districts (*okresy*) into the higher territorial self-governing tier.[40] The main variants included the retention from the communist era of the nine districts of the Czech part of the former Czechoslovakia plus one new one for Moravia, or alternatively, 17 new regions based on large urban centres. Another proposal was that the country be regionalized or federalized based on the 'historic' districts of Bohemia and Moravia. Some opponents of regionalization argued that the Czech Republic should be considered one region comparable in size to Bavaria and therefore did not need to be further sub-divided.[41] A Constitutional Act on the Formation of the Regions was approved by both chambers of the parliament by the end of 1997, by which time the Klaus government had lost power, although it did not enter force until 1 January 2000. The act established 14 regions (*kraje*), but it was only in 2000 that the legislation on the powers of the regional assemblies and rules for their election was passed. Subsequently, in 1998 eight so-called 'cohesion' regions conforming to NUTS II criteria were formed, each overlapping with one or more of the *kraje*.

Hungary

In the post-1867 Habsburg era, the Hungarian kingdom of the dual monarchy instituted a centralized hierarchical system of territorial administrative structures leaving little place for autonomous local self-government. Following the accession to power of the communists in Hungary a two-tier soviet-type system of sub-national government was introduced in 1950 with soviets at the county and local level. The county (*megyek*) system, which has its roots in the Middle Ages, was largely left unchanged at that time, though county borders were changed subsequently. Under Kadar, the public administration system was reformed in 1968 to introduce a degree of electoral competition at the local level. However, although compared with other Eastern bloc states more competences were increasingly devolved to the sub-national level in the late communist period, the essence of the centralized, hierarchical communist system remained unchanged until the collapse in 1988–89.

Local government reform was a key element of the transition in Hungary. The 1990 Local Government Act was preceded by three years of policy debate and preparation which was supported by the reformist wing of the Communist Party.[42] It resulted in the establishment of a two-tier, non-hierarchical system of self-government at both the county and local levels, with each level of government enjoying its own separate mandate and jurisdiction.[43] The stipulation in the constitution that any enfranchised citizen of a village, town or county is entitled to local self-government resulted in the mushrooming of local government units. The number of municipalities virtually doubled between 1991 and 1998 from 1607 to 3154.[44] At the county level, 19 self-government units with councils – initially elected indirectly by representatives of local governments but post-1994 by direct voting – were formed with a four-year mandate. Local authorities have extensive constitutionally protected powers over local affairs. In addition provision was made for a network of state administrative offices, independent of the county and municipal governments and responsible directly to the central government. These deconcentrated state administrative offices operating at the county level manage administrative matters that fall outside the authority of local self-governments in several areas, including land registration, tax administration and public health.[45]

A third short-lived institutional feature of the Hungarian system was the establishment in 1990 of the 'Commissioners of the Republic' who were appointed by the president for seven 'regions' and the capital. In effect, these regions were created on the basis of the communist-era planning regions.[46] Their main responsibilities involved prefect-like supervision of the legality of the operations of local governments and the coordination of the activities of the local state administrative authorities. Given the fragmentation and lack of capacity of local self-government units, the number of state administrative offices proliferated and the Commissioners of the Republic became powerful and proactive actors at the regional and local levels, to the increasing disgruntlement of the municipal and county governments.[47] In 1994, when the Hungarian Socialist Party came to power, the Commissioners of the Republic were abolished and replaced by a system of public administration offices (PAOs) in the counties and the capital which had essentially the same functions although heads of PAOs were henceforth to be appointed by the Minister of the Interior. At the same time greater responsibility was handed over to county-level self-governments. Under the two-tier system established in Hungary, there is a high degree of jurisdictional autonomy between central and local affairs and also between the two tiers of local government (see Chapter 5).[48]

Poland

Prior to Poland's formation in 1918, the country had been divided between three different empires – Russia, Germany and the Austro-Hungarian empire – each of which had different governance systems and operated different degrees of central control at the sub-national level. Government was more authoritarian in the eastern part of Poland, which was part of the Russian empire, while in Galicia the dual administrative system of the Austro-Hungarian empire was in place, and in the areas that were part of the German Reich (Posen, Western Prussia and parts of Pomerania) a more centralized system was in place based on the two-tier Napoleonic structure.[49] With the accession to power of the communists, these differences were subsumed under the soviet system of rule. Poland had a three-tier sub-national governing structure – *gminy* at the local level, the *powiaty* at the district level and *województwa* at the regional level – which formed the integrated, centralized hierarchy that was a characteristic of all soviet type party-state systems. While there was a certain degree of continuity in the territorial organization of Poland in the early communist years some changes were introduced. For example, administrative changes were introduced at the municipal level, the larger local units (the *gminy*) were split into smaller units, and rural administration was carried out by the *powiaty* which in practice meant the amalgamation of smaller units.[50] A comprehensive territorial reorganization was introduced in 1975 resulting in the restructuring of the *województwa* and *powiaty* levels. The historic appellation *województwo* was retained but the new regions were much smaller (a third of their former size) and the *powiaty* were totally abolished. Rather than facilitating central economic and political management, the 1975 reforms actually weakened the communist system owing to the disruption caused by the abolition of the deep-rooted *powiaty* which was a key level for securing communist control.[51] The reforms were soon abandoned and followed by a cycle of recentralization that was spurred on by the rise of Solidarity and the imposition of military rule in 1980–81.[52] Thus the basic centralized top-down approach remained largely unchanged until the collapse of the communist government.

Local government reform was on the agenda at the round-table talks between the Communist Party and Solidarity in 1988–89. Following the accession to power of the Mazowiecki government in August 1989, legislation was quickly passed to re-establish self-government at the local level.[53] The 1990 Local Government Act transformed Poland from a three-tier system into a two-tier system with strong central government and local government limited to about 2500 local authorities responsible for all public activities that were not assigned to other public institutions.[54] In the initial post-communist period, the meso-level remained weak, dominated by state deconcentrated organs: 49 regions remained as institutional appendages directly subordinate to the central government, as did 287 district offices of state administration that retained responsibility for the most important services. Assemblies of representatives from the municipalities were established in the 49 regions, but their powers were limited.[55] A Task Force for Regional Policy was established by the Mazowiecki government in 1989 to draw up plans for the reconfiguration of territorial government in Poland. There was interminable wrangling over the shape of a future meso-level tier of government, and given the instability of governments in the mid-1990s the reform was continually postponed. The Polish Peasants Party, for example, which formed part of the governing coalition from 1993 to 1997 vigorously opposed the reinstatement of self-government at the *powiaty* level for fear of losing power and alienating their supporters in rural areas and small towns.[56]

Thus, paradoxically, in the first decade of Poland's post-communist rule, while there was a consensus about the desirability of decentralization, what transpired was a process of centralization.[57] While some new responsibilities were decentralized to the local level following the 1990 reform, the capacity of municipal governments to act was constrained by their weak fiscal position resulting in a return to some of the operational practices of the communist era. In particular, there was a resurgence in the power of sectoral hierarchies directed by the central government at the meso-level as regional administrative branches of particular economic ministries were established in some areas. Finally, in 1998, a year after the accession to power of the Solidarity Electoral Alliance-Freedom Union government (AWS-UW), a series of laws were passed that paved the way for a three-tier self-governing system, including the re-establishment of the *województwa* level, but this time with elected regional self-governments. Moreover, the new regions were demarcated to comply with the EU's NUTS II criteria (see Chapter 5).

Slovakia

As part of the Hungarian kingdom in the late Habsburg period, Slovakia was subject to hierarchical centralized rule from Budapest. During the communist period as part of the Czech and Slovak Socialist Republic, the three tiers of sub-national governance in Slovakia were structured along the lines of the soviet model. Following the collapse of communism, the key regional tier of government in Czechoslovakia, the national committees, was dissolved. Under the municipal law passed in the autumn of 1990, local self-governments (with limited competences) were established in Slovakia with state administrative units at the district and sub-district level. As in other states, the number of poorly resourced local self-governing units mushroomed. Though the creation of a second tier of self-government units and a new territorial division were proposed in the concept of public administration reform drawn up by the government of prime minister Čarnogursky in 1991, the final decision was left until the dissolution of Czechoslovakia was agreed and the new parliament of an independent Slovakia was in place. After the June 1992 elections, the government was preoccupied by the political and economic problems of separation, as a result of which the problems of public administration were pushed further down the political agenda. The accession to power of the nationalist and highly centralizing government of Vladimir Meciar (1994–98) led to a further delay in the introduction of decentralizing reforms to the regional and local levels.[58]

In 1996, the law on the territorial and administrative arrangements of the Slovak Republic and the law on local state administration were approved. The reform was essentially a state administrative rather than a decentralizing reform. The number of state administrative regions was increased from four to eight and the number of districts was doubled from 38 to 79. Thus, Slovakia had four levels of administration (central, county, district and local level). The county and district levels were state deconcentrated units rather than self-government structures. The counties were headed by a 'principal' appointed by the government. Regions and districts had no independent resources as their budgets were drawn up by the Ministry of the Interior and funded exclusively from the central treasury. Meanwhile, the 2850 local units enjoyed the rights of self-government but were weakened by their lack of independent financial resources. The regionalization process was further complicated by the presence of a territorialized Hungarian minority in the south-west of the country, bordering Hungary. Consequently, regionalization became a highly politicized issue due to Slovak fears about Hungarian separatism, and Hungarian demands for autonomy. Meciar's regional demarcation of 1996 drew the regional boundaries in a way which gerrymandered the Hungarian minority, splitting its population across several regions and thus weakening its political presence in the regions.[59]

The EU was sharply critical of the perceived authoritarianism of the Meciar government and accession negotiations with Slovakia were frozen. When the more liberal and pro-EU government of Mikulas Dzurinda came to power in 1998, the decentralization of public administration was a key aim because of the pressures to accelerate Slovakia's EU accession process. Nevertheless, the reform was delayed by coalition disagreements about the number and shape of the regions. There were those that supported a four-region structure as under the former communist system, the opposition favoured eight regions to match the existing state administrative regions which they themselves had set up while in government, and the centre-right governing parties and the Hungarian coalition partner party had proposed a twelve-region solution (as this would have made one Hungarian-dominated region a certainty).[60] Finally, in July 2001 the Slovak parliament passed the new law on local public administration which provided for the devolution of government prerogatives to eight regional self-governing entities which conformed with EU NUTS II criteria. Although the government itself had, in the end, approved the establishment of twelve new regions, this proposal was defeated by a temporary coalition of nationalist opposition and governing parties. The demarcation of the new regional structures ensured that the power of the Hungarian minority would be diluted across several predominantly Slovak populated regions.

Slovenia

Although a centralized planning economic management and political system was established in Yugoslavia in 1945, from the early 1950s onwards measures leading to the decentralization of political and economic decision-making began to be introduced. In 1949 a quasi-federal system was introduced with six republics and two autonomous provinces. In 1952 the multi-tier sub-national governance system was streamlined into districts and communes, the latter being based on the amalgamation of smaller towns and villages. In 1963 the central government went a step further, abolishing the districts and thus leaving the system of communes as the main unit of sub-national self-government. Accompanying economic reforms granted greater independence to enterprises and opened the way for the market to play an expanded role in the Yugoslav economy.[61] Perhaps the most important difference between Yugoslavia and the other communist countries in the region is that public administration was separated from the economy and in addition, both administrative and economic organizations at the sub-national level over time enjoyed substantial autonomy.[62]

As part of Yugoslavia, Slovenia was divided into 65 relatively large municipalities and communes, which performed the functions both of central state administration and of local authorities and enjoyed considerable political power.[63] During the 1970s twelve functional planning and administrative units managed the increasingly mixed economy. Despite the institutional legacy of Yugoslav federalism, its close geographical proximity to EU and West European states with federal or highly decentralized systems of local governance (Austria, Italy and Switzerland), and to post-communist transition states such as Hungary that were engaged in rapid decentralization to the communal level, Slovenia exhibited no contagion effects to reform its local government system. After independence, the state-directed fused system in which municipalities typically performed both state administrative and local government functions was retained. The new constitution of Slovenia, enacted in 1993, made provision for self-government at both the local and regional level, but it was not until the passage of the 1993 Law on Local Self-Government that the path was cleared for the establishment of local self-governments at the municipal level. At present there are 192 municipalities (11 of which are urban municipalities). These vary considerably in terms of size, population and economic power. In addition, there are 58 state administrative units whose jurisdiction may extend over several municipalities depending on the specific competences.[64] No further steps have been taken to establish a meso-tier of self government. Article 143 of the constitution gives the *obcine* (communal municipalities) the right to join together to create regions on a voluntary basis but no attempt was made to do this until 1998. Slovenia, like Estonia, is a small country with no historical tradition of regional governance and no obvious political functional need for it. Nonetheless the debate over the possible territorial breakdown of a regional self-governing tier has surfaced on a number of occasions. In particular, successive Slovenian governments have been concerned at the prospect of losing structural funds due to the wealth concentration around Ljubljana. Consequently, to avoid this problem Slovenia tried to demarcate two NUTS II regions but has been blocked by the Commission (see Chapter 3).

Estonia

As one of the republics of the former Soviet Union, Estonia had its own republican Supreme Soviet in Tallinn, with the dual structure of soviets and party organs extending from the Estonian capital down to the counties and localities. The revitalization of 'socialist self-government' during perestroika provided a catalyst for movements for autonomy and independence in the Baltic republics, ultimately contributing to the break-up of the Soviet Union.[65] In Estonia, the democratization of local government proceeded slowly at first, but accelerated as the republic moved towards independence in 1989–91.

From 1989 to 1993 Estonia had a two-tier system of local self-government comprising units at both the municipal and county level. In 1993 Estonia rationalized this into a single tier that was organized in a vertical, centralized structure. The elected intermediary structure at the county level was replaced by an appointed stratum of state administrative officials. The single tier system of local self-government includes 253 municipalities (46 urban and 207 rural). Local authorities enjoy considerable autonomy, are responsible for administering public services and have their own budget, although they remain fiscally dependent on the centre since 65 per cent of local government resources comes from a share of state income taxes and grants. County-level governance is an appendage of central government. The 15 county governments (the territorial division has not been amended in the course of the transition) are responsible for organizing and coordinating the work of national institutions at the local level and for implementing national policies in accordance with the law and instructions of the government. They also exercise a supervisory role over local self-government institutions. The county governor is a political appointee of the prime minister (in consultation with local government representatives), and serves for a five-year term. In addition, county assemblies made up of representatives of local self-governments have minor competences.

In 1995 the Estonian government introduced a policy encouraging the voluntary merger of local governments, with the aim of reducing the number of units from 247 to around 100. The first amalgamation took place in 1998.[66] Given the extremely slow progress on the voluntary merger scheme a set of financial incentives has been introduced to foster greater uptake of this option.[67] There is no regional self-government in Estonia and little evidence of elite support for meso-level government, although this is not to say that the question of regionalization has been absent from the political agenda. Perhaps the most controversial aspect and greatest disincentive to reform is that regionalization may result in local political power shifting to the territorialized minority of russophones (mainly ethnic Russians) in a few areas, such as Narva, and even possibly the capital Tallinn, a prospect that generates fears about Estonian ethnic hegemony and the territorial integrity of the state.[68]

Romania

From its formation in 1919–20, Romania was administered in a very centralized manner, with a system of counties and prefects. With the establishment of communist rule, a system of *rayon* (or territorial production complexes) and provinces was set up in 1950 to carry out planning and public administration tasks. Intermittent reforms and territorial reorganizations took place throughout the communist period with the aim of increasing political control and improving economic management although the intrinsic hierarchical structures of administration remained unchanged. The most far-reaching reform was introduced in 1967 when the *rayon* system and provinces were replaced by a system of counties *(judet)* and communes, a process which included the forced mergers of villages to form the smallest units of public administration. This reform instituted a system of subnational territorial arrangements along the lines of the former pre-communist monarchical model. A limited decentralization of management which took place in the wake of the 1967 reform was largely undone in 1980 when there was a further retrenchment of the central planning system by making county-level party committees fully responsible for economic performance in their respective regions.[69]

The collapse of the Ceaucescu regime in December 1989 did not lead to immediate reforms to the system of governance at the regional or local levels as the first reforms came only in 1991. This time-lag in comparison to other post-communist states reflected both the country's historic centralist traditions and its hesitant post-communist transition path. The first local elections were held in the autumn of

1992, embedding a two-tier non-hierarchical system of administration. At the local level there are 2688 communes (made up of one or several villages) and 263 towns of which 84 have the status of a municipality. In each local unit, there is a directly elected council and mayor, which enjoy powers of self-government. Despite the passage of the Local Public Administration Act (1991) there are few safeguards of the independence of local governing units against control from central authorities.[70] The 41 counties plus Bucharest make up the intermediary tier and form the basic architecture for deconcentrated public administration. Each county is headed by a prefect who acts as the central government representative at the local level, and thus oversees the implementation of government policy at the sub-national level. At the county level there are also directly elected councils which coordinate the activities of local administrations. The county council elects a president from its ranks to perform executive functions at the county level although in practice the prefect tends to dominate at the county level.[71] Following the 1996 amendments to the law on public administration, additional responsibilities for regional development were devolved to the counties (including spatial and economic planning and investment programmes). The financial instruments available for regional development initiatives are extremely sparse, and the problematic financial relationship between central and local levels of government has undermined the supposedly non-hierarchical relationship between the different levels of government and between the state deconcentrated and self-governing organs.[72]

Ultimately Romania remains a highly centralized country and despite its size, no moves have been taken to introduce an intermediary self-governing tier between the centre and the local level. As in Slovakia, the reluctance to establish elected regional governance is largely politically motivated by the fear of separatism from the territorialized Hungarian minority.[73] Indeed, when PHARE coordinated the establishment of eight macro-regions in Romania under the Law on Regional Development of July 1998, it proved to be too controversial as it was seen as empowering the territorialized Hungarian minority and constituting a threat to the territorial integrity of the state.

Conclusion

While regional and local governance under communism was relatively uniformly structured, it was subject to strong political controls from the centre and was driven by predominantly functionalist goals, with sub-national units acting as an organizational pillar of the one-party state and central planning. Two main contradictory trends were evident in the post-communist era: decentralization versus recentralization. The decentralizing impetus occurred in those states which tolerated a fragmentation of state authority leading to a proliferation of local governance units (Hungary, Czech Republic, Slovenia) as a key means of overcoming the authoritarian legacy of communism and accelerating transition. This trend was characterized by four features: first, new local government self-financing regulations provided an incentive for fragmentation in local government that led to the proliferation of municipalities and communes; second, it was partly an opportunistic reaction and assertion of power by sub-national elites to the weakness of central states in the early phase of transition; third, the competition between central and local elites over distributive issues, in particular the rush into 'nomenklatura privatization' was reflected in ideological and institutional struggles between reformist central governments and more conservative regional and local authorities; and fourth, this trend was a democratizing reaction to the overly-centralized and functionalist 'command-administrative' communist system. This reaction resulted in the abolition or diminution in the role of regional government, a level which under communism had been a critical link in the authority chain between central and local rulers. Significantly, in many states post-communism led to a revival of the political mobilization of local identities within historically bounded sub-national government, as in Hungary where the counties are resisting efforts to politically regionalize the country. Elsewhere, new functionalist criteria were developed in the organization and orientation of regional and local governance, as in the new regions of Poland.

The second trend involved a reconcentration of power to the centre, though the reasons for this varied. The reimposition of strong central governance was driven by authoritarian reactions by central elites to democratic transition (Slovakia), or was impelled by the need for strong central government in states where sovereignty was perceived to be threatened by territorialized internal minorities or an external power (as in Estonia). In some states it was motivated by a combination of authoritarian reaction and fear of territorialized internal minorities (as in Romania). In their search for a new institutional architecture of regionalization, policy-makers in the CEECs were influenced by a number of push and pull factors. On the one hand, the resonance of the pre-communist and communist-era legacies tended to frame the political debates over policy options. A desire to combat the power logic of the communist system of control promoted in many states a drive for decentralization to the local level rather than the regional. On the other hand, the existence of the framework of economic and planning regions inherited from the communist era and its functional logic, compounded by the pressure from the Commission for a regionalization that matched the technical standardization of the NUTS system, exercised an enormous pull for regionalization to proceed, particularly in the larger countries. Consequently, the imperative of finding appropriate organizational forms and of developing adequate administrative capacities to meet the requirements for EU regional policy acted as a catalyst for the reform of regional government in the CEECs. The reforms, however, as we shall see in Chapter 5, were shaped in the main by the domestic constraints and context of transition.

3
The Commission, Conditionality and Regional Policy

When the EU first acknowledged that those associated CEECs that 'so desire' could become members, at the Copenhagen European Council meeting in June 1993, it expressed the political and economic conditions for membership in vaguely worded and normative statements of intent in the 'Copenhagen criteria'. As we discussed in Chapter 1, the criteria laid down three conditions for applicant states (the stability of their democracy, the proper functioning of their market economy, and their capacity to integrate with the EU) and a fourth condition related to the EU's own capacity to absorb the new members (see Box 1.1). Although the details of how these conditions were to be met were not elaborated at the time, by implication it was understood that some objective criteria would be devised by which to evaluate applicants. The fourth condition gave the EU a pocket veto on the accession of new members, since it would take the final decision on whether it was ready to enlarge. The Copenhagen Council also ordered organizational changes to progress the accession including a reinforcement of the PHARE programme of aid and technical assistance which had been established in 1989 and was already managed by the Commission, the establishment of a 'structured' multilateral dialogue of high-level meetings between the Council, Commission and the candidate countries (at the level of heads of state and government once a year, and ministerial level once or twice per year depending on issue area), and the creation of a special task force to train officials from the candidate countries in EU law and operational procedures. By these means the convergence of the candidate countries' legislation with the *acquis* would be accelerated and their national elites could be acculturated into EU norms and mindsets.[1]

Following the Copenhagen summit, the Commission pursued a 'pre-accession strategy' for enlargement which focused on bilateral relations with the national governments of applicant states.[2] The strategy formulated at the Essen European Council 1994 was built around the by now four established pillars of the EU-CEEC relationship; the 'Europe Agreements' on the liberalization of trade which were negotiated in 1991–92 (signed between 1991–96, but came into force between 1995–98), PHARE, the 'structured dialogue', and legislative alignment. The bilateralism inherent in the strategy for enlargement was steadily reinforced both at the Essen European Council in December 1994 and the Madrid European Council in December 1995.[3] What is striking about this cumulative bilateral strategy is that the process of enlargement was structured as one for negotiation between the EU and the national elites of the applicant states. While this approach made sense – the EU is, after all, a union of sovereign states – it did leave an Achilles heel in the process by excluding other elites (notably in our case, the regional and local elites) and the wider public from participation at all stages of the process. These actors would only be included in the final stage, after the negotiations had been concluded and the decision required ratification by the people of each candidate country.

Though in line with previous rounds of EU enlargement, the lack of involvement of sub-national actors in the preparation of the candidates for EU regional policy is indicative of the Commission's 'top-down' approach to the processes of enlargement and 'Europeanization' in the CEECs and constituted a 'regional deficit' in enlargement.[4] The paradox is that while the EU marginalized the participation of sub-national elites in its enlargement strategy, among its main concerns over integration was the issue of how best to organize and involve regional and local governments in the implementation of EU policy. After all, the administrative and 'absorption' capacity of these levels is seen as critical for the success of the whole enlargement project. At the Essen European Council 1994, for example, issues of regional cooperation and infrastructural integration via trans-European networks were introduced into the pre-accession strategy, and regional development became one of the priorities of PHARE. The regional dimension of enlargement was also discussed at the Madrid European Council (1995), not surprisingly as Spain was a major beneficiary of EU structural funds and it put on the EU agenda the implications of enlargement for the allocation of structural funds. The Madrid Council introduced a supposedly clarifying condition to the effect that the candidate countries must have the 'administrative capacity' to implement the *acquis*.[5] It was only at this stage, two and half years after the Copenhagen criteria were formulated, that the Commission was charged to prepare a detailed analysis of the impact of enlargement on the EU (especially agriculture and structural policy) and draft 'opinions' evaluating each applicant country individually.

The Commission's report 'Agenda 2000 for a Stronger and Wider Europe', published in July 1997, formulated a 'reinforced pre-accession strategy', which sidelined the 'structured dialogue' and introduced a strategy shift from multilateralism to bilateralism in the negotiations over accession negotiations. The shift was explained as offering a better mechanism for addressing the country-specific needs identified in the Commission's Opinions on the preparedness to join of each applicant country which were published contemporaneously. There was barely any reference to the regional or local dimensions in the Commission's evaluation of the fulfilment of the Copenhagen criteria. The shift in focus from the national level as the unit of analysis was evident only in the Commission's Opinions on the readiness of each applicant state, as only here, for the first time, was regional 'capacity' identified as a heading for the underlying lack of preparedness of the CEECs for membership.[6] Consequently, instruments such as the 'reinforced pre-accession strategy', 'Accession Partnerships' between the EU and applicant states, the 'National Programme for the Adoption of the *Acquis*' (NPAA) to be implemented in each candidate country, and PHARE aid, were targeted to building or developing the 'capacity' for integration.

Hereafter, enlargement was viewed as a monogamous affair based on the new 'Accession Partnerships' between the EU and applicant states. The Accession Partnerships were designed as multi-annual structuring devices, detailing priority areas and PHARE programming. They were initially tied to the Commission's 1997 Opinions and were to be reviewed and revised as necessary. The candidate countries signed their Accession Partnerships in 1998, and they were subsequently revised in 1999 and 2002. The revisions were adopted by the Council based on the proposals made by the Commission which, in turn, were tied to the assessments presented in the Commission's annual monitoring device, the Regular Reports. While emphasizing that the processes of 'deepening' and enlargement were complementary and feasible within the EU's resource ceiling, 'deepening' in this sense referred to the nebulous expectation that candidate states must have the capacity not only to adopt but also to implement the *acquis*. Not surprisingly, the vision of enlargement that was promoted by the EU and the governments of applicant states was of a 'national' one, symbolized by the

NPAA. Moreover, the short- and medium-term priorities under the NPAA did not focus on regional policy issues, as the Regular Report sections on the NPAA demonstrate.

The 'Agenda 2000' and the 'Opinions' provided the basis for the decisions at the Luxembourg European Council in December 1997 to proceed with enlargement by commencing accession negotiations with five of the CEECs (the Czech Republic, Estonia, Hungary, Poland, Slovenia), plus Cyprus.[7] The basis for the negotiations with these 'in' states, which opened on 31 March 1998, was the general Copenhagen condition that they must adopt the *acquis*. Their progress in this regard was to be monitored by the Commission in Regular Reports on each country. This condition was also the basis for the extension of the accession negotiations to a further five CEEC states (Bulgaria, Latvia, Lithuania, Romania, Slovakia), plus Malta, agreed at the Helsinki European Council in December 1999. Essentially then, by making the adoption of the *acquis* the touchstone for enlargement to proceed, the EU set the membership hurdle for the CEECs and other applicants at a height that existing EU member states had achieved mostly only after a long period of life within the EU. Only Austria, Finland and Sweden, all advanced industrial countries, adopted most of the *acquis* in advance of accession to the EU. Moreover in all previous enlargements prior to the commitment to establish the single market, the scale and complexity of the *acquis* and necessary adaptation rates were much smaller and more manageable. This has made the challenge of the transposition of domestic legislation even greater for the CEECs particularly given the simultaneity of the EU alignment process with the massive political and economic transformations which have been underway in the region since the collapse of communism.

After 1998 regional policy became one of the most important aspects of enlargement for the Commission given its substantial financial implications (as we discuss later). Consequently, both the Commission and the CEEC governments had a strong incentive to pay particular attention to the arrangements for managing regional policy during and post-enlargement. The Commission's approach to its conditionality on this issue was, however, divided and inconsistent over time. During the early enlargement phase the Commission focused on the institutional territorial-administrative configurations in each candidate country, but as the process progressed to a conclusion it became increasingly more concerned with the 'capacity' of the CEECs to access and manage the funds at central and regional levels and deliver effective use of them.

Costs and benefits

During the enlargement process of the latter half of the 1990s only very modest sums were expended by the EU to assist the CEECs in their adjustment to the demands of accession. The main cost to the EU came through the PHARE programme funding commitments which led to expenditures of just under 5.6 billion ecus in fourteen countries in Eastern Europe and the Balkans in the period 1990–98 (see Table 1.2). The enlargement completed on 1 May 2004 produced a sharp increase in budgetary subventions from the EU to the new members of almost €24.5 billion over a two-year period in Structural and Cohesion Funds alone (see Table I.1). Considerable strains will arise from enlargement on the EU's funding of regional policy through the structural funds and many current regional beneficiaries will lose out if the present system for allocating funds is not reformed. Currently, the EU allocates funds on the basis of two key identifiers of regions that are 'lagging behind' and in need. Priority regions and areas (that is, 'Objective 1' regions) are identified on the basis of the NUTS II classification system. Such regions are identified as those with a per capita GDP of less than 75 per cent of the Community average. The sums involved are huge; in the period 2000–06 the total budget allocations for regional policy in the EU amount to €213 billion, of which €195 billion are structural funds, 69.7 per cent of which are allocated to Objective 1 regions.[8] The vast majority of the 53 NUTS II level regions in the CEECs have per capita GDP levels well below the threshold of 75 per cent of the EU average to qualify for Objective 1 funds, and with the exception of a few areas they are likely to continue to benefit for a long period.[9] The enlargement of ten new members will lower the EU average GDP and will thus eliminate mathematically many (perhaps as many as 27) of the 46 regions from the existing EU-15 which qualify for structural funds under the present arrangements (see Map 2).

The financial implications of enlargement have been a major concern for the existing member states, particularly with regard to the consequences for CAP and regional funds. The Berlin European Council in March 1999 agreed expenditure ceilings for the post-accession period which envisaged, assuming enlargement would occur in 2002, that about €40 billion would be committed to the potential new members between 2002–06.[10] The 'big bang' enlargement agreed at the Helsinki Council, including the ten countries of the CEEC group plus Malta and Cyprus (the 'Helsinki Group'), has had to be managed

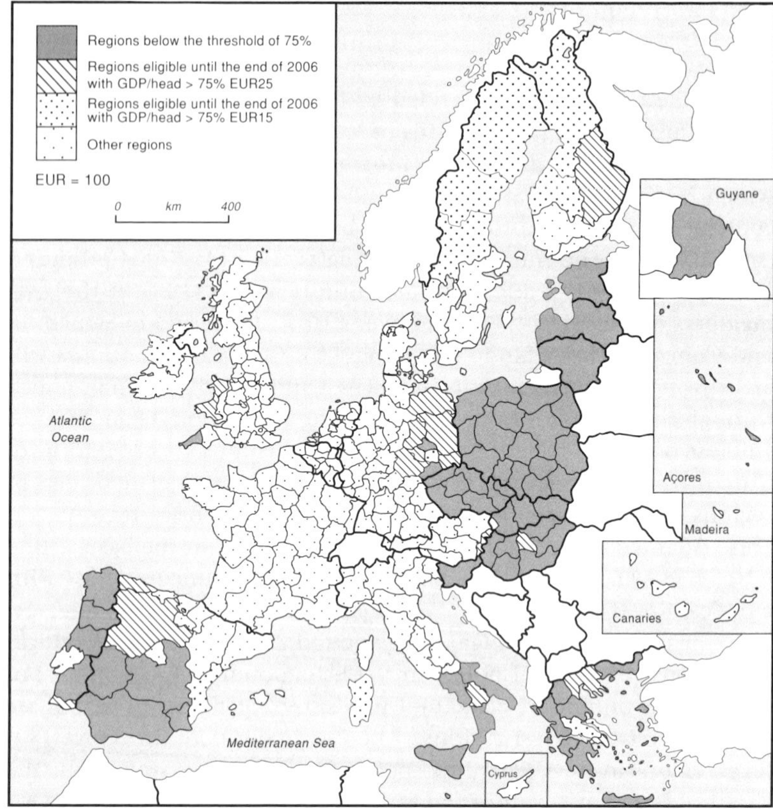

Map 2 Regions with GDP/head less than 75% of the EU average (1997–98–99)

within the Berlin expenditure ceilings.[11] The financial package agreed at the Copenhagen Council in December 2002 essentially adhered to the Berlin ceilings by committing €40.8 billion to the ten CEECs in 2004–06, over half of which (€21.7 billion) was to be spent on 'structural actions' which will largely be shaped by and benefit regional policy.[12] Some economic models suggest that the CEECs will, on average, benefit up to ten times more from enlargement than the EU-15.[13] In contrast, the political and economic costs of enlargement will affect the EU-15 'asymmetrically', with negative impacts felt most in those countries such as Spain and Portugal that are the current major recipients of Structural and Cohesion Funds and whose geographic location makes them less likely to benefit from increased trade with the

CEECs. Although the new member states will have to contribute some €15 billion in membership contributions to the EU budget while having a limited absorption capacity in the initial post-enlargement phase, and they will lose out from the staggering of the CAP funds to the new members over a ten-year period, the Copenhagen Council also agreed temporary budgetary 'compensation' to ensure that the new members would be 'no worse off' after joining.

The costs of enlargement look very different depending on how they are calculated.[14] For example, in the absence of budgetary reform, the increased costs of the enlargement countries through structural funds alone are projected to account for about 25 per cent of the total EU budget and will have to be sustained over a long period of time since GDP per capita in the CEECs is now and will continue to be significantly lower than the EU average.[15] This perspective on the costs is clearly politically sensitive. In principle, however, the EU can easily cope with the net financial costs of enlargement. The current cap placed on funding which limits the combined total annual receipts from structural and cohesion funds to a maximum of 4 per cent of national GDP is not optimum for the developmental needs of the CEECs and would slow down economic convergence.[16] The options that the EU will have to address with regard to regional funding reforms before the end of 2006 for the next financial perspectives (2007–13) are threefold. First, there is a reform option. This would rationalize, reduce and target funds to the poorest countries (the so-called 'cohesion model') or to the poorest regions (the so-called 'concentration model'). The underlying idea behind reform is that the richer EU states would manage the costs of their own regional development problems and thus curtail the Commission's influence, and in return they would reduce their contributions to the overall EU budget. Second, there is the status quo option. This would maintain the existing system more or less intact, preserve the Commission's role in regional policy, but with some reformulation of the thematic and/or territorial priorities. Third, there is an expansion option. This would see the funds for regional policy increased to ensure that the existing beneficiaries (the so-called 'statistical effect regions') do not lose out by moving above the GDP threshold after enlargement, while the new members also benefit fully.[17] Such options will put the GDP threshold and the ceiling of the EU's total budget spending (currently 1.24 per cent of GDP) at the centre of negotiations. The financing of regional policies could also change to a system in which each country pays or receives proportionally to its distance from the average EU per capita income level.

A Commission model of regionalization?

The institutional architecture of regional policy within the EU is highly diverse and flexibly arranged. The implementation of regional policy is overwhelmingly a competence of the member states and their 'own rules' (see below). Consequently, how regional policy functions in the EU is essentially determined by how the government of member states is spatially and institutionally organized, varying widely along a spectrum from unitary-centralized states to federalized-decentralized states. The Commission's role in regional policy while largely being concerned with the dispersion and management of funds also interacts with its other more powerful roles in competition policy and state aid regulations where it has established 'guidelines' for state aid to underdeveloped regions. The Commission's effect on institutional models of government is indirect. The divergent models of sub-national government inside the EU and the absence of clear institutional requisites are evident in Chapter 21 on 'Regional Policy and Co-ordination of Structural Instruments', which is one of the thinnest parts of the *acquis* as organized for the enlargement negotiations. The thinness of the *acquis* in the field of regional policy contrasts with the centrality of this policy domain during enlargement, and in particular its budgetary implications. In general, it has been regarded as one of the most problematic areas for fulfilment of the *acquis* by the CEECs.[18] The structural thinness of the *acquis* in regional policy constituted a formal conditionality gap. How did the Commission respond to the weakness of leverage provided by the *acquis*? We can assess this by examining three questions. First, when formal conditionality was weak did the Commission employ informal or 'soft' conditionality to influence institutional choices in the CEECs? Second, how consistent was the Commission in dealing with the CEECs over a content-poor part of the *acquis*? Third, how effective was the Commission in shaping domestic agendas and institutional choices in this policy area?

A further paradox of enlargement is that while parts of the Commission seem to have been influenced by the ideal of 'multi-level governance' and in particular by the desirability of institutional change in the candidate countries which would build 'participation' at the regional level in the making of regional policy, concurrently, sub-national actors were by and large structurally excluded from the enlargement negotiations. The interactions between the Commission and the CEECs over compliance with Chapter 21 of the *acquis* led to a general perception among key actors in the CEECs that the Commission was attempting to foist an EU 'model' of regionalization on them.

The perception of an 'EU model' arose in a context where many of the Commission actors involved in the technical aspects of enlargement in PHARE and the Commission's 'country teams' had been influenced by the ongoing debates within the Commission over the reform of regional policy in the early 1990s. Contemporaneous with the institutional changes introduced at Maastricht, the early 1990s saw a major debate in the then EC over the issue of which institution, the Commission or member states, was best positioned to deliver 'value for money', while also developing norms of 'partnership' and 'subsidiarity' in the use of regional funds. For the advocates of the multi-level governance approach, the boost to regional funds from the 'Delors packages' were attempts to empower regional actors. In practice, intergovernmentalism prevailed as the implementation of the 1993 reform followed no single model or template, with regions being more or less empowered depending on the national political institutional arrangements of member states and their 'own rules'.[19] The diversity of regional and local government in the EU, spanning the spectrum between federal and unitary states, evolved largely on the basis of country-specific historical factors and the interaction of European, national and regional and local politics. Similarly, the procedures for using structural and cohesion funds are not uniform, but rather they vary according to the institutional arrangements for regional and local government in each member state. Regional policy and the dispersion of regional funds per se, therefore, may not necessarily connect regional elites and networks either with each other or with EU institutions, in particular where such funding is absorbed into national government budgets.[20] The extent to which sub-national actors have become engaged with EU policy-making institutions, instruments and processes varies widely, both within and across member states.[21]

The Commission has repeatedly complained about its lack of power in regional policy in the member states and criticized the weak 'partnership' between central and sub-national authorities in the operation of structural funds.[22] Although the Commission was itself internally divided in the struggle over competences and by different visions of regional policy based on departmental interests, parts of it appropriated the concept of 'multi-level governance' to describe its overall mission in regional policy.[23] These debates over institutional reform within the EU were an immediate frame of reference for Commission officials when the drive for enlargement began in the mid-1990s.

There is evidence to suggest that Commission officials who had been frustrated in an attempt to extend the Commission's competences in regional policy by the 1993 reform, were motivated to use enlargement conditionality to pursue their particular agenda for the implementation of regional policy in the candidate countries. The *acquis*, however, offered them little by way of leverage to assert conditionality, since there are few areas of the *acquis* as 'thin' as that of Chapter 21 dealing with regional policy. In particular, EU law, regulations and guidelines are sparse on the institutional requirements for the implementation of regional policy. For example, the general provisions on the structural funds state: 'In application of the principle of subsidiarity, the implementation of assistance shall be the responsibility of the Member States, at the appropriate territorial level according to the arrangements specific to each Member State, and without prejudice to the powers vested in the Commission, notably for implementing the general budget of the European Communities.'[24] This regulation clarifies that there is no EU legal template for institutional or other aspects of regional policy and regionalization.

When the Commission assumed responsibility for enlargement in 1994, it did so with weak administrative resources for dealing with the CEECs. A new Directorate General had to be established (DG Enlargement) and its staff was recruited largely from other DGs (DG Regio, DG External Affairs) and departments in national governments with relevant expertise in delivering technical and structural assistance, often at the regional level. Some of DG Enlargement's functionaries had career tracks specializing in development aid. The modus operandi in regional policy during enlargement was one where the Commission and the private sector consultancies employed through PHARE stressed the 'partnership' between the public and private sectors at the EU, national and sub-national levels at both the programming design and implementation stages. Furthermore, the Commission's track record of involvement in the operation of structural and cohesion funds demonstrated that states with weak administrative capacity and poor control at the regional and local levels were more likely to have serious problems with the mismanagement of funds or even with accessing them in the first place. Moreover, the Commission had become used to interacting with institutions, networks and lobbies of organized actors from the sub-national level which had mushroomed in Brussels, despite the apparent strengthening of the role of the member states in this policy area after 1993.[25]

Thus, the enlargement process from 1994 onwards became infused by a carry-over of policy practices and preferences within the Commission from earlier debates about regional policy in the EU. Some actors in the Commission favoured a more inclusive approach to the 'participation' of regional institutions in regional policy, and acted as if conditionality for enlargement gave them a power asymmetry vis-à-vis the CEECs which could be applied as a lever to ensure compliance. As a PHARE official put it: 'We do not impose, but we expect candidate countries to come up with a compatible structure.'[26] He did not define, however, what 'compatibility' might entail in this respect. Moreover, the Commission was caught up in the general drive from Western governments and international agencies in the mid-1990s for a speedy transformation in the CEECs, viewing these states as an experiment for the implementation of neo-liberal policy and institutional models. The weakness of the formal conditionality in Chapter 21, given the sparse content of the *acquis*, meant that key actors within the Commission employed informal conditionality in the pursuit of their policy objectives in the CEECs.

The 'capacity' issue

The notion of 'capacity' as part of the conditionality for membership was first addressed, though not elaborated, in the Copenhagen criteria (see Box 1.1). It was most explicitly linked to the second Copenhagen criterion which referred to the existence of a functioning market economy and the 'capacity to cope with the competitive pressure and market forces within the Union'. However, the third and, to a lesser extent, the first Copenhagen criterion are also informed by the notion of capacity. The third criterion refers to the 'ability' to take on the obligations of membership including adherence to the aims of the political, economic and monetary union. The word 'ability' could have easily been replaced by a further reference to 'capacity' and, in fact, in the French version of the Copenhagen Council Presidency Conclusions, the term '*capacité*' is employed throughout.[27] The first, political criterion, asking for 'stability of institutions guaranteeing democracy, rule of law, human rights and the respect for and protection of minority rights' also implies a notion of institutional capacity. Finally, the fourth condition, aimed at the EU itself, also used the term 'capacity', highlighting the need for the Union's 'capacity' to absorb the new members. There was ambiguity as to what 'capacity' meant and what the CEECs were required to do. After the Opinions and pre-accession strategy of 1997, the 'capacity' issue was expanded wholesale to include elements such as legislation and regulation, and in particular with regard to Chapter 21 the idea of 'regional administrative capacity'. Weak administrative 'capacity', particularly at the regional level in relation to Chapter 21, has been repeatedly highlighted in the

Regular Reports as one of the key shortcomings of the candidate countries throughout the negotiation process. If taken cumulatively, the Regular Reports may be seen as an attempt by the Commission to give some coherence to the notion of building 'administrative capacity' in the candidate states by linking it to the requirements of the *acquis* in specific policy areas, such as sectoral capacity, effective structures and personnel for coordinating the negotiation process and adoption of the *acquis*, administrative and judicial reforms, and the preparation for the implementation of structural policies.[28]

The paradox is that despite the financial implications and thus critical importance of regionalization in the CEECs for the EU, and despite the Commission's use of language about institutionally embedding 'partnership' in regional policy and demanding greater regional 'capacity', the participation of the regional elites and institutions of the CEECs in the enlargement process was marginal. The Committee of the Regions repeatedly highlighted this structural flaw and argued that the negotiations were a 'state monopoly' with regions largely excluded.[29]

Nevertheless, as greater knowledge about candidate countries and experience of managing their differences emerged during the process of enlargement, it was to be expected that a more differentiated policy approach would evolve, and this was bound to affect, in particular, the grey zone of informal influences on the CEECs emanating from the Commission. As noted earlier, the shift in the Commission's policy approach occurred in 1997. From generally ignoring the implications of its own rhetoric about the need for 'partnership', and structurally excluding the key elites and actors at the sub-national level in the negotiations on regional policy, the Opinions of 1997, for the first time, identified weak regional 'administrative capacity' as a key problem for enlargement in many of the country reports.[30] In the Opinions, and thereafter in the Regular Reports, the Commission cited the requirements of Chapter 21 of the *acquis* as if it provided clear 'EU standards' that were either a lever for the Commission or an incentive for the CEECs to develop regional policy and institutions. The formulaic criticism that the candidates suffered from problems of 'weak' or inadequate 'administrative capacity' at the regional level became a mantra for the Commission. It did not, however, set explicit benchmarks for measuring progress toward an appropriate level of such 'capacity'. Thus, in regional policy an absurd situation arose where the Commission was pursuing a form of conditionality that had a very weak legal basis in the *acquis*, and no definable benchmarks by which either the Commission or the CEECs could measure compliance.

The thinness of Chapter 21

The Commission's official guide to the negotiations stresses that there is no Commission 'model' of regionalization: 'The *acquis* under Chapter 21 does not define how the specific structures for the practical management of Structural and the Cohesion Funds should be set up, but leaves it up to the Member States.' To comply with Chapter 21 the candidates must have in place an 'appropriate legal framework' to implement the specific provisions for regional policy, and agree a NUTS territorial classification with the Commission (via Eurostat). They must demonstrate 'programming capacity'. This includes the design of a development plan, procedures for multi-annual programming of budgetary expenditure, the implementation of the partnership principle at the different stages (which envisages the involvement of regional administrative, social and economic actors in the management of structural funds), ex-ante evaluation of the development plan, and compliance with the Commission's evaluation and monitoring requirements. In addition, they must demonstrate 'administrative capacity', which means they are to 'define the tasks and responsibilities of all the bodies and institutions involved in the preparation and implementation' and ensure 'effective inter-ministerial coordination'. Finally they must show sound financial and budgetary management (control provisions and information on co-financing capacity and level of public or equivalent expenditure for structural action) that complies with the provisions in this area, and demonstrate the 'additionality' provided by their co-financing arrangements.[31] In sum, Chapter 21 of the *acquis* is concerned with the procedural rather than the institutional mechanisms for regional policy, reflecting the Commission's lack of competence in this area.

Much of the content for Chapter 21 came from the Framework Regulation on the Structural Funds, which does not require transposition into national legislation.[32] The weak legal content and nebulous language used in Chapter 21 reflects the fact that it is a member state competence. Nevertheless, the Commission made the issue of 'capacity' in administrative, programming, and financial management key aspects of the Regular Reports and the negotiations over Chapter 21 with the CEECs. The Regular Reports tended to concentrate on the adoption and amendment of laws, regulations and regional development programmes as well as the establishment and reorganization of ministries and coordinating units, while also making very general references about the need to 'further enhance' administrative capacity.

The Regular Reports of 2001 and 2002 make the most explicit use of the structural funds criteria for measuring progress, referring systematically to 'territorial organization', 'legislative framework', 'institutional structure', 'programming', 'evaluation and monitoring', 'financial control and management' and 'regional statistics' (see Chapter 4).

The Commission has tried to build administrative capacity in the candidate countries for the implementation of regional policy by a number of pre-accession instruments (PHARE, SAPARD and ISPA) as well as through specifically targeted projects. About 30 per cent of the PHARE budget has been allocated to 'institution-building' since the reorganization of PHARE in 1997. While 'institution-building' is defined by the Commission as 'adapting and strengthening democratic institutions, public administration and organizations that have a responsibility in implementing and enforcing Community legislation', only a tiny proportion of funds have actually been devoted to these areas (see Table 1.1). In 1998 the Commission also employed a new device, termed 'twinning', which involved the secondment or employment of specialists from member states in key administrative posts in candidate countries as pre-accession advisers with the mandate to assist in the transposition, enforcement and implementation of specific parts of the *acquis*. 'Twinning' was extended to the regional level, however, only in the 2000 programming round.[33] Thus, there were no clear benchmarks for measuring progress by candidate countries towards achieving an acceptable regional administrative capacity beyond the vague and brief statements in the Regular Reports and any unrecorded advice given by 'twins'.

In the absence of a 'thick' *acquis* in Chapter 21 the Commission also employed the baseline criteria for administrative reform developed by the SIGMA (Support for Improvement in Governance and Management in Central and Eastern European Countries) group of the OECD to define 'administrative capacity'. These criteria focused on macro-level administrative reform, highlighting the establishment of an independent and professional civil service and judicial system, without issuing detailed recommendations as to the form of sub-national governance. The timing and nature of the civil service legislation passed in the CEECs after 1997, for example, is clearly correlated with the Commission's increased emphasis on administrative reforms. As a result, some have argued that the public administrative spaces in the CEECs converge more with each other and norms of 'Europeanization' than is the case in the EU itself.[34] This understanding of the public administrative space, however, is focused on the national executive level. The issue of regional administrative capacity, after all, is a fundamental part of the horizontal and vertical configuration of a country's administrative space, both with regard to its territorial form and power allocation. In these latter respects the CEECs diverged widely from each other, though in this they mirrored the differentiated systems of the EU member states.

It appears that there were competing views within the Commission over whether Chapter 21 entailed a 'model of regionalization' and how it should be implemented by the CEECs. The differences were within and between DGs, and views changed over time. The issue hinged on how to create and standardize regions in the CEECs at the NUTS II level, the critical level for regional policy, and whether the Commission should pressure the CEECs to install elected authorities at the regional level or administrative agencies or quango-type boards. The key question was whether regionalization was to be political, statistical, or both (that is, that NUTS II statistical regions would be overlapped by an elected tier of government). The study by Hooghe and Marks of multi-level governance and the wide variations in regional policy across member states demonstrates a strong correlation between 'regional influence in structural programming' and strong 'regional governance'.[35] This correlation seems to have informed DG Enlargement's views that the 'partnership' principle in EU regional policy practices constituted best practice for the CEECs. The goal was to develop multi-level governance with the appropriate 'partnership', 'programming capacity' and 'administrative capacity', with funds allocated to member states on criteria derived from socio-economic development at the NUTS II territorial level. The question is whether these officials saw this requirement as entailing 'strong', preferably elected, regional governance?

The NUTS statistical classification system of Eurostat has been an important tool for the Commission in its attempts to shape and standardize regional policy. The NUTS system consists of three key levels (NUTS I, NUTS II, NUTS III). The NUTS II level is the crucial one for regional funds. It provides not only the statistical information and analysis for regional development planning and programmes, but also defines the administrative level at which structural funds and other regional and cohesion funds are managed. The existing NUTS II regions in the EU were drawn up independently, largely on the basis of designations arrived at by individual member states and subsequently approved *pro forma* by Brussels.[36] The Commission even refers to this EU-15 process as one that is based on 'gentlemen's agreements' between the member states and Eurostat.[37] Equally, the manipulation of NUTS regional demarcation to maximize regional funding opportunities is not without precedent in the EU as the creation of the two NUTS III level regions (Border-Midland-Western region, and Southern and Eastern region) in Ireland in 1997–99 demonstrates.

In contrast to Ireland, conditionality has allowed the Commission to intervene directly in the designation of NUTS regionalization in the CEECs. Attempts by candidate states to manipulate the NUTS system to maximize funding opportunities were rejected by the Commission. For example, it rejected Slovenia's proposal to create two NUTS II regions, which would disaggregate its wealthy capital from the rest of the country, and forced it to adopt one region for the whole country.[38] Furthermore, Eurostat has systematically employed NUTS categories in its interactions with the statistical offices of the candidate countries to promote a technocratic standardization.[39]

Consequently, one of the reverse effects of the operation of conditionality in regional policy is that it has intensified the Commission's attempt to strengthen the legal basis of the *acquis* for a standardized NUTS classification scheme for the Union as a whole. A draft regulation on NUTS regions prepared in 2001 noted that regions were conceived in the existing member states as 'normative regions' (sic) which reflect 'political will', and further states that the tensions between the Commission and the National Statistical Offices, in particular during enlargement, demonstrate the need for clear guidelines on the criteria for NUTS classifications. The regulation was enacted in May 2003 after the enlargement negotiations had been concluded.[40]

The perception of conditionality

Interviews with regional officials in the CEECs and with CEEC delegations in Brussels revealed that there was a widespread perception, both among the Commission and the CEEC actors involved in the enlargement process, that the Commission was pushing for a particular model of decentralization in regional policy in the CEECs. While the candidates set their legislative machinery to work to rapidly secure the adoption of many aspects of the *acquis*, regional policy was a key area where there was open resistance to the Commission's attempts to interfere. Such interference impinged upon issues of territorial governance that overtly and directly were sensitive for political sovereignty.

Before 1998, according to a senior official in the Polish delegation in Brussels, there was no formal written exchange between the Commission and the candidate countries on the content of regional policy. The Commission's formal views were set out in the Opinions of 1997 and subsequent Regular Reports which, while they have not been consistent in recommending that the candidates should adopt a particular model of institutional governance at the NUTS II regional level, have commended states which have made progress on developing what the Commission termed 'active' regional policy, that is, one which involves all government levels, establishing acceptable NUTS II regions, and building regional 'institutions'. This practice constituted an incentive structure and sent a strong signal that countries which promoted regional participation in regional policy and engaged in institution-building at the regional level were making progress on accession.

Initially, Hungary was top of the Commission's chart for progress on Chapter 21 as the Opinions singled out the 1996 Law on Regional Development and Physical Planning which established seven planning and administrative-statistical regions as the first in a candidate country to adopt 'a legal framework closely in line with the EU Structural Policy'.[41] Equally, Poland's proposed development of a democratized level of regional self-government was commended for moving towards a 'modernized regional policy closer to that of the EU'.[42] At the same time, Slovakia suffered from a general EU critique of the Meciar government. However, while the Commission criticized its regional self-government reform of 1996 for still leaving regional policy decisions 'overly centralized with all major decisions taken directly by the Government', no mention was made of the gerrymandering of the Hungarian minority.[43] In the case of the Czech Republic the Opinion's verdict is even harsher: 'Currently, the Czech Republic has no regional policy.'[44] The Commission's criticism directly stressed the fact that regional development initiatives in the Czech Republic were implemented via sectoral policies at the national level. The problem for the Commission was that 'there exists no *elected* [authors' italics] body between the State and the communes although the constitution foresees the establishment of the so-called territorial units of self-administration' and that the districts are 'bodies of state administration with general competences (*no self-government*) [authors' italics]'.[45]

The Commission's preferences were also transmitted through other channels: PHARE, some working papers, speeches and bilateral meetings at ministerial and expert level.[46] Interviewees at the CEEC missions to the EU were forthright in expressing their frustration with what was perceived to be an overly interfering approach from the Commission in regional policy. An interviewee at the Hungarian Mission explained how there was 'amazing pressure from the EU because Hungary does not have regions. We think there was no real need to set up a regional structure. We have regions – the counties. We have been trying to organize at the NUTS II level. It is driven by Structural Funds. They [the Commission] may deny this fact of imposition. Internally you can see maps though the Commission won't admit to it.'[47] Hungary went from 'ice-breaker' to laggard within a year. The 1998 Regular Report criticized its failure to further develop 'institutional and administrative capacity in regional development'.[48] An interviewee at the Romanian Mission described how Commission officials pressured them to 'design NUTS II level regions, which we did not have in Romania ... because the Commission tends to favour decentralized management of funds'.[49] In the 1998 report on Romania the Commission openly acknowledged its direct involvement in the design of the country's Law on Regional Development adopted in July 1998.[50] In fact, PHARE showcased its involvement in Romania's Green Paper on Regional Development (1997) which was the basis for the law, and which had tied the establishment of a number of macro-regions as planning units to associations of elected county councils.[51] The perception of a power asymmetry meant, as a high-ranking official at the Estonian Mission to the EU explained, that the Commission saw candidate countries as 'mice in laboratories ... anything could be asked of them'. He observed that the pressure to regionalize was 'only because of EU policy principles and in particular money channels'. He noted the key role of PHARE in applying direct pressure: 'approval of a particular programme is their mode of influence, their way of interference'. While he accepted that it was in Estonia's national interest to rationalize the division of local authorities, he resisted the Commission's interference on the question of how many levels to create.[52]

Thus, in a policy domain where formal conditionality was weak or virtually non-existent, there was a general perception among those CEEC officials closely involved in the negotiations that the Commission relied on informal conditionality by carrot and stick methods, whether by signalling criticisms and approval for compliance in the Regular Reports, channelling PHARE funding to promote particular types of institutional development and regionalization, or by the positive reinforcement of compliant rhetoric and behaviour through personal interactions between Commission officials and their CEEC counterparts.

Commission officials are naturally defensive when charged with an attempt to impose a particular model of regionalization in the CEECs. When questioned on this issue they tended to refer to the requirements of the *acquis* on regional administrative capacity for managing structural funds (though as we noted earlier such requirements are extremely vague in the *acquis*), while they also emphasized that no single template for administrative reform was being imposed. An official from the Slovenia team at DG Enlargement, who had chaired the negotiations over the regional chapter, was insistent that 'no one has told anyone to establish regional administrations though some people in Eastern Europe have gone around suggesting that this is the case. Regions have to be naturally grown products in Eastern Europe. All the candidate countries have to do is guarantee that they can manage the Structural Funds. They could opt for decentralized organs of central administration. All that is needed is interlocutors – for the "partnership" prerequisite. No schema has been proposed from Brussels. All you can say is that the candidate countries have responded to incentives.' When asked to clarify the intriguing nature of the 'incentives', since if an incentive structure is to work there must be an objective or policy outcome envisaged, he admitted that there had been a push from the Commission for a particular template of regionalization in the CEECs: 'Some people here in the Commission think that you can jump stages. In terms of regional policy, there are some who think it should be aimed at the sub-national level.'[53]

An official in the Polish team at DG Enlargement was even more explicit and stressed that in their work with national agencies on the introduction of public administration reforms, including civil service reform, 'decentralization was the most important objective'.[54] PHARE was the instrument to achieve this by providing the technical expertise to promote institutionalization at the regional level. In the opinion of this official, had the Suchocka government survived in 1993, the Polish reform would have gone ahead much earlier under PHARE's guidance. Similarly, senior officials at DG Enlargement's Romania team expressed their views of regionalization in unambiguous terms: 'We are looking for a mode of decentralized implementation. This is problematic because of the history of the country.' They stressed that the development regions introduced in Romania in 1998 had been 'designed with the Commission'. When asked to explain the objective of the Commission's role in Romania's regionalization, an experienced official who had been transferred from DG Regio to assist with enlargement in the Romania team declared: 'We have always been looking for a mode of decentralization, but we have not found a satisfactory formula ... the search continues [since] this is *le clef d'or* for successful regionalization.'[55]

Policy contestation within the Commission

The Commission itself appears to have undergone a policy learning curve in the mid-to-late 1990s over enlargement, as evidenced by the reform of PHARE in 1997–98. Changes in the Commission's approach to regional policy in the CEECs came later, but were, nevertheless, part of the policy learning process. Within the Commission, the tension between conflicting policy positions and objectives became more apparent over time and as the enlargement process progressed. On the one hand, the early pressures from the Commission were driven by preferences among some key officials within DG Enlargement and DG Regio for an institutional design in the CEECs that would embed decentralization and partnership with the regions, and on the other hand, there was a belated realization that efficiency and 'value for money' concerns must impel the Commission to rely on the most reliable, efficient and most easily monitored mechanism of dispersion of funds, namely central ministries. As one senior official in PHARE explained: 'In the smaller countries, structures are being set up at the national level. It doesn't make sense to set up regional structures ... in Hungary, Estonia and Slovenia. However, Poland and Romania are too big to be run from the centre in terms of the practical implementation of Structural Funds ... Ten years of work in Eastern Europe has given us experience in knowing what sort of level is needed. We do have some doubts about whether the necessary administrative capacity will be in place.' This Commission official admitted that a 'top-down approach' had been imposed from Brussels in the early years of the accession process, particularly through PHARE's multi-country programmes. He acknowledged that 'in the early years PHARE made the mistake of telling them [the candidates] what to do ... the evaluation reports demonstrated the unsustainability of the programmes ... Since 1997 the emphasis is on a national approach.' According to the official the main problem by late 2000 was how to make the candidate countries assume 'ownership' of their projects to ensure their sustainability. It had become clear over time that the Commission had to differentiate more between the candidates and between large and smaller countries in particular. The Baltic states and Slovenia, for example, would not be expected to manage programmes at the sub-national level. This differentiated approach to regional policy, as the official admitted, 'emerged over time' and led to the closure of PHARE Management Units and the move to a much more consolidated system. As the official put it: 'Regional focus does not mean that everything has to be managed at the regional level. This was not made very clear in our programme in previous years ... in the Programming Instruction Guidelines, [we were refused access to these documents: authors].[56]

Inexperience on the part of Commission officials was also partly to blame. As a senior official in ISPA observed with regard to the Commission's role in the regionalization of Hungary: 'Colleagues from Structural Funds [that is, DG Regio] pushed for "regions". They under-estimated the political games and the intricacies they got involved in.'[57] As another Commission official explained, the regional level in Hungary was considered to be 'highly corrupt', as it was manipulated by the Fidesz government of prime minister Viktor Orban to secure its patrimony: 'all the PHARE projects are located in the municipalities' party structures and all the heads of the regional development councils are from the governing parties'.[58]

Officials in the Commission's Forward Planning Unit accepted that a major problem with the regional dimension of enlargement was that there are 'conflicting visions of what the requirements are for having an appropriate institutional set-up for Structural Funds'. There were, apparently, competing democratizing and technocratic visions. Many in the Commission, they observed, favoured a more decentralized approach because they saw it as the 'more efficient way of taking into account specificity ... and the more democratic'. After the corruption scandals in the Commission in 1999 (leading to the resignation of the Santer Commission) policy changed, according to these officials, to emphasize management of funds from the national level rather than the regional or local for fear of mismanagement. The view of these officials was framed by the notion of 'multi-level governance', as for them the 1988 reform of the structural funds 'placed a new emphasis on decentralization as a way of elevating the position of the Commission vis-à-vis the member states as well as empowering the local level. Twelve years on this has been seen to be very successful.' At the same time they recognized that the Commission's leverage on the CEECs to develop regions had been applied 'in heavier ways' than in previous waves of enlargement.[59]

As enlargement neared its conclusion the Commission modified its own mantra of problems with 'regional administrative capacity' in the candidates for new ones that stressed the need for strong 'managing authority' and 'inter-ministerial coordination' in regional policy and structural funds as part of a general concern with post-accession imple-mentation. In working documents and seminars on regional policy in February and early March 2001, the Commission clarified that, given its concerns about the weak regional administrative capacity in the candidates, it wanted centralized management of funds so as to maximize efficiency, streamlining and control of expenditures. According to an official in the Polish Mission in Brussels this policy shift caused 'a significant and noticeable dispute between our country and the Commission'.[60] Having introduced regional self-government in 1999, and given its great regional disparities between well-developed and under-developed regions, a general backwards shift in the organizational principle of the state to a reconcentration of power in regional policy to central ministries was a great reverse in Poland. As an official in DG Regio explained, the Commission was suggesting in effect that Poland 'delay their process of regionalization a bit' so that there would be 'progressive decentralization'. The Commission's concern with the 'absorption capacity' in structural funds meant that it was a case of: 'If you want to have decentralization – fine, but make sure you can use the money well. Start at the central level and progressively go where you would like to.'[61]

In the final Regular Reports in 2002 candidate countries with non-existent regional government, such as Hungary, that have 're-defined' their financial management and control for structural funds and regional policy towards a heavily centralized approach have been praised by the Commission, while Poland, the candidate with the strongest and most democratized regional government level, was criticized for its lack of 'vigour' in such central controls.[62] It seems that the closer the reality of enlargement became the greater was the concern in the Commission to anticipate problems previously encountered in structural funds with Spain, Greece and Portugal, where regional policies and the institutional capacity to manage them, both centrally and locally, was constructed virtually from scratch and there was initial significant mismanagement of funds. For one Commission official one of the most serious failures of the PHARE programme was precisely its lack of impact on the 'organization of the state' in the CEECs: 'it has not contributed to management at the central level. We created capacity at the local level ... but errors are unavoidable and there is a learning curve during the enlargement process'.[63]

The competing visions and shifts in approach within the Commission to regional policy in the candidates reflect this learning curve but also genuine differences in the remits and opinions of the various departments of the Commission, in particular differences within and between DG Enlargement and DG Regio over whether to promote centralized or decentralized management of regional policy in the CEECs. The process of EU enlargement confirms that the Commission has not been a unified actor in the application of conditionality. The Commission did not have a consistent or well-defined institutional preference for regional policy, though in some countries its actors did pressure for decentralization. The message from the Commission changed over time not only in response to practical experience, but also depending on which officials were most engaged, which also fluctuated over time. Those most closely involved with the enlargement project within the Commission do appear to have preferred a decentralized democratic regional variant in the early stages, but the ground shifted in favour of more centralized management in the latter stages. In such a fluid situation, where the absence of formal conditionality in regional policy made benchmarking of clear and consistent rules and evaluation of outcomes against such benchmarks difficult to achieve, the way was opened for a heavy reliance on informal conditionality by the Commission. Moreover, the informal conditionality was employed in an ad hoc fashion, thus making for a strong perception in the CEECs that conditionality existed but was inconsistent.

Conclusion

Given that regional policy is a competence under EU law where the national governments decide the institutional framework and means of implementation, the Commission lacked a repertoire of legal instruments to enforce a particular institutional model on the candidates, even if such a uniform 'EU template' had existed – which it did not. The lack of leverage from formal conditionality meant that in this policy domain elements with the Commission resorted to informal conditionality vis-à-vis the CEECs to push their normatively driven preferences for a model of regional decentralization. In this respect the context in which the enlargement process began is crucial. EU enlargement conditionality for the CEECs in the area of regional policy was implemented in a context of a spill-over of policy contestation within the Commission, where earlier divisions over the reform of regional policy in the Union still resonated. This spill-over informed the early stage of the enlargement process and strongly influenced perceptions in the candidates that there was a Commission 'model' of regionalization that favoured democratized regional governance and sought to reconfigure the governance of the CEECs in this image. Over time, however, it has become obvious that the Commission itself has been divided. From early 2001 the

Commission began to stress more systematically and proactively a clear preference for the centralized management of structural funds in the candidate countries.

Most of the CEEC states began to regionalize only once the enlargement negotiations were underway, thereby affirming a strong temporal correlation. The following three chapters test whether there has been a general pattern of causal links between EU conditionality and policy, institutional and attitudinal change in the CEECs. Chapter 4 analyses the Commission's monitoring function during enlargement through the Opinions of 1997, the 1998 Accession Partnerships and the subsequent annual Regular Reports, to evaluate what conditionality was applied in regional policy. Chapter 5 then examines how the CEECs responded to the pressures from the Commission in regional policy, while Chapter 6 examines the impact of enlargement on the norms and identities of the elites at the regional level.

4
Monitoring Conditionality and Compliance

For conditionality to be credible, it must be clearly benchmarked and be applied with consistency. Similarly, commitment to conformity and compliance with conditionality must be fairly evaluated. Regular monitoring was chosen by the EU as the means to communicate the criteria of accession and assess progress and to highlight shortcomings in adaptation by the CEECs. The Opinions of 1997 and the five sets of annual Regular Reports from 1998 to 2002 were the main outlets for the Commission's monitoring process. These documents are the only official and transparent public statements of the Commission's assessments of the progress of the candidate countries over time. The Reports fell within the remit of DG Enlargement where the monitoring process was overseen by the Horizontal Co-Ordination Unit that also produced a manual for the country desks highlighting the issues to be covered. On the basis of reports from the EU delegations in the candidate countries, complemented by information supplied by other international institutions, NGOs and some member states' governments, the country desks produced the drafts of the annual Reports. The Co-Ordination Unit had the task to streamline all of the draft reports in terms of substance, language, and comparability and to communicate with the various relevant line DGs, country desks and the legal service in performing this role.

The political salience of the Commission's reporting was characterized by peaks and troughs. The zenith of their political salience occurred at the beginning and the end of the enlargement process. For example, prior to the beginning of the accession negotiations in 1997, the Opinions were employed by the EU to legitimate the 'queuing' system for enlargement which centred on the selection of the 'Luxembourg Six', that small group of candidate countries that were permitted to enter negotiations with the Commission over membership in 1998.[1] This hierarchy of 'ins' and 'outs' among the candidates created an atmosphere of competitive emulation, transforming enlargement into a scramble for accession. Some countries, in particular Hungary, saw itself as an 'ice-breaker' leading the pack. Some of those relegated to the 'out' group, such as Slovakia, made an immense effort to catch up by signalling commitment and compliance in the two-year period between the Luxembourg Council of 1997 and the Helsinki Council of 1999, when the scale of the enlargement was revised upwards to include Bulgaria, Latvia, Lithuania, Romania, Slovakia and Malta. Overall, the 'pull factor' of EU conditionality seems to have been strongest in the pre-negotiation phase, in particular in the case of the Baltic states, Bulgaria, Romania and Slovakia. During this phase, the EU's rhetoric about conditionality primarily centred on the fulfilment of the vague first political Copenhagen criterion, which had to be met before the accession negotiations could begin. Over time the eponymous 'progress' Reports essentially became increasingly characterized by 'spin' and became an attempt to extol the cumulative success story of enlargement. The political salience of the Reports also peaked at the end of the process in late 2002, when they were employed to deliver the EU's official seal of approval for the political decision to accept ten candidate countries as new members from 1 May 2004. The 2002 Reports and, in particular, the follow-up Comprehensive Monitoring Reports of 2003 were qualitatively different from previous reports in that rather than presenting fairly general assessments and vague recommendations, they offered detailed criticism and policy advice.

The Commission's reporting mechanism, consequently, served three main goals. First, it mapped out each country's trajectory towards EU membership and provided a base point of reference for the pre-accession and accession negotiations and the Accession Partnerships. Second, as the only benchmark for the comparison and ranking of the candidate countries available to the Commission and to the candidates, the Reports, which were keenly awaited by the accession countries each autumn, were a key commitment device for generating competitive 'European' emulation among the candidates. Third, the Reports allowed the Commission to highlight and prioritize its own areas of concern over compliance. Moreover, the monitoring structure tracked the Commission's own learning curve towards the CEECs, beginning with the elemental data and formulaic comments in the Opinions and early Reports but becoming more detailed, differentiated and nuanced over time. In particular in policy areas where the *acquis* is thin, the Regular Reports became the default mechanism for the Commission to define and communicate standards of compliance. The Reports attempt to compensate for such 'thinness' of the *acquis* by cross-referencing other EU regulations or norms and recommendations of other international institutions and 'European standards'. Given the thinness of the *acquis* in the area of regional policy the Reports became critically important for the Commission to showcase its policy preferences and for the candidates to identify what the criticisms of them involved. In particular, as we shall discuss below, the sections of the Opinions and the Reports dealing with Chapter 21 were generally highly formulaic in their content and tended to focus on the Commission's vaguely defined notion of 'weak capacity' to implement the *acquis*.

In the absence of detailed *acquis* criteria, there were three obvious sources the Commission could turn to in its attempt to define measures and benchmarks: the Europe Agreements, the Accession Partnerships (from 1998 onwards) and the Regulations on Structural Funds. The Europe Agreements provide the framework for bilateral relations between the EC and their member states on the one hand and the partner countries on the other hand. They cover trade-related issues, political dialogue, legal approximation and other areas of co-operation, such as industry, environment, transport and customs and ultimately aim to progressively establish a free-trade area between the EU and the partner countries. The EU itself describes them as preparing 'the way for the EU and the partner countries to converge economically, politically, socially and culturally'.[2] The Agreements commit the partner countries to the approximation of their legislation to that of the EU, in particular in areas relevant to the internal market. The bilateral relations are channelled at three institutional levels: the Association Councils denote bilateral meetings at ministerial level reviewing all areas of legal approximation; the Association Committees (and sub-committees) convene meetings at senior official level to review individual areas in more detail; and the Joint Parliamentary Committees bring together members of the national parliaments of the partner countries and members of the European Parliament. The Europe Agreements became the framework within which the CEECs prepared for EU membership, and PHARE was the main financial instrument tied to the Europe Agreements.

The Europe Agreements with all the CEECs include an almost identical article on 'Regional Development'. It asked both parties to strengthen cooperation in the field of regional development and land use and lists a number of measures that 'may be undertaken' to achieve this goal, such as the exchange of information by national, regional or local authorities on regional and land-use policy; the provision of assistance to the partner country for the formulation of a regional development policy; joint action by regional and local authorities in the area of economic development; the study of coordinated approaches for the development of border areas, areas with regional disparities and interregional cooperation; exchange visits to explore opportunities for cooperation and assistance; the exchange of civil servants and experts; the provision of technical assistance; and the establishment of programmes facilitating the exchange of information and experience.[3] Thus, the Europe Agreements defined the parameters very widely and had little to contribute to the definition of benchmarks in the field of regional policy.

The Accession Partnerships, one of the three cornerstones of the 'reinforced pre-accession strategy' proclaimed by the Luxembourg European Council in 1997 (the others being PHARE and participation in Community programmes), were drawn up for each candidate country in 1999 (and revised in subsequent years).[4] They identified the priority areas in which a country had to make progress in order to prepare for accession, and the ways in which PHARE was to support these preparations. The priority areas in the National Programmes for the Adoption of the *Acquis* (NPAA), drawn up by each country individually, spell out more precise commitments on the part of the candidate states. The Accession Partnerships, which are only about 15–20 pages long, frontload the three Copenhagen criteria as their 'principles' and explicitly build on the Opinions and Regular Reports. This link is further highlighted by the fact that the Regular Reports sum up the short-term and medium-term priorities of the Accession Partnerships. Under Chapter 21 the Accession Partnerships emphasize the preparation of a national policy on social and economic cohesion; a monitoring system; institutional and administrative capacity of the bodies involved in programming and managing funds 'in line with the Structural Funds approach', including the definition of managing and paying authorities; 'a clear division of responsibilities at national and regional level'; the improvement of administrative capacity through recruitment and training and inter-ministerial coordination; and financial control provisions.[5] In the majority of cases, a brief reference to the preparation for structural funds and administrative capacity is included under 'medium-term priorities' in the subsequent Accession Partnerships.

Over time the cross-references to the Structural Funds Regulations (see Chapter 3) in the Accession Partnerships became more explicit, but it is obvious also that they were the only available source for a somewhat more detailed description of EU requirements and were the main basis for conditionality in the area of regional policy.[6] Nevertheless, the tension remained in this 'thin' part of the *acquis* between, on the one hand, very brief regulatory recommendations given that this was a competence that was in the domain of member states and 'their own rules' – and, on the other, the Commission's attempts to build regional administrative and institutional capacity in the candidate countries. In part, as we discussed in Chapter 3, this included a normative drive from some actors in the Commission to create regional self-governments.

The Opinions of 1997

Since statistical measures of wealth and poverty underpin the EU's own methodology for regional policy, it is not surprising that the section on 'regional policy and cohesion' in the Opinions of 1997 presents basic descriptive statistics about each candidate country, in particular the average GDP per capita and unemployment rates as well as specific sectoral and regional disparities. Against this background of poverty and regional disparities the need for an effective regional policy is both legitimated and emphasized. The Opinions also acknowledge existing EU activity in this field through the Europe Agreements, which provided for cooperation on regional development and spatial planning, in particular through the exchange of information between local, regional and national authorities and the exchange of civil servants and experts. No further details on the extent and depth of these links were provided.

As discussed in Chapter 3, the Opinions offered a snapshot of the candidates' standing on regional reform. Two elements that drew the particular attention of the Commission were, first, the extent to which regionalization in the candidates was a good fit with 'EU standards', and second, what plans or prospects, if any, were there for regional self-government. Initially, Hungary was the clear leader of the Commission's chart for progress on Chapter 21 as the Opinions singled out the 1996 Law on Regional Development and Physical Planning (which established seven planning and administrative-statistical regions) as the first in a candidate country to adopt 'a legal framework closely in line with the EU Structural Policy'.[7] Equally, Poland's proposed development of a democratized level of regional self-government was commended for moving towards a 'modernised regional policy closer to that of the EU'.[8]

In the case of the Czech Republic the Opinion's verdict is even harsher: 'Currently, the Czech Republic has no regional policy.' The Commission's criticism directly stressed the fact that regional development initiatives in the Czech Republic were implemented via sectoral policies at the national level. The problem for the Commission was that 'there exists no elected body between the State and the communes although the constitution foresees the establishment of the so-called territorial units of self-administration' and that the districts are 'bodies of state administration with general competences (no self-government)'.[9] Similarly, in the case of Bulgaria, the fact that the Commission's Opinion stresses favourably that there is the possibility of the new districts, which are envisaged to replace the existing nine regions, gaining self-governing powers is a form of implicit encouragement. This impression is reinforced by the Commission's view that the draft legislation on regional policies is 'based on EC practices', while its criticism of Bulgaria's sectoral approach to regional development stressed 'the need for an active regional policy involving all government levels'.[10]

At the same time the Commission did attempt to differentiate among the candidate countries according to size. In contrast to the bigger candidate countries, the Opinion on Estonia makes explicit reference to Estonia's size and the fact that regional policy 'should continue to constitute an integral part of the national development strategy'. Smaller countries, such as Estonia, were not expected to regionalize but they were expected to develop 'regional policy instruments' and make 'progress in establishing a regional development policy'.[11]

The Opinions contrasted the increasing awareness in the CEECs of the need for an effective regional policy with their weak 'capacity' to deliver it through a coherent strategy, administrative framework and budgetary instruments. The Commission's carrot and stick incentive structure, however, was ambivalent. Rather than offering specific policy recommendations, strategies, structures and instruments, the Commission employed nebulous phrases such as referring to the need to adopt the 'necessary reforms', make a 'major effort of reform', and remedy 'the deficiencies'. The Opinions pointed to general failures in the broadest of terms.[12] Bulgaria, for example, was called upon to improve 'its administrative capacity to manage integrated regional development programmes', and specifically in the areas of administrative and budgetary procedures, inter-ministerial cooperation and co-financing arrangements.[13] In some cases the Commission stressed the need for new political thinking about regional policy. In the Czech case the Commission not only censured it for weaknesses in administrative and budgetary issues, but also implicitly criticized its uncertain constitutional framework and called for action to 'determine the legal basis of a Czech regional policy'. In contrast to other CEECs, an optimistic spin was given to this lack of compliance: 'Given the Czech Republic's administrative capacity and with the necessary political awareness, this should be achieved within a reasonable time-frame.'[14] Estonia was evaluated in very similar terms, highlighting the need for 'political support' for regional development policy. As regards regional institutions and policy-making the Opinions' observations confirmed the overall differentiation between the frontrunners and laggards.

The Opinion on Slovakia contains the most explicit criticism. Among the 'serious deficiencies' in the organizational framework of regional policy it criticized the high degree of centralization: 'Regional policy decision-making is overly centralised with all major decisions taken directly by the Government.'[15] The controversial Slovak law of 1996 on territorial-administrative reform, which divided the country into eight regions (and 79 districts) was only briefly mentioned, yet without any comment on the gerrymandering of the regionalization to minimize the influence of the Hungarian minority in the southern regions. In fact, Slovakia was prima facie in breach of the Copenhagen political criteria as regards the 'respect for and protection of minorities'.[16]

Consequently, from the outset the ecology of the enlargement process was one characterized by a readiness on the part of the Commission to criticize the candidate countries for their failures and weaknesses, while at the same time it was less willing to spell out what reforms should be undertaken and what benchmarks should be followed. The Opinions did, nevertheless, signal to the CEECs that the Commission's preference in terms of the institutional architecture for regional policy was for a momentum towards some form of regional 'self-government'.

The Regular Reports 1998–2003

The prominence of the Copenhagen criteria 1998–99

The 1998 and 1999 Regular Reports followed a similar format to the 1997 Opinions by using the first three Copenhagen criteria as their main structuring device for the negotiations. Each country was assessed according to the political criteria, economic criteria, the ability to assume the obligations of membership, and, in line with the Madrid Council (1995) conclusions a fourth section on 'administrative capacity to apply the *acquis*' was added. Regional policy fell under the economic criteria in the reports, and together with employment it formed the section on 'economic and social cohesion'. It was also considered separately, again under the heading 'economic and social cohesion' where it formed part of the section on 'administrative and judicial capacity'.

The 1998 Reports reinforced the directional impetus provided by the Opinions for the establishment of an institutional architecture for regional policy in the CEECs. In general, the entries under 'regional policy' are very brief in the 1998 Reports, often amounting to no more than a few lines. The less progress an accession country made in this regard, the briefer was the Commission's reporting and evaluation. Lithuania's Report attributes 'little progress' and merely refers to the need to implement the country's general regional policy guidelines of 1998.[17] In the case of Bulgaria, for example, which the Opinion did not credit with the capacity to participate in the EU's structural policy, the cryptic reference to 'some progress' is accompanied by one basic recommendation, namely the advice that the relevant ministry needs to be strengthened.[18] The adoption of key legislation or development concepts and the establishment of relevant institutions were evaluated positively, and the failure to do so was criticized, such as in the case of Slovenia: 'It is regrettable that a law on regional development has not yet been adopted.'[19] Similarly, Slovakia is seen to have made 'limited concrete progress' beyond the recognition of a need for legislation on the basis of a general state plan on regional policy.[20] More generally the Commission also demanded a 'strengthening' of the administrative structures without spelling out what this meant in practice. Furthermore, for the first time the Commission referred to the need for attention to be paid to the question of the 'implementation' of laws and frameworks.[21] The Commission's approach, consequently, maintained the vague and reactive character of the Opinions rather than evaluating according to clearly defined standards or benchmarks and proactively detailing policy recommendations.

The question as to the causal relationship between the regional self-government agenda set out in the Opinions and the development of regionalization in the CEECs will be discussed in Chapter 5. There was, undoubtedly, a temporal correlation. The Reports commended developments in institution-building at the regional level such as the Czech parliament's approval of the territorial division of the country into 14 regions in December 1997, and Romania's Law on Regional Development of July 1998 which created eight development regions. Romania in particular was seen as having made 'notable progress'. Its legislation had been drafted with EU assistance, and thus it was regarded as offering a solid basis for defining national and regional-level policy and programming structures.[22] The 1998 Report on Poland explicitly states that the territorial state administration reform, due to enter into force in January 1999, 'should have a significant positive effect on the development of a genuine regional policy approach in Poland' even though Poland's regional development strategy was 'still at a conceptual stage' and there remained 'administrative deficits in the elaboration, co-ordination and implementation of regional policy'.[23] The signal was reiterated by a shift in the Commission's view on Hungary's progress on regional development and administrative capacity. In the eyes of the Commission Hungary went from being an 'ice-breaker' to a laggard within a year precisely because it was not developing regional-level institutions. For despite the Hungarian parliament's approval of a 'National Concept on Regional Development' in March 1998, according to the Commission it had 'not adequately addressed the short-term Accession Partnership priority relating to the reinforcement of institutional and administrative capacity in regional development'. From the Commission's standpoint Hungary had made advances in legislation and in developing concepts in regional policy objectives, but the 'accompanying structures and institutions' were still too weak and this was what was critical for the management and implementation of Community assistance.[24] In particular, the Commission identified 'difficulties in making use of EU funds (PHARE) for regional development' to illustrate the need for strengthening the country's project development and management capacity, which would allow for a greater absorption of pre-accession aid and prepare for the participation in structural funds.[25] Latvia's assessment stood out in the 1998 round of Reports. The Commission's reference to 'significant progress' on the way to participation in the EU's structural policy was a strong indication of what benchmarks it was employing: a 1998 government concept of regional policy, followed by legislation to accelerate regional development, as well as the establishment of a Regional Development Council for the coordination of regional policy at the central, regional and local level were singled out as the positive developments in Latvia.[26]

Over time the content of the Regular Reports that was dedicated to regional policy and its institutional environment expanded, reflecting the growing importance of this policy domain for the candidate states and the Commission. Equally, the Commission's criticisms become more explicit and more specific, though the lack of detail in its policy recommendations remained. A distinctive focus of the 1999 Regular Reports was on the candidates' attempts to define regions in line with the EU NUTS classifications. Thus, the Report on Bulgaria hailed the new law on regional development and the law on the administrative-territorial division of 1999 as a 'significant step', while highlighting that within this framework clarification is needed with regard to the six NUTS II macro-regions and 28 regions at NUTS III level. This reference to the preliminary NUTS classification is complemented by a more general reminder that particular attention has to be paid to the implementation capacity of the central coordinating unit in the Ministry of Regional Development at national and regional level.[27] In the case of Latvia and Lithuania the Commission clearly states that according to EU methodology the whole country will be considered as one NUTS II region.[28] In the preceding years the candidate countries had debated different options for NUTS territorialization, principally with the aim of creating a coherent structure of statistical units which would also maximize the potential receipts from structural funds. In the 1999 reports, for the first time the Commission revealed its concerns over the relationship between regional self-government and the effective management of structural funds. There was not a significant shift from the Commission against regional self-government at this time, but its previously strong signal was becoming adulterated.

We can analyse the mixed signals by examining the Reports on the two countries which were gradually developing forms of democratized regional self-government: the Czech Republic and Poland. In the case of the Czech Republic the Report referred in critical terms to the decision to divide the country into 14 regions matching NUTS II criteria and eight regions akin to those of NUTS III by 2000. The Commission required 'clarification' as to the 'division of responsibilities between the political (NUTS II) level and the administrative (NUTS III) level in order to ensure smooth implementation'.[29] In contrast, Poland, having introduced its regional reform in January 1999, received the most emphatic endorsement in the 1999 Reports. Under the section on the 'political criteria', the Commission applauded the 'reforms of impressive scope and depth' over the previous twelve months, including regional administrative reform.[30] Compared with the Commission's evaluations of 1997–98, the 1999 Report commends Poland for making 'major progress' in strengthening the legal, institutional and budgetary framework for the implementation of structural actions despite the fact that regional policy strategy is still at a 'conceptual stage'. In particular, the Commission expected that Poland's 16 new regional governments (coinciding with the NUTS II level) would have 'a significant positive effect on the development of a genuine regional policy approach'. As with the Czech Republic, however, the Commission made the clarification of the relationship between the new political regions and the lower level authorities (at the NUTS III level) an 'urgent priority'.[31]

Romania and Slovenia were also favourably commented upon in 1999 with regard to their progress in the legislative and specific institutional frameworks for regional policy at the national and regional level.[32] The Report on Slovenia illustrates that the Commission's initial emphasis on basic legislation is gradually being replaced by a stronger concern for capacity issues. Thus, Slovenia is urged to 'rapidly' establish the institutions ensuring administrative capacity, which is needed for the efficient management of the pre-accession instruments as well as subsequent EU structural policy.[33] There is an apparent contradiction between the glowing treatment of Romania and the quite severe criticisms of Hungary. Both countries opted to form their county-level governments into administrative-statistical development regions with appointed boards (voluntarily in Hungary, by law in Romania) rather than establish elected regional self-government bodies. In the case of Romania, the Report is extremely vague as to what should happen next, stating merely that 'further efforts are required to ensure effective implementation of structural policies including in the area of budgetary and financial procedures needed and in building the necessary administrative structures and management capacities, both centrally and regionally'.[34] The Report on Hungary acknowledges that it has reached an 'advanced state of preparation for the implementation of structural funds', but states that there has been little progress on the 'concrete implementation of regional policy objectives'. The institutional framework for regional policy is classified as 'weak' overall, even though the linking of the funding of the regional development boards with the central finance ministry is seen as a positive development in the area of fiscal management and coordination.[35]

The concern about the administrative coherence and functioning of regional and local tiers of government was repeated in the Report on Slovakia. As in 1998, Slovakia is identified by the Commission as having made 'no concrete progress' either in legislation or institutional framework in preparation for the implementation of structural funds, despite the fact that it had by now demarcated four NUTS II regions and eights NUTS III regions.[36] The Commission simply noted that the territorial and administrative reform process remained 'unfinished'. The Commission recommended that Slovakia create 'an independent co-ordination structure with the capacity to implement and monitor regional policy' but it did not clarify whether this meant at the regional or national level, or both. Echoing the advice given to the Czech Republic and Poland, the Commission wanted 'a clear separation of administrative and political functions' at the regional level.[37]

The emphasis on the *acquis* and capacity, 2000–02

The 2000 Reports

From 2000 onwards the structure of the Regular Reports changed significantly to reflect a much greater attention to the 'capacity' of the candidate countries. The Commission now systematically commented separately on each of the chapters of the *acquis* under the section heading 'Ability to assume the obligations of membership'. This consolidated the evaluation of capacity into one main section whereas previously it had fallen into several sections, including the previous fourth section on 'administrative capacity'. In addition, in 1999 and 2000 there is an increasing emphasis on the Commission's own efforts to raise the capacity level of the CEECs through 'Twinning' projects, which are detailed and given more prominence by including them in the introductory sections to the Reports. Thus, while 'administrative capacity' to apply the *acquis* is no longer treated as a separate issue in the Reports, the theme is evaluated as an integral part of all sections and policy areas. The capacity issue becomes the key thread linking all aspects of enlargement. A significant inconsistency in the reporting mechanism was also much more evident from 2000 in that the Reports did not employ a consistent time frame for the measuring of 'progress'. The Reports routinely opened with a reference to the level of progress achieved since the last Regular Report. In determining whether a country made progress or not, however, it is not always clear whether the Commission is measuring solely against the previous year or over a longer span of previous years. This ambiguity also changes depending on the country being reported on.

In 2000 the evaluation of developments in regional policy draw explicitly from the criteria laid out in the Structural Funds Regulations since they, in fact, constitute the *acquis* in this area. While the regulations are 'thin' and thus do not make for precise benchmarks, they do at least provide a structuring device for the evaluation. The categories for evaluation that are drawn directly from the regulations on structural funds include an agreed NUTS territorial organization, legislative framework, preparation for programming, administrative co-ordination, evaluation and monitoring systems, financial management and regional statistics, followed by a brief 'overall assessment'. The overall thrust of the Reports is on whether the CEECs have complied with these requirements for national-level oversight of implementation and management in order to ensure fiscal rectitude.

Indirect references to regional capacity issues are also made in the sections on 'short-term priorities', and under the 'Reinforcement of administrative and judicial capacity' in the section on 'Accession Partnership and National Programme for the Adoption of the *Acquis*', mostly in connection with the management of ISPA and SAPARD funds. Under the 'medium-term priorities' regions are increasingly mentioned under 'economic and social cohesion' and in relation to improving the NPAAs. The Reports on many smaller countries repeatedly noted that the regional and local levels had not been covered at all or not sufficiently detailed in the NPAAs.[38] The NPAAs are also linked into the Commission's positive reinforcement strategy for enlargement. When NPAAs copied the structure of the Regular Reports, the Commission demonstrably approved of them in the Reports.

As with the 1998–99 Reports, the terminology employed in the evaluation of progress in the Reports for 2000 was generally imprecise. Typically nebulous comments included references to 'no substantial progress' or 'more work is needed' (Bulgaria), and to 'no particular progress' or the fact that 'a number of difficulties remain' and 'efforts need to be continued' (Estonia). Nevertheless, the 'capacity' issue was the main theme that imbued the Reports and indicated the priority for the Commission. Specifically, this entailed a concentration on concepts such as 'coordination' and management 'structures'. A clear distinction between larger and smaller countries emerges in the way that the Commission addresses these issues, and there is also for the first time a clear demarcation between the 'ins' and the 'outs' among the candidates, with Bulgaria and Romania increasingly marked down for lack of 'progress' and placed in the 'out' category.

The 2000 Report on the Czech Republic recognized that 'over the last three years' the Czech Republic had made 'significant progress' overall.[39] The positive developments for the Commission included several capacity strengthening measures: the Act on Support for Regional Development which defined the competences at national, regional and local level; government guidelines on the management and organizational structures for the implementation of EC pre-accession assistance; the legal basis for regional development, especially budgetary rules; the contribution of the National Development Plan 2000–06; the programming documents for SAPARD and ISPA; and increased staffing levels in the Ministry for Regional Development.[40] The Commission reports, but does not evaluate, the completion of territorial organization in the Czech Republic (14 regions similar to NUTS III and eight regions corresponding to NUTS II became operational for statistical purposes in January 2000, and for legislative purposes in January 2001). Rather the Commission reverts to the default routine call for 'administrative strengthening' and 'further efforts'. It also recommends obtusely that 'communications between the central and regional levels could be improved'.[41]

While there is some confusion in the Report on Hungary as to whether it had made 'some progress' or 'significant progress' overall, the Report repositioned it among the frontrunners with regard to the adaptation to EU regional policy.[42] Since the harsh criticisms of the 1999 Report Hungary had adopted the 1999 Law on Regional Development which strengthened the seven Regional Development Councils at NUTS II level (they were transformed into compulsory bodies with a legal status) and improved coordination by entrusting one ministry – the Economics Ministry – with the control of regional policy. The Commission appears satisfied that Hungary is progressing on the 'partnership' principle with local, regional and economic and social partners now being involved in the planning and implementation of programmes through the National Regional Development Council and the seven Regional Development Councils. Unusually for the Commission the report analyses in some depth the positive and negative features of the 1999 Law on Regional Development. The Commission welcomed the fact that the law had 'increased the importance of the regions which correspond to NUTS level II' and 'further clarified the role of different institutions', but remained critical of the capacity of the framework at the regional level to deliver 'efficient decision-making and respect for programming principles'. Consequently, the Report called for Hungary to strengthen the 'working capacity both at national and regional level enabling the implementation of Structural Funds and the Cohesion Fund' and the financial structures at the regional level. This was understandably interpreted as Commission pressure for a shift to political regions in Hungary (see Chapter 3).

In the Report on Poland the Commission's view of 'significant progress' overall was linked to the passage of the new Law on Regional Development and its definition of a two-tier regional government system. Poland now had a clearly demarcated, institutionalized and democratically elected administrative-political framework at all territorial levels. Furthermore, it had developed the concept of a 'regional contract' to be negotiated by the national government and the 16 *województwa* as the basis for funding regional development programmes. The Commission expressed some concern about the contracts and wanted more clarification. It was more concerned, however, with the financial arrangements between the national government and the regions. Poland's new regions had no separate tax-raising powers and thus depended wholly on the centre. The Report appeared to suggest that a separate budgetary basis for the regions 'should be carefully examined'.[43] The apparent overlap in the responsibilities of the two leading officials in the regions, the marshal and the *wojewoda*, is mentioned without comment (these reforms are discussed in more detail in Chapter 5). While the Report did raise concerns about capacity and implementation, the weight was on a positive evaluation of Poland's democratized regional governance.

Slovakia's progress was classified as 'limited'. In particular, the Commission criticized Slovakia's incomplete and unbalanced territorial and administrative organization. The new territorial-administrative organization introduced in June 2000 after a heated political debate which was fuelled by the conflated issues of the territorialized Hungarian minority and the regional boundaries, created twelve disparate units corresponding to NUTS III regions. The Commission considered that this configuration was dysfunctional.[44] Furthermore, Slovakia was regarded as lacking some basic coordinating institutional structures such as a 'lead ministry', and the competences on regional policy were 'scattered among different institutions'.[45] Slovenia, in contrast, received one of the highest evaluations by achieving 'significant progress' in the field of regional policy. The number of implementing acts and secondary legislation adopted to build the legal and institutional framework in this policy area are commented upon favourably. The Commission's main complaint about Slovenia was that it was attempting to maximize its potential receipts from structural funds by anachronistically dividing the country into two NUTS II level regions (separating the wealthy capital Ljubljana from the rest of the country).[46]

With the exception of Slovenia, the Regular Reports for 2000 indicate that progress in the field of regional policy is slower in the smaller

CEECs, most notably Estonia, Latvia and Lithuania. In these states the legislative framework and government decisions lag behind the bigger candidate countries, largely because the order of domestic political priorities is such that regionalization is perceived to be less relevant. The Reports on Estonia and Latvia, for example, highlighted that the Commission was concerned about the slow rationalization of local self-government by a reduction in the number of units. Estonia, according to its Report, lacks 'administrative co-ordination' in regional policy and 'the current structures do not yet seem to provide an appropriate framework'. Similarly, Latvia is told of the 'urgent need' to put in place legislation preparing for the future use of structural funds.[47] This Report provides one of the more specific references to the Commission's primary concern with the central level of funds management a priori to regionalization: 'The strengthening of regional structures should focus on the establishment of local and regional partnerships, which may contribute to planning and project design within the overall partnership structure ... To this end, it is of the utmost importance that the necessary structures for co-ordinated programming, management, monitoring, evaluation, financial management and control of Structural Fund assistance are established at the central level, before a stand is taken on whether a further decentralization is feasible or advisable.'[48] The Report proceeded to state that the main concern is with 'effective financial management structures' and 'operational and transparent financial control' for EC funds and national resources. That the Commission was attempting to steer regional policy towards strong central control in the Baltic states is explicitly stated in the report on Lithuania, where the law on regional policy is criticized: 'Above all, the strong element of decentralization contained in the Law raises some concerns with regard to the administrative capacity to meet the requirements of the implementation of future Structural Funds assistance.' The Commission wanted a strong 'concentration' of the responsibility for the preparation for the structural funds to the Ministry of the Interior, and the primary goal of the 'utmost importance' was to strengthen 'capacity for the regional development planning process at central level' and not at sub-national levels.[49]

Two larger candidate countries, Bulgaria and Romania, are strongly condemned for the slow speed of development in regional policy. This was a sign that the Commission had already consigned them to the 'out' category as far as the next wave of enlargement was concerned. Bulgaria, for example, was criticized because although it had introduced six planning regions corresponding to NUTS II the 'responsibilities at the regional level are not very clear'. It was told to 'speed up the implementation of administrative reform'.[50] The 2000 Report on Romania reversed sharply from the Commission's previous positive evaluations. Even in the introductory section on twinning, which usually confines itself to the latest update on the number and type of projects funded and sometimes lists the member states involved in twinning, the Commission has added an unusually explicit and detailed critique, pinpointing the lack of commitment on the part of Romania's national authorities: 'The success of twinning projects in Romania depends on the national authorities' contribution to smooth implementation. In addition to assigning adequate staff and providing operational facilities, full participation of the senior management of the beneficiary institutions is necessary in order to deliver meaningful institutional and policy reform.'[51] The signal the Commission appeared to be sending was that Romania lacked commitment to the enlargement process. The Report emphasized the weakness of administrative capacity at both the central and the regional level. Exceptionally, here the Commission attempted to sketch out what its understanding of 'administrative capacity' entailed: 'the main priority is to strengthen co-ordination and management structures in order to allow an efficient and partnership-based decision-making process, at regional and local level, that is coherent with national regional policy. A clear and balanced allocation of responsibilities should be implemented: at national level, between national administrations involved in the future management of structural funds (National Agency for Regional Development and line Ministries); and at macro-region level between all the participants involved in the Regional Development Boards.'[52] Our interviews with officials in DG Enlargement suggest that the explanation for this reversal in the estimation of Romania was undoubtedly related, among other issues, to the coming to power of a new nationalist government and its suspension of the controversial macro-regional bodies set up with PHARE assistance.

The 2001 Reports

In the 2001 Regular Reports the Commission shifted its focus once again. Whereas in the 2000 Reports there had been mixed signals on the issue of 'capacity' and centralized and regionalized forms of managing regional policy were evaluated without prejudice towards one form or the other, in 2001 the Reports concentrated on the capacity of central governments to manage programming and budgeting, whether the levels of staffing and training were adequate, and whether central governments had provisions for the monitoring and evaluation of the use of funds. The gap between the candidates most likely to join in a first round of enlargement and those relegated to a later second round is also much more clearly reflected in the assessment of progress. Most of the first-round accession countries are classified as having achieved 'good', 'some', 'further', or even 'limited' progress, whereas the others are evaluated as having made 'little' or 'no' progress.

Hungary is acknowledged to have made 'good progress'.[53] Hungary's positive evaluation is linked to its compliance with the Commission's expectations in several key areas, in particular by the appointment of the Ministry of Finance as the future managing authority for structural funds, the reinforcement and training of staff in the relevant ministries and agencies, a simplified National Development Plan with a limited number of operational programmes, including a single, centrally managed Operational Programme for Regional Development, and the confirmation of the NUTS classification agreed with Eurostat in 1997.[54] The Commission concluded that 'programming is progressing well in Hungary', though the 'administrative capacity', in particular with regard to the future managing and paying authorities in the ministries, still 'needs to be considerably strengthened'.[55] Areas that are identified for improvement include 'inter-ministerial co-ordination' and 'an even wider application of the principle of partnership'. The Commission, however, also wanted the partnership principle activated at the regional level: 'Genuine partnership structures at regional level, including the regional and local authorities and other competent public authorities, the economic and social partners and any other relevant bodies (e.g. minority groups), should be established, and a strong input of the regions into the programming process taking place at the national level should be ensured.'[56] The Report on the Czech Republic was also generally positive as it was deemed to have made 'further progress'. The key question for the Commission was how it would define the financing arrangements for the new regional governments, which became operational in 2001, to guarantee their ability to contribute to the co-financing system for the structural funds.[57] The self-governing regions also had yet to be included in the National Development Plan as part of the partnership principle. The unanswered question arising from these reports was what kind of regional inputs could be achieved in a context where the Commission's emphasis was being placed on centralization, and in the absence of functioning regional self-government.

The Report on Poland went some way to answering this question. Despite the development of strong regional self-government in Poland, its Report recognized only 'limited' and 'no particular progress' since the last report. By 2001 the 16 regional self-governing units, created in 1999, are seen to be operational and 'effectively carrying out regional policy functions', but the report claimed that 'developments in this area have largely stalled'.[58] In fact, Poland was making significant and experimental reforms to its regionalization. Further institutional changes were to be made from January 2002 including the creation of seven new districts (NUTS III level), and changes in the borders of six districts and two regions. Most importantly, a new system of 'regional contracts', concluded in mid-2001 between the elected head of each *województwo* and the Minister for Regional Development, now determined the amount of financial support provided to each regional self-government in 2001 and 2002, though the funds were under the control of the *wojewoda* (the regional representative of the central government). For 2001–02 a small budget of just under 1.5 million euros had been earmarked for the implementation of regional development priorities as detailed in the 'regional contracts'. The Commission stressed that 'these funds constitute grants towards earmarked projects and do not for the moment imply a decentralization of public finance in the absence of amendments to the law on the income of regional self-governments'. While the Report recognized that the contract system 'has the potential to play a key role in the preparatory process and, in the medium-term, in Poland's socio-economic development', and despite the fact that the regions had newly established 'steering committees' to involve social partners in the use of funds, it was not deemed an adequate mechanism for fulfilling the 'partnership' requirement.[59]

The 2001 Report on Poland sent the clearest signal yet that the Commission did not want a decentralization of the management of regional funds at this stage, even where regional self-government was operational. The primary concern was with national-level preparations for structural funds and regional inputs into that level: 'At the regional level variable progress has been achieved with programming, while at the national level no positive new developments can be reported ... A strong input of the regions into the programming process taking place at the national level should be ensured.' Yet, the section on twinning make some interesting observations about the distinctiveness of Poland's regionalization, noting that projects under PHARE 2000 included twinning with regional administrations to enhance their preparations for structural funds management.[60] Moreover, the report uniquely and enigmatically admits to the reality of divergent models within the EU and the candidates, commenting that 'nearly all Member States are or will be engaged in twinning, allowing Poland to benefit from a variety of administrative models and cultures in the European Union'.[61]

In response to previous criticism Slovakia had again reformulated its territorial organization in July 2001, after more heated domestic debates, into four regions approximating to NUTS II and eight districts similar to NUTS III, but this configuration had still to be finalized with the Commission.[62] In fact, the Commission regarded these structures as incomplete: 'On the regional level no structures exist which could assume in a credible manner significant management tasks in the near future.'[63] Like Poland, Slovakia was seen to have made 'little progress' since the last report and had 'little advanced' in 'developing the necessary structures for the implementation of Structural Funds after accession'. In the case of Slovakia the Commission alternated between emphasizing the policy process and the institutional basis on which it should operate. It accepted that 'procedures for financial control ... are being put in place' (for example, the Ministry of Construction and Regional Development was established as the future managing authority, and a new implementing agency will be the paying authority), and that 'the first steps' have been taken on programming by the drafting of the NDP.[64] Nevertheless, the key issue was the establishment of 'a clear and reasonable division of responsibilities on the central level and between the central and regional level'.[65]

According to the 2001 Report, Slovenia made 'limited progress' or 'very little progress'.[66] This Report records no particular developments and even 'no progress' under key sub-headings of the evaluation of Chapter 21, such as territorial organization and institutional structures, and notes fairly modest changes under the rest, for example staffing increases, the establishment of working groups or a supervisory board for the preparation of the NDP, and includes the routine reminder to strengthen the administrative capacity of the ministerial units designated as managing and paying authorities. Slovenia is most directly criticized for its proposal to create two NUTS II level regions, which the Commission flatly rejected.[67]

Despite the recognition of 'some progress' in both Estonia and Lithuania since the last Reports, criticisms in these cases focused on the weak capacity of the programming and managing authorities for structural funds.[68] The Commission was particularly concerned that there should be a strong centralization of management in both countries and thus approved readily of the designation of the Ministry of Finance as the future managing authority and paying authority for some funds.[69] Lithuania remained one of the few accession states to agree its provisional NUTS classification with the Commission. Latvia's assessment is much more critical. It had made 'limited progress' since the last Report.[70] The criticism extended to the whole gamut of legislative, institutional, structural and administrative issues.[71] Despite the criticisms, the Commission considered that 'an important step' had been taken by entrusting the Ministry of Finance with the future responsibility for structural funds.[72]

Political divisions within Romania in 2000–01 meant that its regional policy was in a state of flux. As noted above, the change of government resulted in the dissolution of the National Agency for Regional Development and the suspension of the macro-regions designed in cooperation with PHARE. These were replaced by a Ministry of Development (with two of the ministry's state secretaries in charge of regional policy). Given that the Commission had recommended the centralization of financial controls and managing authority in other accession states, it would have seemed incongruous not to classify Romania's centralization as a positive development. The new ministry qualified as 'some progress' in the eyes of the Commission.[73] This must have been difficult for the Commission officials who had been deeply involved in the regionalization scheme of 1998 and had seen it fall victim to nationalist paranoia about separatism.

Romania had agreed its NUTS classification with Eurostat (42 counties (*judet*) similar to NUTS III, and eight 'development regions' similar to NUTS II), but the Report stated that the responsibilities of the ministries and other bodies involved in the preparation of structural funds assistance was under-defined both at the national and regional level. In a similar vein, the report makes a value-neutral reference to the Law on Local Public Administration of 2001, which defined the new responsibilities for local authorities and placed coordination power with the prefects, the local representatives of the central government. The Commission made oblique references to the political situation in the country. It observed that a 'political consensus' is the basis for efficient inter-ministerial coordination and advised that the role of regional structures in programme development and implementation needed to be 'further clarified'.[74]

Bulgaria made only 'little progress' since the last Regular Report. As with Romania, Bulgaria had established administrative structures at the regional level, namely six planning regions corresponding to NUTS II level, but the Commission was dissatisfied with weak definition of their role and responsibilities. In particular the 'transparent involvement of the regions in programming, implementation and evaluation of EC assistance' was deemed to be too weak and thus not in step with the 'partnership' principle. It is clear from the report that the Commission was thoroughly dissatisfied by the weak capacity and poor coordination within and between central ministries. Moreover, as with Romania, the report noted the lack of a political consensus in the domestic politics of Bulgaria over the adoption of EU norms and regulations.[75]

The 2002 Reports and the accession decision

The Regular Reports of 2002 were the final Reports before the EU took the decision on the scale of the enlargement at the Copenhagen Council of December 2002. The Reports were structured as an overall evaluation of the progress made by the candidate countries since the Opinions of 1997, and were much more concise in analysing compliance with the chapters of the *acquis* than any of the previous Reports. Two features of the Reports stand out. Firstly, there was an attempt to minimize the differences between those candidate countries that were considered to be eligible for the first wave of enlargement. The political logic here is evident, for how could there be significant differentiation in the progress if they were all to be accepted as new members. Conversely, the gap in progress between the first-wave accession countries and Bulgaria and Romania is much accentuated in the Reports. Again, the logic was to more fully differentiate those who were not to be granted membership. In comparison with the previous Reports, those of 2002 also elaborate more precise recommendations regarding the outstanding shortcomings of all the candidates. A new feature in the Reports is the addition of Action Plans, which are meant to provide guidance to the candidates on how to close the last remaining gaps. Nevertheless, there are apparent contradictions and tensions in the Reports over the need to sanction accession and the findings of little progress on the key questions of capacity and implementation.

In 2002 Hungary is simply mentioned to have made 'progress' without any further classification of its achievements. The key elements of this progress included the final confirmation to Eurostat of the NUTS classification in January 2002, the concentration of control to the Ministry of Finance as the single future paying authority for the Structural and Cohesion Funds, and the introduction of a consultative forum for the presidents of the Regional Development Councils to meet the 'partnership' criteria.[76] These were hardly radical changes, even compared with the 2001 Report. The Report was contradictory. On the one hand, we are told that Hungary 'has met the priorities of the Accession Partnership in the area of Regional Policy only to a very limited extent'.[77] On the other hand, Hungary was now applauded by the Commission for 'generally meeting the commitments it has made in the accession negotiations on this chapter', for its 'high degree of alignment with the *acquis*' and for 'achieving adequate administrative capacity to implement the *acquis*'.[78] There is also a repetition of the formulaic demands for greater attention to inter-ministerial cooperation and partnership in programming and implementation.

Poland is deemed to have made 'important progress' since the last Report. As with Hungary, this evaluation is based on fairly basic developments which had not radically altered from the position in 2001, such as the agreed NUTS classification, the designation of the Finance Ministry as the paying authority and a framework for multi-annual programming. Whereas the 2001 Report had been less than complimentary about regional self-government in Poland, the 2002 Report emphasized the 'important roles' to be played by the elected and appointed structures at the regional level.[79] While the legislative alignment with the *acquis* was considered 'reasonable' by the Commission, it wanted the 'current level of administrative capacity needs to be substantially improved'. As with previous Reports no specific recommendations are made with regard to the criteria or measurement of the 'level' of administrative capacity.[80]

The Report on the Czech Republic acknowledged that 'further important progress' had been made. Several basic developments receive the Commission's approval: the finalization of the Objective 2 eligible area in the region of Prague; legislation on financial controls in public administration; the establishment of all the Regional Councils and the operationalization of the new regional governments at NUTS III level; the restructuring of the ministries; a revised NDP; compliance with the partnership principle; and the introduction of a pilot version of the new monitoring system.[81] The Commission was positive about the level of 'administrative capacity' but called for strengthening of financial control, and communication and coordination channels in order to enhance 'project development capacity at national, regional and local level'.[82]

Slovakia's 2002 Report is also premised on a formulaic and largely unsubstantiated certification of 'progress' made over the past year. Again the progress is hinged on agreements on the creation of four NUTS II regions, the establishment of the managing and paying authorities, the beginning of the programming process in January 2002, and a regulatory framework allowing for multi-annual budgeting and internal audits. The Commission remained critical, however, about 'transparency, efficiency and reliability in the implementation of programmes' and administrative capacity more generally.[83] Obvious weaknesses in the readiness of Slovakia were glossed over. Thus, the overall verdict in the 2002 Report reads: 'Slovakia has aligned itself with the *acquis* in the field of regional policy and co-ordination of structural instruments but effective administrative structures are only in place to a limited extent.' A clear definition of the implementation structure for structural funds was also considered to be 'still missing'.[84] Under the section on the Accession Partnership, the tone is even more hesitant, indicating that even the legislative framework is only 'almost completed'.[85]

Whereas serious weakness had been identified with Latvia in the 2001 Report, its evaluation by the Commission in 2002 improved impressively. The Report recorded 'important progress' which as elsewhere hinged primarily on the designation of the Ministry of Finance as the future managing authority for structural funds, the reorganization of this ministry and the passing of a Regional Development Law in March 2002.[86] Despite the fact that Latvia was now considered to be among the first wave candidates and ready for membership, the Report states that weak administrative capacity is 'a matter of concern' for the Commission, which must be addressed if Latvia is 'to be ready for membership'.[87] Similarly, Estonia is considered to have made 'important progress' in preparing for the implementation of the *acquis* and structural policies through developments in its legislation and administrative capacity.[88] At the same time, the Report notes that the accession priorities in the area of regional policy have been only 'partially met', though the implementation of the Action Plan to remedy this 'is on track'.[89] As with the other reports, Lithuania's 'significant progress' is overstated. The key elements noted were the agreement with Eurostat on the NUTS classification, a new legislative framework allowing transfers between different budget lines for EC-funded projects, explicit programmes on strengthening administrative capacity and partnership, the submission of the NDP 2002–04 to the Commission and internal financial audits in all ministries and bodies involved in Structural and Cohesion Funds. The Commission's evaluation of Lithuania's administrative capacity to implement the *acquis* is, however, hesitant as this aspect is evaluated as being 'sufficient, though still rather fragile'.[90]

The Report on Slovenia suggests that it is best prepared for the implementation of regional policy, as it had made 'major progress' since the last reporting round. The elements identified by the Commission as meriting this evaluation – such as designating the Economics Ministry as the future managing authority and the Finance Ministry as the future paying authority, ongoing preparation of the Single Development Plan, the establishment of a monitoring committee to oversee the implementation of the NDP and the partnership principle and no new developments with regard to territorial organization and financial control – are not measurably different from those developments in other candidate countries noted earlier but which merited a less complimentary evaluation of 'progress'. The Report praises Slovenia for being 'well advanced in the field of financial control and management', while also observing that there had been 'no significant developments' in the area of regional policy.[91]

The two candidate countries that have been relegated out of the advanced group, Bulgaria and Romania, are treated the least generously in the 2002 Reports. Although Bulgaria is credited with 'some progress' in preparing for the implementation of structural funds, a categorization that by comparison with other Reports suggests a tangible improvement since 2001, the language of the Report is harsher than before, including a reference to the 'rather unsatisfactory management of some of the pre-accession funds that help Bulgaria prepare for the Structural and Cohesion Funds'. Later in the Report, the Commission concludes that overall 'since the Opinion Bulgaria has made little progress reaching a low level of readiness for the *acquis* in this area'.[92] The core weakness as far as the Report was concerned was the weakness of administrative capacity in key ministries, in particular at the central level, 'to design strategies and to implement and evaluate projects for regional development and economic and social cohesion financed by EC and national funds'.[93] Equally, Romania is declared to have made 'limited progress'. No substantive developments are commented upon, yet there are vague criticisms. For example: 'Considerable additional preparation is needed to improve the quality of the existing NDP before it can serve as a basis for a future development plan', and 'the capacity to discuss and clarify development priorities is very limited both at the national and regional levels'.[94] Romania is urged to focus particular attention on 'clarifying the role of the regional levels' in the management and implementation of structural funds as well as inter-ministerial coordination and partnership.

These Reports were of critical importance to the final decision on enlargement taken at the Copenhagen Council in December 2002, when all of the CEEC group (except for Romania and Bulgaria) were given an accession date of 1 May 2004. The decision was legally ratified in the Accession Treaty signed in April 2003. Equally, the Reports of

2002 demonstrated that the Commission still acknowledged that there were serious weaknesses in the CEECs as a whole with regard to fulfilment of the accession criteria.

The Comprehensive Monitoring Reports

Arguably, once the decision on accession had been taken, the Commission's leverage over the candidates and the power of the Reports to generate compliance was significantly weakened. To highlight the most important remaining gaps in the new member states and to maintain the credibility of the monitoring process, the Commission amended the format for the final round of the pre-accession reports. These reports were termed 'Comprehensive Monitoring Reports' (CMRs) and were to be published for the Council and the European Parliament six months before the accession date, and thus after many of the accession referenda had taken place in the candidate countries. The Thessaloniki European Council 2003 stated that 'In the coming months, the ten acceding countries are encouraged to keep up their efforts so that they are fully prepared to assume the obligations of membership by accession ... With a view to making a success of enlargement, the monitoring of these preparations has been intensified on the basis of the reports submitted regularly by the Commission.'[95] The process of compiling the information and the drafting resembled that of the preceding Regular Reports, though they were more concisely tied to the *acquis* and excised altogether the section on the political conditions. After all, the political criteria were considered 'fulfilled'. Despite some dissenting voices, there was a consensus inside the Commission that a political section in the CMRs 'would have been an anomaly'.[96]

Before the publication of the CMRs the Commission issued a Communication to the European Parliament and the Council 'On the Implementation of Commitments Undertaken by the Acceding Countries in the Context of Accession Negotiations On Chapter 21 – Regional Policy and Coordination of Structural Instruments'.[97] The Commission had committed itself to this specific report together with the CMRs at the Brussels European Council in October 2002. The fact that regional policy was singled out is a belated urgent recognition in the reporting mechanism of its salience for the performance of an enlarged EU. The Communication laid out the requirements and gaps in compliance more systematically and concisely than in any of the previous Reports or Accession Partnerships. It was as if transparency in the reporting could be allowed only once the political decision on enlargement had been taken.

The CMRs are organized under six headings (legislative framework, institutional framework, administrative capacity, programming capacity, financial and budgetary management, future project pipeline), which somewhat diverged from the usual sub-headings in the Regular Reports but provided for a more appropriate summary of the main tasks and problem areas. The Commission Communication of 16 July 2003 for the first time gave the CEECs a clear and detailed schema of the requirements under each heading. As for the legislative framework, the transposition of the *acquis* in the areas of public procurement, state aid/competition, environment and equal opportunities is highlighted as being essential for the implementation of the Structural and Cohesion Funds. With regards to the institutional framework the Commission's key areas of concern were inter-ministerial coordination, the institutional arrangements of the implementation system, the number and role of the intermediate bodies, the independence of the certifying role of the paying authority, financial control requirements and internal audit arrangements. The section on 'administrative capacity' was one of the few explicit attempts by a Commission document to detail the content of this concept. Obviously, this was a rather late stage in the accession process to do this. The content specified staff recruitment and training plans in administrative and executive institutions, the clarification of the responsibilities of the actors involved in the project application flow and the development of guidelines and manuals for operational programmes. Programming capacity here referred to the submission of the programming documents without delays and within 'a coherent strategic framework', the definition of the monitoring indicators and a computerized system for the collection and exchange of data. Under 'financial and budgetary management', the clarification of the flow of funds, verification checks by staff independent of the managing and paying authorities and the provision of appropriate and separate accounting systems for the structural funds and the cohesion fund are mentioned. As for the 'project-pipeline', the project preparation and national co-financing remain the Commission's primary concern.[98]

Each country CMR is structured around the chapters of the *acquis*. For each chapter the CMR identifies the areas in which a country 'is essentially meeting the commitments and requirements arising from the accession negotiations'. It is noteworthy that accession conditionality is defined purely in terms of the *acquis* and without reference to the Copenhagen criteria. The Commission's wording seems to reflect a realization that conditionality has been an evolutionary process and by 2003 is very different from that formulated in 1994. Each CMR then moves on to the areas where important further action is necessary to meet the 1 May 2004 deadline. In the overall conclusion, the CMR systematically groups the chapters or sub-areas within chapters in which a high level of alignment has occurred, areas where 'enhanced efforts' are needed to complete preparations for accession and 'issues of serious concern' which could persist until after accession unless immediate action is taken. These summaries are, in essence, an audit for enlargement that provide balance sheets of strengths and weaknesses.

Each CMR's review of Chapter 21 began with an important clarification, which is given to the candidates for the first time:

> The *acquis* under this chapter consists mostly of regulations, which do not require transposition into national legislation. They define the rules for drawing up, approving and implementing Structural Funds programmes and Cohesion Fund actions. These programmes are negotiated and agreed with the Commission, but implementation is the responsibility of the Member States. It is essential that Member States respect Community legislation in general, for example in the areas of public procurement, competition and environment, when selecting and implementing projects, and have the necessary institutional structures in place to ensure implementation in a sound and cost-effective manner from the point of view of both management and financial control.[99]

Ironically, the post-enlargement evaluation reporting in the CMR is much clearer on the essential elements of regional policy than the Regular Reports had been. Progress was determined under five key headings: territorial organization, legislative framework, institutional structures, programming and financial management and control. The NUTS classification had always been clearly marked as a priority under 'territorial organization', but the ability to ensure multi-annual budget planning had not previously been singled out yet now it was declared to be '*the essential feature of the legislative framework*' (authors italics).[100] Under 'institutional structures', the report emphasizes the need for a human resource strategy, and specific financial control provisions, internal audit units and inter-ministerial coordination. The 'programming' requirement includes the submission of a range of documents, such as the Development Plan, the Operational Programmes and the Single Programming Documents, a monitoring system and a mechanism ensuring the application of the 'partnership' principle. The CMRs also pay more attention to consequential cross-referencing under related chapters, thereby underlining the concrete links between different areas of policy-making.[101]

The vast majority of countries (Czech Republic, Estonia, Hungary, Latvia, Poland, Slovakia, Slovenia) were deemed to be essentially complying with the requirements concerning territorial organization and programming, whereas the requirements in relation to the legislative framework, institutional structures and financial management and control were only partially met. Only in the case of Lithuania was the legislative framework considered to be satisfactory. Moreover, the improvement of project pipelines, implementation structures, staffing and training as well as the alignment with the public procurement norms and rules are common themes running through all the conclusions to the CMR's evaluation of compliance with Chapter 21.

The importance of administrative and judicial capacity for the implementation and enforcement of the *acquis* was highlighted and addressed in a separate section at the beginning of each CMR. In the introductory section on 'public administration' each CMR conveyed additional information on local and regional governance in the CEECs.[102] The CMR on the Czech Republic included a reference to 'the decentralization to the regional and local level', which was nearing completion with the abolition of the old districts on 1 January 2003. The 14 regions were seen to have received 'considerable powers', including in the area of territorial planning and directly elected regional assemblies provide for regional self-government. The Commission remained concerned, however, about the need to clarify the division of competences.[103] Hungary's section included a reference to the ongoing debates in Hungary about regionalization, with a new reform proposal of August 2003 to reorganize the counties into economic and geographical regions, with elected regional governments and regional public administration offices. The current statistical-planning regions, which, as the CMR noted, were set up for structural fund purposes, would serve as a basis for regional public administration. Parts of the reform require a two-third majority in parliament, but the Hungarian plan was to finalize the reforms by the time of the next general elections in 2006.[104] The Commission restricted itself to summing up the reform proposal without passing judgement on it, though its non-disapproval, given the broad context of the reporting instrument, could reasonably be seen as approval.

The CMR on Poland briefly described the existing three-tier governance structure introduced in 1999, complemented by the rather opaque criticism that it lacks 'a clearly oriented, long-term programme for local and regional self-government' which 'could complicate the further implementation of the decentralization process'.[105] In the case of Slovakia reference was made to the constitutional amendment of 2001 which introduced eight self-governing regions with elected assemblies. The CMR stressed that the implementation of the regional reform was incomplete, in particular concerning fiscal decentralization which is due to be in place by 2005. In this case the Commission added a more detailed reminder: 'It is important that the transfer of functions and fiscal decentralization go hand in hand, ensuring a timely and proper functioning of a democratic, efficient and sustainable self-administration.'[106] In the case of Estonia, Latvia and Lithuania the CMRs stressed the limited outcomes of the reform of local government which had aimed to reduce the high number of municipalities. The failure was seen as posing difficulties for the financing and implementation of structural funds.[107]

The 2003 Reports on Bulgaria and Romania

For the second-wave countries, Bulgaria and Romania, the Commission continued the practice of issuing Regular Reports. Although they followed the structure of the preceding Reports, they showed some influence from the CMRs and a more acute awareness of the need to differentiate between the first- and second-wave countries. Compared to previous Regular Reports, the 2003 Reports on Bulgaria and Romania were more explicit in their description of the requirements and contained somewhat more focused guidance on the methods for compliance. In terms of the legislative framework for multi-annual programming and financial control and central-level institutional decisions like the designation of units within the Finance Ministry as managing and paying authorities, the 2003 Report on Bulgaria noted 'some progress'. As regards 'administrative capacity' the report clarified that this would hinge on 'credible human resources and career development strategies' and 'qualified and experienced staff'. Particular emphasis was put on the need for 'effective co-operation and communication between central and regional level implementing structures and to a substantial strengthening of the capacity of potential final beneficiaries at the regional and local level'. The conclusion included a strong rebuke of the political intent in Bulgaria: 'Greater appreciation of the scale of the task ahead is necessary, as well as a firm commitment to draw on the lessons to be learned from implementing the pre-accession instruments.'[108]

The 2003 Report on Romania reflected the fact that Romania's basic political institutions were still in flux. In particular there was instability on the arrangements for structural funds because of the merger of ministries and a reallocation of competences, specifically the dissolution of the Ministry of Regional Development and Prognosis and the transfer of regional development responsibilities to the Ministry of European Integration. The Commission remained sceptical about a government decision to set up partnership structures at national and regional level. In each area of regional policy Romania was urged to improve, but the overarching institutional 'uncertainty' was identified as the most fundamental problem the country needed to resolve. As with Bulgaria, the report implicitly concluded that there was a lack of political will for accession.[109]

As a follow-up to the Regular Reports of 2003, the Commission issued a 'Strategy Paper and Report of the European Commission on the Progress towards Accession by Bulgaria, Romania and Turkey' in November 2003.[110] It was an attempt to reassure these three countries that negotiations 'will continue on the basis of the same principles that guided the negotiations with the ten acceding countries, without calling into question the results achieved' and confirms that 2007 as the accession date for Bulgaria and Romania 'has now become a common objective of the Union'.[111] The striking aspect of this report is that it reverted to the format of the Opinions and early Reports by structuring the evaluation under the three Copenhagen criteria. With regard to the third criterion – the adoption of the *acquis* – regional policy was one of the areas Bulgaria was asked to concentrate on, alongside the reminder to build up the administrative capacity for fund management. In the case of Romania, the overall weak capacity of the public administration to implement adopted legislation was highlighted as an even more profound problem which, in the eyes of the Commission, would require 'a comprehensive, structural reform of both public administration and the judicial system'. The Commission emphasized that 'these concerns extend beyond adoption of the *acquis* and also apply to the management of EU financial assistance'.[112]

Conclusion

By systematically analysing the Commission's monitoring mechanism, in particular the Reports, we have attempted to demonstrate how nebulous and oscillating it was in many of its fundamental aspects. In the absence of a detailed *acquis* on regional policy, the Structural Funds regulations provided the only regulatory basis for the Commission to measure progress by the candidates. The problem for the Commission was that these regulations provided normative guidelines rather than explicit legal and institutional benchmarks. The Commission, nevertheless, examined specific laws on territorial-administrative reform, regional development, and ministerial organization to evaluate progress. Both conditionality and compliance, however, escaped clear definitions and consistency in the process. Ironically, after the accession negotiations had been completed the Commission provided much more precise recommendations for the successful candidates. In particular the Commission's Communication of July 2003 and the Comprehensive Monitoring Reports, but also the 2003 Reports for Bulgaria and Romania (and Turkey) and the Commission's Strategy Paper on these three countries defined the essence of 'administrative capacity' in the field of regional policy much more systematically than all the preceding Reports.

The Opinions and Reports also map a gradual shift in the Commission's focus from the norms of the Copenhagen criteria, and especially the political criteria, to a technocratic emphasis on the formal adoption of the *acquis*, and then to an emphasis on managerialism (the administrative capacity to effectively 'absorb' funds). The Reports also provide further evidence of the Commission's ambiguous signals regarding the form of institutionalization of sub-national governance discussed in Chapter 3. While the Opinions and the 1998 Reports contained some encouragement for decentralization and regional government, from 1999/2000 onwards, the Commission stressed the need for central control over regional policy.

This analysis suggests that there was a learning curve during accession, which generated a higher level of professionalization in the interaction between the Commission and the candidates over time. Equally, the greater clarity of the Commission's monitoring in the period after the political decision to enlarge had been taken is indicative of the extent to which the enlargement monitoring process was constrained by political factors. The poor clarity and flexible interpretations that characterized the Commission's monitoring during the enlargement process allowed for a wide latitude of political manoeuvrability over the application of conditionality and the evaluation of compliance. The absence of clear benchmarks blurred substantive cross-country comparisons. As we have discussed, the Commission qualified the degree of 'progress' in each case in a remarkably imprecise manner, but this progress was sometimes relative to that achieved at the last round of monitoring, and sometimes relative to some new non-transparent measure. Consequently, whether it was concerned with new legislation adopted or institutional change initiated, the monitoring did not allow for a consistent and cumulative evaluation and ranking of the candidate countries. For all the ambiguities of the process, however, there remains the question of how effective the Reports were in securing compliance with EU regional policy requirements by the candidate countries, and it is to this issue that we turn in Chapter 5.

5
Transition, Enlargement and Regionalization: a Comparison of Hungary and Poland

During the initial post-communist transition years in most CEECs the issue of local government reform was high on the political agenda as a central theme of democratic state-building. As discussed in Chapter 2 most countries introduced democratizing and decentralizing changes to the structure of local government (see Table 2.1). In formulating these reforms domestic policy-makers looked to their historical legacies of pre-communist experiences, to the transferability of systems of local government in Western Europe and beyond, as well as to the 'model(s)' promoted by the Commission and its actors. The framing of regional reform had normative and functional dimensions. As discussed in Chapter 2 some of the CEECs were formerly part of the Austro-Hungarian empire and thus had experience of a system of self-government and autonomy dating from the mid-nineteenth century and enduring in some cases until the 1930s. The functional legacy of communist-era planning regions provided a geographic template for the NUTS regionalization. The policy issue of whether to opt for political or statistical regionalization was also subject to an important territorial and functional constraint in that the former was most obviously relevant to big countries rather than to smaller countries such as Slovenia, Estonia, Latvia and Lithuania. In these countries debates about regionalization were primarily spurred on by the exogenous pressures of EU accession. In Poland, the Czech Republic and, to some extent, Slovakia regional reform had been a salient and controversial issue in the early years of post-communist transition during the constitution-making process, and even in these cases the implementation of regional self-government was postponed. Thus, while regionalization became a key issue in most CEECs during the enlargement process, the temporal correlation should not deflect us from the domestic factors in the debates in countries like Poland or Hungary, and key structural determinants such as size of country.

This chapter investigates the extent to which the developments in regional policy that emerged in the CEEC states from the second half of the 1990s, and which were temporally correlated with EU accession, were also driven by EU conditionality. The Commission's Opinions of 1997 identified 'regional administrative capacity' as a core requirement for accession and thereby galvanized latent debates over regionalization. As we have discussed in previous chapters, the formal EU conditionality for regional policy as embodied in Chapter 21 (regional policy and coordination of structural instruments) of the accession negotiations was weak on regulatory content. As we discussed in Chapter 3, some sections of the Commission attempted to apply an informal conditionality in the form of a preference for a regionalization that involved not only compliance with NUTS II standards but also included a form of regional self-government. Our concern here is with two main questions. First, was there a causal linkage between EU conditionality and policy and institutional outcomes in the CEECs in the regional policy domain? Second, to what extent was regionalization shaped by path-dependent factors located in domestic political settings rather than external pressures for compliance? In particular, we examine the impact of post-communist transition on regional reform. We present a comparative case study of developments in Poland and Hungary to analyse these questions.

These countries have been selected because they have been among the most important candidates for EU membership from several viewpoints. They are two of the most powerful economies of the CEECs, are generally regarded as having the most successful transition records, were the main beneficiaries of the EU's technical transition assistance programmes delivered by PHARE (and also of EBRD funds), and were the politically most important states of the CEECs during the enlargement process.[1] They share certain additional key features that we might expect to influence regional reform. On the one hand, they both have a tradition of regional identities, while exhibiting a low salience of politically significant ethno-territorial cleavages that might complicate or deter regional reform. On the other hand, they have both experienced repeated changes of government across the left and right of the political spectrum during their transitions in the 1990s which have helped to delay reforms in this area.

Against this background of similarities, the institutional choices for managing regional policy have been very different in Poland and

Hungary. They illustrate well the two ends of the spectrum of institutional change that has occurred in the CEECs: democratic regionalization in Poland, and administrative-statistical regionalization in Hungary. Against a comparable structural background Hungary and Poland have chosen highly divergent approaches to the issue of building 'regional administrative capacity', and thereby generated very different institutional settings for regional policy-making. The following analysis traces the reform process in both countries. We examine the actions of the key actors and evaluate the relative importance of the EU's external incentives and pressures compared with the domestic political structures, conditions and preferences. This comparison will help to 'bring transition back in' to the discussion about EU enlargement and conditionality by demonstrating their overlaps and interaction.

Hungary: administrative-statistical regionalization

In 1990 Hungary took a lead on its transitioning neighbours by becoming the first post-communist country to introduce local self-government reforms, the provisions for which were among the most liberal in the region.[2] The plans for reforming the hierarchical centralized socialist system had been discussed among reformist members of the Communist Party, the leaders of the pro-democracy movements, and academics, since the mid-1980s.[3] The Hungarian Democratic Forum coalition government (1990–94) held only 54 per cent of the seats in parliament, and given that a two-thirds majority of the parliament was needed to ensure the passage of the new local self-government legislation, the government was compelled to compromise with the opposition of both the former communists and the liberals. The government wanted to replicate the democratic local self-government of Western Europe, but also structured the new institutional architecture around Hungary's historically rooted *megyek* (county) level sub-national governance.[4] There was a widespread political consensus about the necessity for decentralization to the local level as a fundamental part of post-communist transition.

In theory, local governments at the commune and county level were to coexist in a non-hierarchical relationship to each other, however, the essence of the compromise of 1990 was that county-level governments would be indirectly elected by lower-level local councils, thereby weakening the authority of the counties vis-à-vis the directly elected local (municipal) governments. Broad criteria were drawn up, allowing almost any village or rural settlement to establish its own elected self-governing institutions and granting them a wide range of functions. As we noted in Chapter 2, the reform of 1990 created an incentive structure for a mushrooming of small governing units (to some 3200 units) which often lacked the experience and financial basis to fulfil basic governing tasks. Consequently in the period 1991–94 some of the lowest level units were amalgamated and there was some recentralization of powers. A key change was the creation of eight development regions, each of which was composed of two to three counties.[5] A new tier of central government-appointed bureaucrats, the Commissioners of the Republic, was also established at the new regional level. The liberal opposition, the Alliance of Free Democrats and Fidesz, had pushed for the creation of these quasi-prefects who were appointed directly by the prime minister and whose main responsibility was to supervise the legality of the work of local governments.[6]

Since PHARE had been established in 1989 with the specific aim of prioritizing international assistance to Poland and Hungary, Hungary was one of the first transition countries of Eastern Europe to benefit from aid flows. In 1992, two years after the 1990 reform of local government, Hungary was awarded PHARE money to assist in the country's regional policy, an integral part of which was the development of institutional structures to enable the government to decentralize the formulation and implementation of regional development policy.[7] By this time Hungary had already applied for membership of the EU and had concluded a Europe Agreement in December 1991. The first resolution on regional development, passed by parliament in 1993, displayed some influence of PHARE and was framed in a manner that demonstrated Hungary's commitment to 'Europeanization' by recommending that institutions should correspond to EU systems and practice.[8] Regional reform was politically controversial in Hungary's transition politics and was subject to much bargaining over the boundaries of the regions and their competences. In particular, there was no political consensus over whether the regions should be elected bodies or merely NUTS II compliant statistical regions devoid of political content.

During the communist period, the county-level governments had been a key lever of vertical control for the Communist Party and regional development was often determined by patronage networks within the party rather than on objective need. During the transition, views on regional and local governance reform cut across the left-right spectrum of ideological cleavages. The centrist Hungarian Democratic Forum, and the rightists of the Hungarian Christian Democratic Party and the Smallholders' Party supported the revival of strong county government and argued that both self-government and state supervision offices should be concentrated at this level. This position was opposed by the liberals of the Alliance of Free Democrats, and Fidesz, and by the left in the form of the Hungarian Socialist Party, who feared that the central government and bureaucracy would continue to dominate the localities through the state administrative offices.[9] The party alignment also differed over the proposal to establish regional development bodies. In their 1994 election manifestos the Hungarian Socialist Party, the Alliance of Free Democrats and the Hungarian Democratic Forum had all supported the establishment of regional development bodies, although opinions differed about their composition and functions and the place of the counties within this structure. While the Hungarian Socialist Party, the Alliance of Free Democrats and Fidesz supported the maintenance of strong county-level governments, Fidesz in particular saw the regional bodies as a threat to the power of local self-governments.[10] They also opposed giving the county councils any significant independent status from the municipal and local level.

Confusion and authority leakage resulted from the proliferation in the number of local government units. They became characterized by cronyism and corruption and were reluctant to cooperate or merge for the sake of efficiency.[11] Local leaders often acted, as one interviewee explained, like *'kis kiraly'* (little kings).[12] Their ineffectiveness was persistently criticized by the Commissioners of the Republic. The weak capacity and poor performance of the local governments led to renewed centralization. Competences were taken or eroded away from the local governments by the deconcentration of some forty state administrative departments to the sub-national level, including in key areas such as policing, taxation, education and public health. This gave the central government a tier of administrative control at the local level. These administrative reforms created a highly conflictual situation at the local level which was exacerbated by the alternance of parties in power at the centre and localities, and by the political cycles of transition. There was a political polarization between the centre-right Hungarian Democratic Forum coalition government and the county and local governments, many of which were dominated by members of the centre-right and liberal opposition parties Fidesz and the Alliance of Free Democrats.[13]

Following the elections of 1994 a governing coalition of the Hungarian Socialist Party and the Alliance of Free Democrats had a 72 per cent parliamentary majority. This was a decisive moment for further regional reform since the government controlled the two-thirds majority required for constitutional amendments and thus was in a position to advance or block reform for a regional tier of self-government. The coalition blocked regional self-government and shifted power to the county and municipality levels in a new local government act of 1994 which abolished the Commissioners of the Republic and the eight regions. At the same time, the authority of the county-level governments was enhanced by making them directly elected bodies, and transferring to them key responsibilities for major public services. A new system of centrally appointed Public Administrative Offices (PAOs) was established and located at the county level, though with similar responsibilities to the Commissioners.[14] The PAOs, as one of our interviewees put it, saw themselves as 'a kind of Prefect as in France'.[15] This institutional architecture of two elected tiers of non-hierarchical bodies at the sub-national level (county and local governments), and a system of quasi-prefects, has remained in place, notwithstanding further amendments to the law in 1996 and 1999.

Consequently, there was an extensive political debate and the main parameters of the structure of Hungary's sub-national government arrangements had been largely settled by the time the process of EU accession began to accelerate after 1994. Nevertheless the question of how best to secure and manage structural funds, together with EU pressures via PHARE, continued to keep the issue of centre–regional–local relations on the political agenda in Hungary. The main political parties, however, remained deeply divided over the benefits of establishing a regional tier of governance. The influence of the EU on the development of Hungary's regional policy steadily became more pervasive through the PHARE pipeline of delivering technical assistance. PHARE was instrumental in the preparation of the 1996 Act on Regional Policy and Physical Planning which implemented an administrative-statistical regionalization to make Hungary compliant with NUTS standards. The act laid down guidelines for a National Regional Development Concept which conformed to the precepts of EU regional development policy. The functional logic for the particular configuration of the regions came from the Hungarian Academy of Sciences' Regional Research Centre, which was responsible for drafting the National Regional Development Concept, and recommended the establishment of six NUTS II type regions corresponding to the six economic planning regions of 1971. The regionalization was finalized in a slightly different form, with a seventh region being demarcated in western Hungary, in consultation with Eurostat.[16] The act provided for the establishment on a voluntary basis of Regional Development Councils (RDCs) to assist the government with the management of regional policy. They were composed of representatives of county councils, local government associations, social and civic organizations as well as officials from the Ministry of Environment and Regional Policy. There was no agreement among the main political parties, however, on the exact territorial configuration of the 'development' regions and allocation of powers to the RDCs as most did not want to dilute the power of the counties and municipalities. The governing coalition was itself split over the issue. Whereas some members of the Hungarian Socialist Party favoured large regions, many deputies of the Alliance of Free Democrats favoured bottom-up 'voluntary' regionalization based on groups of counties or local units.[17] The different preferences had informed the decision to establish two different types of regions – statistical planning regions corresponding to NUTS II units and 'development regions', which were a proto-regional administrative structure. Ideally, it was intended that the RDCs would overlap with the statistical regions, though this was not a legal requirement and initially did not happen in practice. As noted in Chapter 4, the Commission applauded Hungary's approach in its 1997 Opinion on Hungary's Application for Membership, stating: 'Hungary is the first among Central European countries which adopted a legal framework closely in line with EU structural policy. Many sections of the new law have been drafted in perspective of taking over the *acquis*.'[18]

Apparently in response to perceived pressures from the Commission, the government rushed through parliament the act on the National Regional Development Concept in March 1998, just prior to the elections. The Regional Development Concept reconfigured the statistical regions and increased their number from six to seven (see Map 3).[19] Since the 'development regions' remained voluntary and lacked resources and powers, the county governments continued to be the dominant players in the preparation of development plans and the distribution of state and EU funding.[20] By late 1999 only five RDCs were established and functioning. Their administrative apparatuses, however, remained skeletal and lacked 'capacity', with few employees and limited financial resources. One county – the Zala county – even opted to join two RDCs simultaneously.[21] Although the Commission's Opinions had clearly welcomed the establishment of the NUTS II compliant statistical regionalization and the RDCs, Hungary was criticized by the EU in the 1998 and 1999 Regular Reports (as we discussed in Chapter 4) for the slow pace at which the RDCs were established, the fact that the councils at regional and county level were not fully operational and a general lag in implementation regarding regional policy objectives.

The opportunity for further reform was presented by the election of a new governing centre-right coalition of Fidesz and the Smallholders' Party in May 1998. Fidesz had been the strongest supporter of local government among Hungary's political parties, yet once in power it began to reverse its position. In general, Fidesz justified its policy shift

HU01 Central Hungary
HU02 Central Transdanubia
HU03 West Hungary
HU04 South Transdanubia
HU05 North Hungary
HU06 North Great Plain
HU07 South Great Plain

Map 3 Regionalization in Hungary (NUTS II regions)

on local government reform by pointing to pressures from the Commission on Hungary to comply with the demands of the EU accession process.[22] The EU simplified and devolved power over PHARE and other aid programmes to the Hungarian government in July 1999, despite charges of cronyism and corruption against the Fidesz government. Aside from EU funding, the RDCs had a very weak resource base and, as unelected quangos dominated by the central government, had difficulties in establishing themselves as effective and authoritative organizations. The 1999 Regular Report criticized Hungary again for not sufficiently addressing the short-term Accession Partnership priority for regional 'capacity'.[23] By instrumentalizing the EU accession pressures as a two-level game playing off external and domestic pressures against each other, the Fidesz-dominated government amended the Law on Regional Development and Physical Planning in October 1999. The central government's control of the RDCs was strengthened, and their status and role was transformed. The government realigned the RDCs to overlap fully with the seven NUTS II level statistical planning regions that had been created in 1998. Now that they were on a statutory footing, the government guaranteed them state funding, and defined more clearly their role in programming and implementing regional development programmes. Though the amendments served to consolidate the legal basis of the new regional institutions, RDC membership was now weighted in favour of central government appointees at the expense of sub-national representatives and civil society, such as the Labour Councils established under the 1991 Employment Act, and chambers of commerce.[24] Consequently, the independence of the RDCs and the government's commitment to the EU principles of 'partnership' and 'subsidiarity' appeared increasingly dubious. Indeed, the whole system of public sector contracting was increasingly seen as a patronage-dispensing mechanism for Fidesz.

The strengthening of the RDCs and the increased importance of the NUTS II regions was welcomed by the EU in the November 2000 Regular Report, although concerns were raised regarding efficient decision-making and programming at the regional level. By late 2000/early 2001, as we discussed in Chapter 4, the Commission's recommendations shifted firmly towards greater central government control and management of regional policy.[25] At the same time, there was increasing domestic political concern about Fidesz's overly-centralized approach and corruption which generated demands from across the political spectrum (including both the Hungarian Socialist Party and the Alliance of Free Democrats) for the introduction of elected regional self-government. Despite these criticisms Fidesz claimed to pursue a long-term policy of 'double decentralization', which would eliminate the counties and replace them by super-regions that would initially be controlled by the central government but ultimately would have elected assemblies, and so-called 'small areas' at the level between the current county and local levels.[26] Interviews conducted with local elites in 1999 in Pécs, one of Hungary's most important self-governing municipalities (which also dominates the county of Baranya), revealed that the elites at this level were overwhelmingly supportive of further change to regional and local boundaries in Hungary as a way of maximizing the receipt of structural funds (see Figure 5.1).

This suggests that even the institutional interests embedded at the county level in Hungary are pragmatically oriented to enlargement and open to further change. The key obstacle remains, however, the consti-

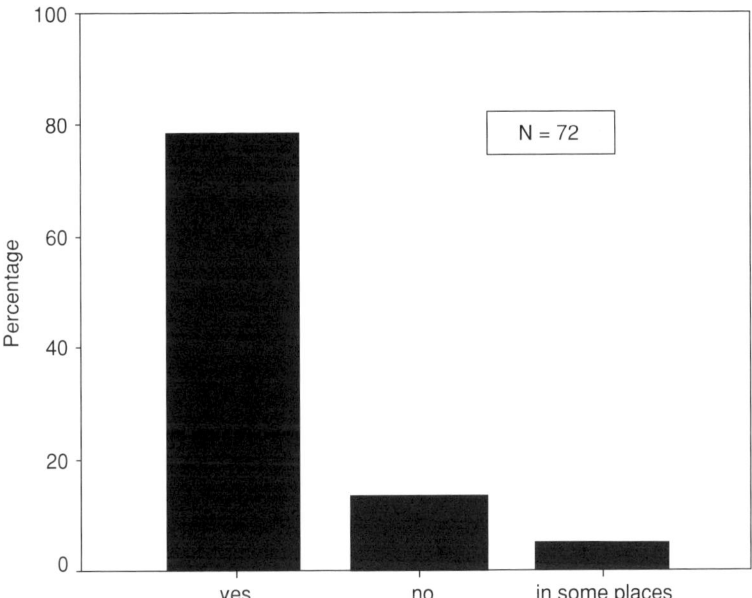

Respondents were asked: Do you agree with the proposition that traditional administrative boundaries should be redrawn, if necessary, to comply with EU funding criteria?

Figure 5.1 Openness to EU influence on sub-national reforms (Pécs 1999)

tutional threshold of a two-thirds majority to enact a new tier of regional self-government. A new reform plan introduced by the socialist government in August 2003 centres on the reorganization of local governments into economic and geographical regions and the regrouping of counties into larger regions. The reform plan even envisages setting up elected regional governments and regional public administration offices. The current statistical-planning regions, which were set up for structural fund purposes, would serve as a basis for regional governments and public administration. These parts of the reform require a two-thirds majority in parliament, which is unlikely to be achieved. The government aims to finalize the reforms by the time of the next general elections in 2006.[27]

The experience of Hungary reveals two trends in its regionalization. In the first half of the 1990s regionalization was overwhelmingly determined by its internal transition politics. Institutional structures were installed and interests were embedded in the period 1990–94, which thereafter greatly complicated additional reforms that threatened these structures. The reforms to regional policy in the second half of the 1990s were shaped by the EU enlargement process. The latter reforms, however, have been influenced less by the vague regulations for structural fund management in the *acquis* and more by the perceptions of pressure from the Commission for certain institutional reforms to enhance regional 'capacity'. Through PHARE the EU influenced the number and shape of the development regions and their organizational structure. Moreover, the EU pressures have not been fed into a vacuum. The institutional architecture and interests that have been embedded by the early transition period are difficult to unpick. Furthermore, Hungary's constitutional amendment threshold is a significant structural hurdle for institutional reform of this kind. The EU pressures for change have also been opportunistically instrumentalized in two-level games by domestic political parties to promote their visions of further regional reforms and defend their local interests. Despite the consensus among the main political parties about securing the country's membership in the EU as quickly as possible, the process of regionalization has been a cross-cutting issue. In the case of Hungary, the enlargement process has sustained the domestic debate on regional governance but it has not surmounted the considerable structural constraints to further institutional reform that were put in place as part of the transition politics of the early 1990s and which predate the EU accession negotiations.

Poland: democratized regionalization

Poland was the first country in Eastern Europe to enact a democratizing reform of regional government. Local democracy and local government reform were crucial components of the round-table talks between Solidarity and the communist government in the late 1980s. Consequently, the issue of state decentralization was high on the political agenda during the immediate post-communist transition period. The debate over centre–local relations in Poland also involved the question of the establishment of a regional tier of government. In contrast to the Hungarian case, where there was a broad political consensus against the formation of a tier of regional government, in Poland there was a consensus about the principle but debate raged as to the shape of the reform. The key cleavage on the issue in the late 1980s was between the old Communist Party elite and the emergent democratic elites around Solidarity. The Communist Party supported the retention of the existing 49 regions as part of a more centralized state structure, whereas Solidarity favoured the establishment of a strong decentralized government tier which would serve as a counterbalance to the centre and the decades of communist centralism.[28]

There were important structural constraints on the potential for regional reform in Poland. Poland was distinctive among the CEECs and many European states in having a polycentric city structure that is characterized by the moderate size of the capital, Warsaw, the industrial dominance of the region of Upper Silesia, and the spread of cities with quite large populations of over half a million inhabitants (for example, Poznań, Wrocław, Łódz). Moreover, for historical reasons concerned with the construction of modern Poland, there is a relatively weak orientation of transport and communications infrastructure towards Warsaw. This is in sharp contrast to a capital city such as Budapest, which is the hub of transport and communications and the economy for Hungary. One of the goals of Poland's 1975 administrative reform (discussed in Chapter 2) which led to the creation of the 49 *województwa* was to strengthen central power, minimize the importance of historically grown regions and promote the layer of larger cities with below half a million inhabitants. Moreover the transition after 1989 saw an increasing east-west divide in Poland, as the more polyfunctional cities located in territories contiguous or networked with the EU were in a position to adjust better to the economic crash of the early 1990s. These factors made the attempt to reform regional government in the 1990s highly contentious.[29]

The lack of a consensus among the political parties about the design of the reform, in particular the number and functions of the new regions, together with a crowded transition agenda in the initial post-communist years, were among the key factors contributing to an almost ten-year gap between the introduction of local self-government at the municipal level in 1990 and the institutionalization of regional government structures in 1999. The 1990 local government reform preserved the 49 communist-era regions as an unelected level of government, where heads were appointed by the government and some competences were deconcentrated from central ministries. At the former *powiat* (district) level a new tier of state administrative districts was established. The main democratizing element lay in the creation of self-governing communes (*gminy*) at the municipal and local levels. As in Hungary, the rapid multiplication in the number of units occupying the lowest level of self-government revealed immense inefficiencies of administration and a lack of adequate funding. The 1990 legislation was intended to be a temporary solution and there was a general political consensus about the need for further decentralization and the introduction of an intermediary tier of self-government.[30]

Throughout the 1990–97 period the national elite in Poland was absorbed by national and international policy issues, and relations with the EU in particular. Public administration was extremely centralized, and also sectoralized, due to the inherited communist legacy of state and economic organization. The centralized administrative structure marginalized the regional elites. It also limited the central elite's capacity effectively to coordinate and manage the regional and local levels. If in the early 1990s the public debate over the regional government reform was dominated by ideological issues concerned with the transition from communist patterns of rule, by the middle of the 1990s functional arguments came to the fore with a growing recognition of the costs and inefficiency of a centralized system that was characterized by large numbers of poorly coordinated state administrative offices, deficient public finances, a lack of transparency and corruption. The reform of 1999 came as the end point of many years of political debate in Poland. Equally, the reform was implemented at this time because of the pressures arising from EU accession. As we discussed in Chapter 3 the pressure from the EU in the early accession period of 1997–98 was to some extent underpinned by a normative push from elements of the Commission for democratized regionalization, though this shifted to a concentration on central control and management in 2000. Both the endogenous long-term and exogenous short-term pressures to institutionalize at the regional level were driven by similar normative and economic logics to promote democracy and participation, while also making for effective integrated regional development. The first serious proposals for regional administrative reform had come from the regional level. For example, the regional elite in Silesia became increasingly frustrated with the failure of the centre to implement urgently needed regional economic restructuring, while Poznań *województwo* even pre-empted national reforms by launching its own regional economic development programme.[31]

The regional government reform was stalled by the leftist governing coalition of the Democratic Left Alliance and the Polish Peasants Party (SLD-PSL) which was in power from 1993 to 1997. The organizational and legislative preparations for a regional reform had been finalized by the short-lived coalition government of seven post-Solidarity and centre-right parties under Hanna Suchocka, which was in power from July 1992 to May 1993. The new PSL Prime Minister Waldemar Pawlak favoured a strong central government and opposed regionalization and the dismantling of the existing 49 regional structures, since his party's political hold was strong in many of these regions. In the 1993 parliamentary elections, the PSL had won in a considerable number of the *województwa* and it was intent on deflecting any threats to these gains by blocking any reform of the intermediary level of government.[32] The PSL proposed the retention of the existing regions but with elected assemblies and a centrally appointed governor (*wojewoda*). Its coalition partner, the Democratic Left Alliance (SLD), supported the establishment of twelve to fourteen large development regions but with self-government concentrated at the district (*powiat*) level. The issue of regional governance reform was a cross-cutting cleavage that divided parties and the left-right ideological spectrum, though to a much lesser degree than was the case in Hungary. Most importantly, the governing coalition was itself split over the issue and it decided to prioritize other reforms in the transition.[33]

The debates re-emerged with vigour only upon the accession to power of the Solidarity Electoral Alliance-Freedom Union (AWS-UW) coalition after the elections in September 1997. Numerous proposals for the administrative subdivision of the country had been circulated among government specialists and academics in the early 1990s with the proposed number of regions varying from six to over forty. There was also an ongoing debate about the functions of the proposed regions and in particular the relationship between self-governing organs and state administrative offices located within the same territories. The three main options which were put forward were: first, to create functional regions that would be dominated by the central government, second, to create self-governing regions within a unitary state, and third, to establish a federal structure along the lines of Germany. The latter was the most controversial idea. Poland, after all, was a territorial construct of the Yalta Agreement of February 1945 and much of western Poland had been annexed from Germany. The issue of federalism, consequently, stoked fears about the danger of sovereignty challenges and the disintegration of the country and enjoyed little support.[34]

As the new centre-right AWS-UW coalition moved to pass the new law on regional government in 1998, an intense party political battle raged over the consequences for party political interests at the regional and local levels rather than a genuine debate on the merits of regional governance and its implications for regional development. The reform was passed as part of a large package of structural reforms of the health care, pension and education systems and the judiciary. Though the reforms were all interconnected, as a package they were overly ambitious and rushed, leaving in their wake a host of unresolved problems.[35] Given that the Solidarity Electoral Alliance was itself not a single political party but an alliance of some thirty political organizations and parties, it is not surprising that differences emerged within the government over the detail of the reform. The majority of mainstream Solidarity parties favoured the division of the country into twelve or thirteen regions that would have both self-governing and state administrative structures. This division was based on the assumption that a region can only function when it has the institutions, intellectual and professional capacity to operate and interact at the domestic and international (especially EU) levels. Nine cities were identified as meeting the necessary criteria to be strong regional centres. Three cities in the poorer eastern part of the country were added to this list in order to achieve a balanced configuration of regions across the whole country. The Regional League, based in Poznań, maintained that there were only eight economically viable regions.[36] At the other end of the spectrum, the more Eurosceptical national-Catholic wing of the AWS (like the old communists) opposed the decentralizing reform altogether, seeing it as a threat to the unity of the state and an unnecessary response to EU pressures.[37] The members of the governing coalition compromised by agreeing to restrict the competences of the new self-governing regional governments, while increasing the supervisory powers of the *wojewoda*, the prefect-like representative of the central government. On the opposition side, the Democratic Left Alliance favoured a return to the pre-1975 division into seventeen regions. At the time of the debate over the reform package, the SLD proposed an assistance programme for those cities faced with the loss of their 'regional status'.

The combined opposition of the PSL and the SLD managed, with the aid of a veto by president Kwasniewski (a leading figure in the SLD), to secure a concession from the government that increased the number of regions to sixteen. These 'extra' regions came out strongly in support of Kwasniewski's re-election in October 2000. The Polish Peasants Party continued to oppose the reform both at the *województwa* and *powiat* levels, fearing a loss of power in their traditional heartlands in the rural communities and existing regions. It argued in favour of a two-tier system based on the existing 49 regions, with the current regions being transformed into self-governing entities.[38] There was also a certain amount of opposition from employees of central ministries and the local administrations in those cities that would lose their regional status. The outcome was a government and opposition compromise on a 16-region configuration that approximated to the pre-1975 communist system.

The two main reform proposals had significant implications for regional development in Poland. A configuration of 'big' regions, for example, the proposal for 10–12 regions centred around regional capitals and similar to the historical provinces would intensify a functional dynamic for growth to be concentrated in the bigger cities and would consequently be more likely to accelerate regional polarization and internal migration, for example, through skilled labour moving to bigger cities. The proposal for a more diffused regionalization to about 25 *województwa* would retain more of the polycentric structure and would assist better with the development of weaker, second-order cities especially in the eastern part of the country.[39]

As a result of the 1998 reform, Poland had a three-tier self-governing system at the sub-national level.[40] The basic units are the 2489 areas and municipalities (*gminy*) at the local level, 308 districts (*powiaty*) and 65 urban municipalities which have been granted *powiat* status, and the 16 *województwa* at the regional level (see Map 4). All three levels of government have a democratically elected council to run the administration in their jurisdictions. The regional level is characterized by a dual administrative structure which one interviewee described as a 'split personality'.[41] A regional governor, the *wojewoda*, is appointed by the prime minister upon the recommendation of the interior minister,

PL01 Dolnośląskie	PL06 Małopolskie	PL0B Pomorskie
PL02 Kujawsko-Pomorskie	PL07 Mazowieckie	PL0C Śląskie
PL03 Lubelskie	PL08 Opolskie	PL0D Świętokrzyskie
PL04 Lubuskie	PL09 Podkarpackie	PL0E Warmińsko-Mazurskie
PL05 Łódskie	PL0A Podlaskie	PL0F Wielkopolskie
		PL0G Zachodniopomorskie

Map 4 Regionalization in Poland (NUTS II regions)

to protect the interests of the state and to coordinate the work of the government administration with the regional government. The elected council in each *województwo* elects a chief officer, the Marshal (*marszałek*), who is responsible for regional development under the overarching management of the Polish Agency for Regional Development. The funding base for the new institutions of local and regional governance was also partially reformed. The key weakness of the reform lay in its failure to immediately devolve sufficient fund-raising powers to the regional level to enable the new governments to function effectively. Critics talk of a decentralization of competences without a corresponding decentralisation of finances since the regional governments are highly dependent on central government funding.[42]

One Katowice elite member described the reform as 'the action of dilettantes, amateurs and improvisation, with a lack of recognition of historic regions and economic, spatial and ecological factors'.[43] There is no doubt that, as in Hungary, the debates in Poland were framed by the political power calculus of the main political parties, whether the aim was to protect whatever stranglehold they had on local and regional levels, or to expand their power at these levels. The perceived preferences of the Commission for a form of devolved regional self-government that was linked to regional development and regional administrative capacity were also temporally correlated with the renewed debates in Poland in 1997–98. Moreover, the 1998 reform was also a response to the criticisms of regional policy and capacity made by the Commission in the 1997 Opinions and in the 1998 progress report. These evaluations asserted that Poland's regional administrative reform was 'incomplete', and complained about the lack of legal basis for the implementation of regional policy and the absence of a mechanism of coordination of regional policy at the national level.[44] Consequently, the impetus for Poland's democratized regionalization was largely an endogenous development that was driven by its transition politics, but the normative and functional design of the reform was also shaped by the accession process.

The reform debate in Poland was framed by this perception of EU accession requirements. During the Sejm debate on the 1998 law, supporters of regional reform stressed its importance for Poland's integration into the EU, maintaining that strong, large regions were important to maximize the benefits from structural funds.[45] This was yet another example of how the enlargement process generated two-level games, as the accession to the EU was instrumentally employed as a legitimating device to advance party political preferences. Our data from local elite interviews conducted in Katowice in 2000–01 revealed that just over 37 per cent of respondents thought that the outcome of the regional reform had been on the whole a product of Polish priorities, 12 per cent thought it was driven by EU conditionality, while 22.7 per cent considered both factors equally influenced the outcome (see Figure 5.2).

The reform design had three main areas of compatibility with the EU's formal and informal conditionality: it strengthened the state's regional administrative capacity through the devolution of power to lower levels; it established a new territorial system that met the NUTS criteria (with the sixteen *województwa* corresponding to NUTS II units), while also combining elements of self-government and administrative deconcentration from the central government; and it advanced the

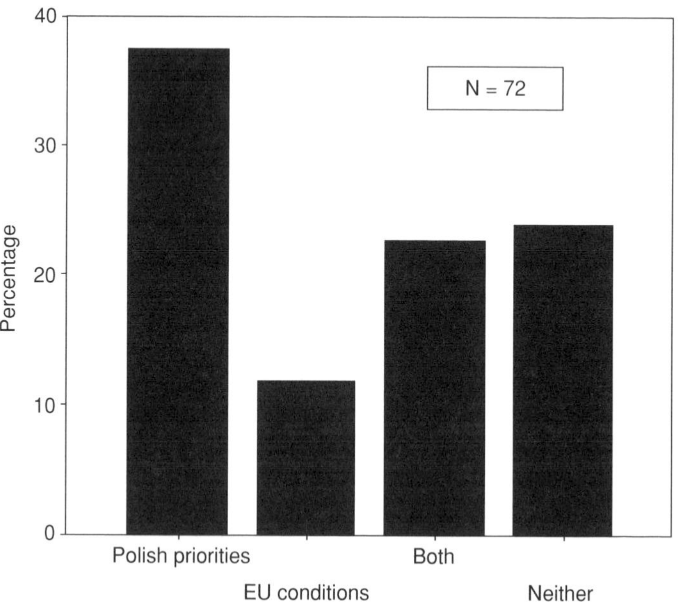

Respondents were asked: Do you think that the reform of regional and district governance structures in Poland in 1999 was on the whole the result of 1. Polish priorities; 2. EU conditions; 3. Both; or 4. Neither?

Figure 5.2 Perceptions of the impact of the EU on sub-national reforms (Katowice 2000)

construction of democratic institutions at all levels of society.[46] Polish lawmakers correctly calculated that the responsibilities of the new regional governments, such as the promotion of economic development, regional public services, environmental protection and the development of regional infrastructure, would satisfy the EU's demand for enhanced 'regional administrative capacity'. Consequently, as discussed in Chapter 4 the Regular Report of 1999 praised the reform as likely to have 'a significant positive effect' on Poland's accession preparations in the area of regional policy. The issues of temporal correlation and design compatibility, however, should not to be confused with direct causal linkages. For example, in the capital of one of Poland's most important regions, Katowice, the question of EU enlargement was rarely raised in the discourse on Poland's regionalization in the early to mid-1990s despite the fact that Poland was receiving PHARE money to assist in the development of regional programmes. The establishment of district and regional self-governing levels was overwhelmingly seen as a progression of the transition from communism which had begun in 1990 with the reform of local government.[47] Thus we can conclude that the impetus for democratized regionalization in Poland predated EU enlargement conditionality, but its timing and design was dovetailed with the ongoing preparations for and perceived prerequisites of EU membership.

The 1998 'National Programme of Preparation for Membership of the EU' drawn up jointly with the Commission assumed that the new regional level would be responsible for the management and supervision of structural funds.[48] With the introduction of the new *województwo* and *powiat* self-governing levels in January 1999, the passage of a law on regional development in May 2000 and the establishment of a Ministry of Regional Development in June 2000, Poland considered itself to be adjusting its regions to 'EU standards'. As one study explained: 'In respect of size they are the counterparts of regions in the countries of the EU, and the government and the Sejm had precisely this in mind when they demarcated and assigned tasks to voivodships.'[49] By late 2000, however, the Commission had become increasingly concerned at the prospect of structural funds being decentralized in any of the new member states given that their 'capacity' was still considered to be insufficient and the division of responsibilities between the centre and the potential new regional managing authorities for structural funds was still largely undefined. In the case of Poland, the lack of regional tax bases for the new voivodships was a severe constraint on their capacity to develop 'capacity' in this area.[50]

Having formally encouraged the development of regional structures at the *województwo* level, and informally promoted a democratized regional government model, the Commission acted in early 2001 to stress the importance of continued central management and of ensuring the necessary administrative capacities at the centre.[51] The 2001 Regular Report on Poland illustrates this change by stating that despite previous progress Poland's preparations for the implementation of structural funds had stalled, particularly as regards developments at the national level. Poland was reminded that 'a clear division of responsibilities must be established at the central level, between central and regional levels and at the regional level between the Voivods and Marshals'. Having previously encouraged Poland's regionalization, the Commission now argued that 'the role of the regions in the management of the funds in the period up to end 2006 requires careful consideration'. The Commission blocked attempts to decentralize operational programmes to the regions.[52] The Regular Reports of 2002 continued to record the Commission's concern about administrative capacity and the problem of weak 'implementation' at different levels of government despite the fact that the negotiations on Chapter 21 had been closed by all the accession countries.[53] Not surprisingly, the conflicting signals transmitted by the Commission gave rise to a great deal of resentment in Poland.

Conclusion

While the causal link between EU enlargement and the establishment of specific institutions for EU structural policy as required by the Structural Funds Regulations was straightforward and primarily a matter of timing, prioritization and government capacity in each candidate country, the design of the wider institutional environment of sub-national government makes for a more interesting and complex testing ground in the search for the EU's impact on domestic structures.

The institutional architecture of regional government in the CEECs is best understood as a development influenced by the interaction of the domestic politics of transition (including historical legacies shaping the debates) and EU conditionality, whether it be formal or informal pressures emanating from the Commission. This dynamic interaction has resulted in a diversity of policy responses and institutional design in the CEECs. While domestic pressures for regionalization might have varied depending on the trajectory of transition, the process of EU enlargement has had a clear temporal correlation with such reforms. The EU acted as a catalyst for change, as debates about local and regional government were galvanized by the Commission's Opinions of 1997, the 1998 Accession Partnerships and the Regular Reports thereafter, and in particular by the Commission's stress on the 'administrative capacity' issue.

This comparative study of regionalization in Hungary and Poland demonstrates that the reform of sub-national self-government was on the whole an endogenous development, engineered by a fairly broad political consensus on the merits of democratization at the sub-national level as part of the post-communist transition. In both cases democratizing reforms of local self-government were introduced within the first years of the transition in 1990. The domestic debates differed, however, in that there was no elite consensus in Hungary over regional self-government, and moreover a structural impediment introduced at the onset of the transition, namely the two-thirds parliamentary majority required for constitutional change, makes such a reform very difficult to achieve. In Poland in contrast the principle of regional self-government was widely accepted but the configuration and power of the new tier was hotly disputed. The institutional design of regional governance in the CEECs can be broadly placed along a spectrum illustrated by the Polish and Hungarian examples respectively: democratic regionalization, where regional institutions are elected and have significant devolved powers, and administrative-statistical regionalization, where regional institutions are quangos with largely advisory status. Most of the CEEC states, with the exception of Poland, the Czech Republic and Slovakia, have opted for a Hungarian type of centrally-controlled administrative-statistical regionalization with Regional Development Agencies (see Table 2.1).

The most obvious relationship between conditionality and regionalization is in the temporal correlation. With the exceptions of Poland, where regional reform was discussed as a fundamental part of the transition process from its outset in 1989–90, and the Czech Republic, where there was a constitutional commitment to regionalization established in 1992, regionalization only became a salient issue in most of the CEECs within the context of an accelerated EU accession process from 1996. It could be argued that the Polish and Czech cases suggest that domestic pressures for regionalization might have accumulated in the other CEECs without EU pressures, as a natural part of their transition politics. The Commission's monitoring and evaluating instruments from 1997–2002 (the Opinions, Regular Reports, CMRs) emphasized the importance of regional administrative capacity for delivering regional policy and thereby created and maintained a momentum for reform and influenced the form and timing of institutional change, but primarily to reinforce existing domestic trends rather than triggering radically different approaches.

As discussed in Chapter 1, the notion of 'Europeanization' suggests that European integration is generating converging institutional or policy outcomes. We should expect this convergence pressure to be even more strongly felt in the case of enlargement countries, given the considerable power asymmetry in favour of the Commission and the context of post-communist transition. This comparative study of a key policy area in two CEEC countries, Poland and Hungary, demonstrates that there has not been a uniform 'Europeanizing' effect. As in the EU member states, the domestic institutional changes in response to the EU's adaptational pressures vary across countries, with considerable room for manoeuvre for domestic actors and institutions as theory predicts. These findings confirm the tentative conclusions drawn from the Europeanization literature, according to which political structures tend to be less 'Europeanized' and exhibit less convergence compared to policy-level studies.

6
Elites and the Normative Capacity for Europeanization

During the EU's eastward enlargement the notion of 'capacity' has been of paramount importance for the Commission and the EU's governing institutions more broadly. As we have seen in Chapter 4, the Commission employed the term as a generic label for the parts of the *acquis* that required new institutional structures, management and organizational arrangements and staffing levels, all of which were often seen as being deficient in the CEECs. 'Capacity' became a catch-all phrase in the accession process, derived from a bureaucratic and technocratic understanding of the concept and, indeed was increasingly over time interpreted in managerialist terms by the Commission. This was, in fact, a narrow understanding of the shortcomings in the CEECs' preparations for EU membership. Getting the appropriate administrative and organizational structures in place is an important but partial step towards the implementation of the *acquis*. The capacity to adopt or implement the *acquis* requires not simply transposition through a domestic legislative gallop, but also a cognitive adjustment by elites who must not only learn to 'speak European', but also become acculturated and assimilated into European norms and 'ways of doing things'. The understanding of 'capacity' that is generally employed in the study of enlargement, consequently, has shorn the notion of its normative content.

To theorize about the institutional, policy and normative convergence entailed in 'Europeanization' requires not only proofs of connectivity to the EU integration process but also of cognitive adaptation to common 'European' values, a collective understanding of how policies are to be framed, and the deployment of both in policy-making and implementation. It presupposes two key conditions: first, it requires that elites in a particular country have some level of connectedness to

EU policy processes; and second, it requires that elites in a country are captured by EU norms and a European identity. Both conditions are usually seen as being facilitated by 'social learning' or 'socialization' of elites from within the EU's institutional environment.[1] Thus, institutional interaction over time fosters institutional and policy convergence. Theories of European integration, Europeanization, and indeed post-communist transition, attach great importance to the role of elites and, in particular, to the process by which elites acquire new attitudinal and behavioural norms and practices which may progress the desired outcome, namely integration and transition. Previous studies of Europeanization in the CEECs infer that the policy push for accession itself indicates a high degree of national elite positive responsiveness but say little about other levels of the elite.

The enlargement process was pervaded by mechanisms of Europeanization which aimed to secure institutional convergence, normative assimilation, communicative symmetry, and network fusion with the elites of the CEECs. Only a few EU instruments, however, were concerned explicitly with the normative conversion of the CEEC elites and knowledge transfer about the EU (see Box 6.1). The 'structured dialogue' of the early 1990s and the accession negotiations themselves, for example, helped to acculturate the post-communist CEEC national elites into 'European' elite discourse, accelerating in the first instance their presentational capacity to 'speak European'. The rapid increase in elite interactions between the EU and the CEECs whether channelled through the inclusion of the CEEC national elites in EU fora and activities or through more penetrative EU instruments that involved sub-national elites, such as PHARE, SAPARD, ISPA and scientific and educational exchanges, were attempts to promote 'Europeanized' thinking in the CEECs. The 'twinning' instrument developed from 1999, whereby EU advisers and practitioners were seconded to ministries in the CEECs to assist with their accession negotiations, was also potentially an important vehicle for normative transfer from the EU to the CEECs. Since many of the 'twins' were experienced retired or seconded career bureaucrats from member states it is not surprising that the folklore about their activities suggests that it could have subversive effects. In particular, it is suggested that they drew on their own experience of interactions with the Commission to infuse the CEEC elites with advice that reinforced perceptions of the predominance of 'national interest' in dealings with the Commission. In addition, there was a spread of business and administrative networks as a result of the opening up of the CEEC economies through the Europe

Box 6.1 Mechanisms of Europeanization

Functional & Normative Goals	Key Instruments
■ Institutional convergence	■ Europe Agreements
■ Normative assimilation	■ Structured dialogue
■ Communicative symmetry	■ Aid/PHARE pipeline
■ Network fusion	■ Delegations
	■ Accession partnerships
	■ Negotiations
	■ EU monitoring
	■ Twinning
	■ Horizontal interactions
	■ EU fora
	■ Convention

Agreements in the early 1990s. Whether such interactions between the EU and the CEECs promoted 'Europeanized' thinking or behaviour should be empirically tested rather than assumed. While our own research is concerned with the overall degree of connectedness of sub-national elites with the European project resulting from the sum of these interactions, ideally the aims and instruments of Europeanization should be differentiated.

Among the main criticisms of the EU throughout the 1990s has been that it has failed to communicate effectively the benefits of the EU to the peoples of member states, and has been reluctant to address its own legitimacy problem in the 'democratic deficit' in EU institutions.[2] The legitimacy problem of the democratic deficit has been replicated in the CEECs. Generally, the enlargement process has further eroded democratic accountability by narrowing the scope for political contestation among parties and national-level actors over key issues.[3] Moreover, despite the financial implications and thus pivotal importance of sub-national elites in the CEECs for the EU, and despite the Commission's use of language about institutionally embedding 'partnership' in regional policy and demanding greater regional 'capacity', the participation of the regional elites and institutions of the CEECs in the enlargement process was minimal. Enlargement has been structurally flawed in that it has been organized as an exclusive competence for the member states, the Commission and the governing national elites in the candidate countries to negotiate. Consequently, while the Commission and the CEEC governments had a strong interest in the particular institutional territorial-administrative arrangements established for managing regional policy, and in the 'capacity' of these institutions to access and manage the EU funds efficiently, a key layer of the delivery mechanism, namely, the elites and actors who will be involved in the programming and implementation of this policy at the sub-national level, had no voice in the accession process. Simultaneously, as we discussed in Chapter 5, the sub-national elites were powerful players when it came to national-level debates over the design of the sub-national administrative-territorial structures, whether in the case of democratic regionalization, most notably in Poland, or in the blocking of regional self-government by local elites as in the case of Hungary.

The attitudes and behaviour of the sub-national elites in the CEECs are important for policy outcomes in three key respects. First, transition produced an enormous attrition on the institutional fabric of the state in the CEECs. The fall of the one-party state was followed by a period of instability that was characterized by institutional weakness. While in most cases the constitution-making process was completed quickly it takes time for new institutions to become embedded in any society, never mind one undergoing the trauma of multiple transitions.[4] One of the characteristics of democratizing transition in the CEECs was a fragile structure of political party competition. Political parties are the key mechanism of political communication, mobilization and representation in democracies, yet in the CEECs they are characterized by organizational weakness.[5] When political parties are weak, political actors become dominant. The organizational and mobilizational weakness of CEEC parties is most exacerbated at the sub-national levels. Consequently, in addition to the prominent role of individual national-level politicians, the importance of regional and local elites as gatekeepers and mediators astride the institutional space between national elites and grassroots public opinion was enhanced by transition. Second, sub-national elites occupy a positional centrality not only for implementing transition choices but also for the successful implementation of key aspects of the *acquis*. In particular, their role is critical for delivering successful outcomes in the implementation of key policies, such as regional policy, in the post-enlargement era. Third, the regional and local elites have increasingly been of normative political importance for the EU's project of democratic self-legitimation.

As we discussed in previous chapters, during enlargement, however, the Commission's views on what constituted best practice in institution-building at this level for the CEECs was contradictory and shifted over time, alternating between decentralized and centralized approaches to regional policy. Nevertheless, the White Paper on European Governance

(2001) expounded rhetoric about the need for a 'multi-level partnership' to involve the regional and local level of governance more fully in EU decision-making.[6] This normative commitment was seriously diluted in the Draft Constitutional Treaty drawn up by the European Convention in 2003 which refers to but fails to clarify or substantiate the even more nebulous notion of 'subsidiarity'.[7]

In this chapter we present a comparative analysis of data from local and regional elite interviews in four CEEC states to evaluate their level of normative Europeanization and their connectedness to the EU integration project. The extent to which the elites in the CEECs have become 'Europeanized' during enlargement has important theoretical and policy implications beyond the ideological aspirational issue of whether this promotes or hinders EU integration. On the one hand, the study of the CEEC elites may confirm or challenge the assumptions about 'Europeanization'. The assumption of 'differential empowerment', in particular, makes significant claims about the impact of Europeanization on the outcome of power games at the domestic level. Furthermore, a key issue for the notion of capacity in an enlarged EU is the extent to which there is a variation in the responsiveness to Europeanization. For example, do sub-national elite values concur with those of the national elite or is there a fissure between the two levels? We can infer that levels of Europeanization will have a significant effect on the operationalization of capacity. The more Europeanized and homogenized the elite values are, the more likely it is that they will adjust well to the performance requirements of post-enlargement, and vice-versa the more fractured the elite structures are, the less effective EU policy implementation will be.

Theory suggests that the articulation of elite preferences will be determined by the elite cleavage structures. The classic elite segmentation includes sub-groups defined according to ideological position (on left/right and pro-EU/anti-EU scales), sociological criteria (age, sex, class or ethnic background, education, career), the interests that they represent, and their networks (local, national and international). Consequently, given the centrality of elites to successful policy outcomes generally, and the crucial importance of sub-national elites for a successful outcome in regional policy specifically, we can infer that the extent and manner by which Europeanization undulates between elite segments will have a significant bearing on their capacity to deliver regional policy. Our data allow us to map the contours of sub-national elite normative Europeanization and to assess the effects on different segments of the elite.

The bifurcated Europeanization of elites

Elite theory suggests that the following groups of factors should be important in shaping the attitudes and behaviour of elites: sociological and socialization factors, elite position, identity and networks. In particular, factors such as age, education and involvement in networks tend to be significantly correlated with attitudes to change. Positive attitudes to change, of course, may not only be a reflection of previous socialization, but also be driven by a structured rational self-interest from those who have most to benefit from the change. From elite theory we can infer that the younger and more educated and more networked internationally an elite member is, the more likely he/she is to have liberal attitudes and adaptive behaviour, and thus be predisposed to Europeanization.[8] We can also infer that the older elites whose careers were rooted in the communist era and who lack the social capital to benefit from Europeanization will be most resistant to it. A robust model of 'Europeanization' in the CEECs would also infer that Europeanized elites exhibit three essential characteristics: first, they would have *good knowledge* about the activities of the EU and its relevance to their own spatial or functional domain; second, they would demonstrate a *good understanding* of what the EU stands for; and third, they would *strongly identify* with the EU and its activities.[9]

Our analysis is based on a large-scale cross-national comparative study of sub-national elites in key regional cities in the CEECs conducted in 1999–2002. The results presented here are based on an analysis of elite interviews (N = 287) conducted using a standardized questionnaire in the following CEEC cities: Pécs in Hungary (N = 74), Maribor in Slovenia (N = 72), Tartu in Estonia (N = 66) and Katowice in Poland (N = 75). We sought equivalence in our cases by using two main criteria in the selection. First, we chose key regional 'second' cities in each country case. By opting for the category 'second' cities we aimed to minimize the effect of variation in terms of the size and importance of the cities relative to the hierarchy of cities within each country. In countries where there was more than one potential option for 'second' city we selected cities that we considered were most geographically oriented to the EU and/or had a reputation for being 'Europeanized' (culturally, economically, politically, historically). Elite members in each city were selected as follows. First, we used positional criteria to identify an initial selection of 20–25 individuals for interviewing who were drawn from senior elected and appointed officials in the executive and legislative bodies of each city. After this initial selection, we snowballed out to other elite members using reputational criteria, by asking our initial selection of elites to identify other leading individuals. Using this method we interviewed as many as possible of the elite members identified, most of whom came from regional and local government, business, the mass media and, to a lesser extent, the cultural intelligentsia, up to a maximum of 75 in each city.

The interviews in Pécs, Maribor and Tartu were conducted in the summer of 1999. The interviews in Katowice were conducted in late 2001 and early 2002 at a more advanced stage of the enlargement process. We recognize that this temporal difference in the fieldwork may affect the comparability of the data but on the whole we do not believe that it has a significant impact on most of the questions that we asked. We have attempted to take account of timing and contextual differences by adjusting questions in a manner that allowed comparison. In addition to collecting key sociological information about the elite members, their activities and networks, the interviews also included a range of questions to test elite opinions on a range of issues including economic and political transition at the national, regional and local level, their attitudes to the EU and the enlargement process.

The data are described in the statistical appendix. Most of the elites that were interviewed came from the administrative segment (64.1 per cent), though many of these were also involved in politics and business or other activities (see Statistical Appendix, A.1). The distribution of the elite segments varied significantly across the cities. In Katowice, Maribor and Tartu significantly more of the administrative elites were among the interviewees, whereas in Pécs there was a significantly higher number of economic and private sector elites (see A.2). The bulk (70 per cent) of the elites interviewed fell within the cohorts aged between 40–59 (A.3). The elites were also highly educated, as the overwhelming majority (67 per cent) had university degrees and postgraduate qualifications, and most of the others had professional and other higher qualifications. Only 1.7 per cent had no further education (A.4). The vast majority of our interviewees (83.3 per cent) were male (A.5).

In the case of attitudes to the EU we found that only a range of network contact variables (travel and visitors from abroad) and age predict or are at least associated with positive attitudes, and moreover are more significant for positive attitudes than other more direct involvement with the EU such as, for example, participation in EU projects (A.6).[10] Thus the 'middle aged' and those who travel abroad more and receive visitors more tend to have a more positive view about the EU and the benefits of their country's relationship with the EU. These findings reinforced the findings about the potential contradictions between the vertical top-down Commission approach to enlargement which seems to rely on the trickle-down effect in its communication strategy, and the crucial role of horizontal engagement and interaction working from the bottom-up in diffusing European norms. Interestingly, those respondents who were dissatisfied with the transition to democracy in their country also tended to have positive views about the benefits of their country's relationship with the EU, suggesting that these interviewees expect that EU membership will have positive effects on the state of democracy at home.

Elite participation in EU enlargement

The EU investment in the accession countries since the early 1990s, both in terms of economic aid (the total sum of PHARE aid amounted to 5589.10 million euros between 1990 and 1998) and organizational time, has been significant (see Table 1.1). The level of elite participation in EU projects has been fairly similar across the respondents in our cases: 48.6 per cent in Maribor, 56.8 per cent in Pécs, 56.9 per cent in Tartu, 58.7 per cent in Katowice. Moreover, when asked 'Generally, what is your opinion of the aims and activities of the EU?', pro-EU views were strongest in Katowice, where 91.9 per cent of respondents held a positive view, none were negative and only 8.1 per cent were neutral. In Pécs, 83.3 per cent of elite members had a positive opinion of the EU, only 1.4 per cent held a negative opinion and 14.9 per cent were neutral; in Maribor, 75 per cent were positive, 8.3 per cent negative and 16.7 per cent were neutral; and in the case of Tartu, 56.9 per cent were positive, only 1.7 per cent negative and a considerable 41.4 per cent remained neutral (Figure 6.1). Some elite members spoke of 'EU colonization' and of accession as a 'forced marriage', but these were a small minority of discordant voices.[11]

While the sub-national elites as a whole were overwhelmingly positive about the EU, enlargement was not a salient issue for them. Rather, these elites were most concerned with the immediate social and economic problems arising from the domestic transition process. In Maribor not one of our elite interviewees cited EU enlargement as an issue of pressing concern for the city. In the case of Pécs only 4 per cent considered it to be an important issue, and in Tartu and Katowice less than 2.5 per cent thought so. The focus on domestic socio-economic policy issues is understandable given the trauma of transition in the CEECs after 1989. Consistently in the interviews the elites in these cities stressed that their

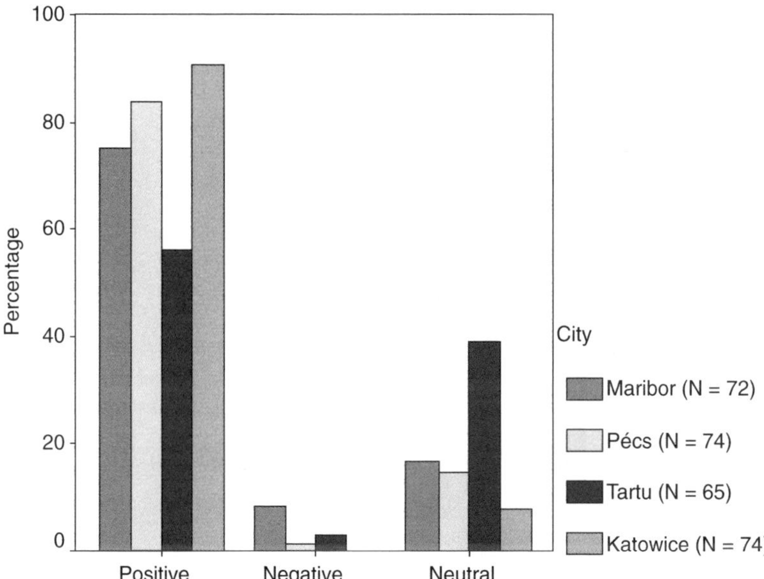

Respondents were asked: Generally, what is your opinion of the aims and activities of the European Union? Is it positive, neutral, or negative?

Figure 6.1 Elite opinions of the EU

overwhelming concern was with the decline of traditional industries during the transition and the perceived failure of central governments to help. What is surprising, however, is that the overwhelmingly positive attitude to the EU in principle was not matched by a recognition of the relevance of the enlargement process and EU membership to alleviating the local problems of transition, in particular through PHARE or even the potential of structural funds. The generally positive attitude to the EU, consequently, masks a deeper cognitive disconnectedness of the elites from the EU that is reinforced by their lack of understanding of how the EU is relevant for their level of governance.

Past or current participation in EU projects or a generally positive opinion about the EU is not necessarily a guarantee of deeper knowledge about the EU's activities even in the local area. For example, one of our interviewees in Maribor had previously been a government minister and had signed a PHARE cross-border project agreement with Austria, but he could not remember the name of it. In fact, there are very low levels of knowledge about the European Union among the sub-national elites in CEECs in general (Figure 6.2).

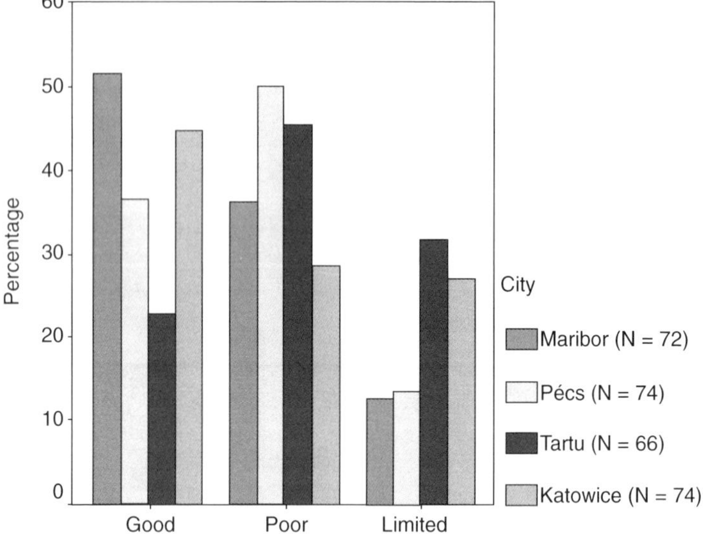

Respondents were asked: Can you name any EU-funded (wholly or partly) projects in your city/region? (Answers were coded 'good' if respondents were able to name any project and the source of funding; 'poor' if respondents were unable to name any projects or sources of funding; 'limited' if respondents showed knowledge of projects, but were unable to identify the source of funding).

Figure 6.2 Elite knowledge of EU-funded activities in the locale

We found the highest levels of knowledge about EU programmes in Maribor (51 per cent), though even here just under half of the local elite members (49 per cent) still had poor or limited knowledge of EU-funded projects under way in their city. The high score was also influenced by knowledge of just one highly visible project ongoing in the city (the modernization of a waste-water treatment plant, partly with EU, but mainly with EBRD funds).[12] In Katowice 55 per cent had poor or limited knowledge of city-based EU programmes, in Pécs, the equivalent figure was 63.5 per cent, and in Tartu, a striking 77 per cent had poor or limited knowledge of EU-funded programmes currently under way in their locale. This suggests that there has been a major communication and recognition problem with the way that EU programmes are delivered at the local level.

It is difficult accurately to assess the level of correlation between the EU financial assistance that has gone into the cities/regions studied and the level of elite knowledge about EU programmes in the cities/regions. The Commission does not disperse its aid on a territorial basis and does not keep records of the amount of EU aid dispersed to particular cities or regions. One plausible reason for this low recognition of the role of the EU lay in the design of PHARE programmes, which were organized and funded through central ministries, associated with the spending of national ministers who supervise the dispersal to sectors (and indirectly to areas) identified as programme priorities. In general such aid was highly politicized and was often distributed as patrimony by governing parties to reward loyal constituencies. Moreover, although PHARE usually had local offices in the cities involved in our research, our observation suggests that these were largely Potemkin-like structures with no permanent personnel present.

The overwhelming reliance on private sector consultants for the delivery of PHARE aid, until the PHARE reforms in 1997–98, was inevitably seen negatively by elites in the CEECs. The private sector 'Marriot brigade' was despised as a siphon for large parts of aid without providing much in the way of practical assistance, and further alienated elite and public enthusiasm for the EU.[13] The lack of direct territoriality in PHARE aid must have contributed to the lack of elite knowledge and poor connectedness to EU activities at the local level. Where EU funds were spent on infrastructural improvements that resulted in a clearly identifiable local and territorialized benefit the EU's activities registered most prominently among local elites.

Regional development agencies established as part of the enlargement process in the CEECs do not promote elite connectedness because they are in most cases skeletal and highly politicized and often corrupt structures with limited administrative capacity. We attribute the significantly weak elite knowledge about the EU primarily to the structural disengagement of sub-national actors in the accession process combined with the failure on the part of the Commission and national political elites to prioritize the communication of knowledge of the benefits of membership within the CEECs. The higher level of elite knowledge of the EU exhibited in Katowice seems to have been the result of institutional factors. In this case the devolution of power to the regional level appears to have acted as an institutional vehicle for connecting the sub-national elite to the wider domestic political process and, by extension, to the EU. Katowice is also located in a region (Silesia) with a strong historical regional identity and connectedness with Germany, and is among the best EU networked cities of western Poland. This combination of institutional development, regional identity and external connectedness through networks has been the driving force of the process of European integration there.

Meanwhile the lack of familiarity with EU institutions and policies stands in sharp contrast to the often detailed knowledge demonstrated during interviews by some sections of the local and regional elites about local government practices and administration in West European countries. This experience and exposure is the result of socialization in extensive professional networks. For example, just under 25 per cent of the elite respondents were members of an international association, just under 62 per cent had travelled abroad within the previous six months and 58 per cent had received visitors from abroad in the same period. Such visits, the transferral of work practices and participation in different Europe-wide networks are signs of the horizontal deepening of the European integration process and the growth of pan-European networks among elites at all levels. However, such horizontal linkages may transfer Euroscepticism as much as they may serve to promote values and behaviour in favour of European integration.[14] Nonetheless, the globalizing effect of increased travel and horizontal contacts among local elites in candidate countries and EU member states would appear to serve as a countervailing force balancing the tendency towards pragmatic caution and limiting the appeal of Euroscepticism.

Understanding the meaning of EU membership

An elite that is cognitively connected to the EU is one that should have a good understanding of what the EU stands for, what its main policy functions are, and what policies to expect once their country becomes a member state. We sought to test this level of understanding among the CEEC sub-national elites by offering our interviewees a list of twelve policy statements, some of which were relevant to EU activities and some of which were not, and some of which inferred integration, and some of which did not.[15] We asked them to make five preferences, which for them best encapsulated what the EU 'stands for' (Figure 6.3). The responses can be grouped into four broad categories that relate to different dimensions of European integration:

1. *Economic integration* Free Trade, Economic Cohesion, EMU, Common Agricultural Policy (CAP).
2. *Political integration* Europe of Nation States (ENS), Federal Europe, Common European Home (CEH).
3. *Security integration* Common Foreign and Security Policy (CFSP), Partnership for Peace (PFP).
4. *Regional policy integration* Europe of Regions, Structural and Cohesion Funds (SCF), Subsidiarity.

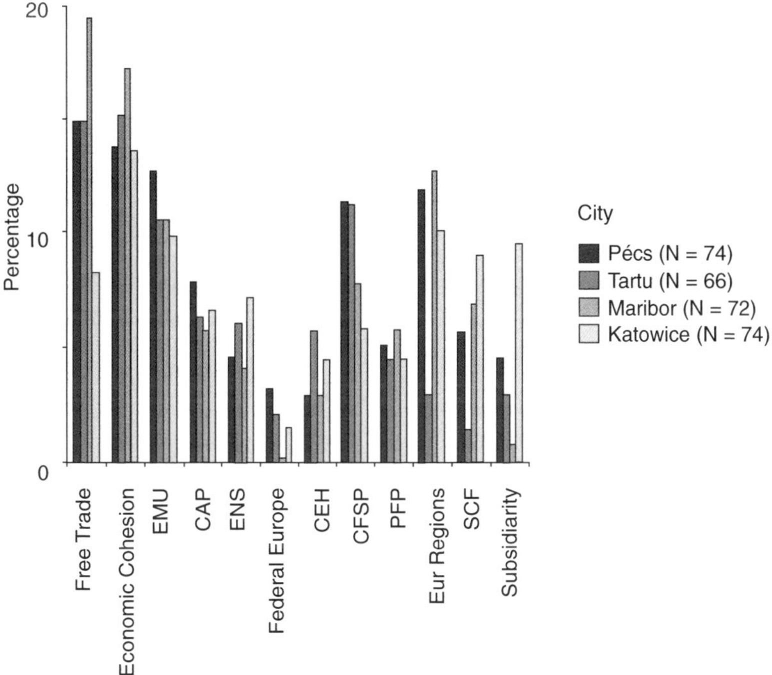

Respondents were asked: Which five of the following phrases best sums up the European Union for you? (The maximum possible score is 20 per cent.)

Figure 6.3 Elite perceptions of what the EU 'stands for'

The limited understanding of the EU among the elites was evident from the difficulty the interviewers experienced with explaining certain terms, such as 'subsidiarity' and 'structural and cohesion funds', which many interviewees did not comprehend even when translated.[16] The overwhelming perception among the elites was that the EU stood for economic integration with free trade and economic cohesion receiving especially high scores. It is striking that the elites lack any vision of the EU as a political integration project. Where respondents did select statements referring to the political project of the EU they tended to choose 'Europe of Nation States'. This preference reflects the determination of the CEEC elites to retain their recently regained sovereignty in the face of pressures for deeper political integration in an enlarged EU. This finding is substantiated further by the fact that the idea of a federal Europe consistently ranked very low in terms of the elites' understanding of what the EU stood for. Moreover, the

Gorbachevian concept of a 'Common European Home' was significant only in Tartu (which had been part of the Soviet Union) albeit still a weak preference. In some cases, particularly in Maribor and Tartu, in countries which at the time the interviews were conducted remained outside NATO, the elites attached high importance to the security dimension of the EU. Even in Pécs (Hungary being in NATO) the security dimension was significant given its proximity to Serbia (and the interviews were conducted in the summer of 1999 at a time of heightened tension over Kosovo). Once more Katowice formed an exceptional case in that here the elites selected regional policy dimension referents such as 'subsidiarity', 'Europe of the Regions', 'Structural and Cohesion Funds' in an informed manner, and ranked them much higher than in other cases. Elsewhere, as regards the regional policy dimension only 'Europe of the Regions' received a relatively high ranking (in Pécs and Maribor), though the term was poorly understood.

While the elite preferences discussed above emphasized the potential economic benefits of entry into the EU, further exploration of the meaning of the EU and the benefits of membership revealed that the elites in most cases saw most benefits accruing to the national level rather than the regional or local levels. The gap between the perceptions of the benefits of enlargement at the national versus the local level was most pronounced in Pécs and Tartu (Figures 6.4–6.6). In Pécs 93 per cent of the members of the local elite considered that Hungary benefited 'significantly' or 'moderately' from its relationship with the EU, whereas only just over 64 per cent believed that the city had benefited similarly, and 36 per cent felt that Pécs had only benefited 'minimally' or 'not at all' from the relationship. Similarly, in Tartu 89 per cent of the local elite considered that Estonia benefited 'significantly' or 'moderately' from its relationship with the EU, whereas 52 per cent felt that Tartu had only benefited 'minimally' or 'not all'. This confirms that the sub-national elites were poorly informed about the potential economic benefits that the EU could bring, and about structural funds in particular.

Even the elite respondents in Katowice, who were more positive about the benefits of EU membership at the local level, felt that in general the EU benefited more from its relationship with Poland rather than vice versa. In Katowice 55 per cent of respondents felt that the EU was the main beneficiary of the relationship, and only 17 per cent considered that both Poland and the European Union benefited equally. In the other cases clear majorities considered that their countries were the key

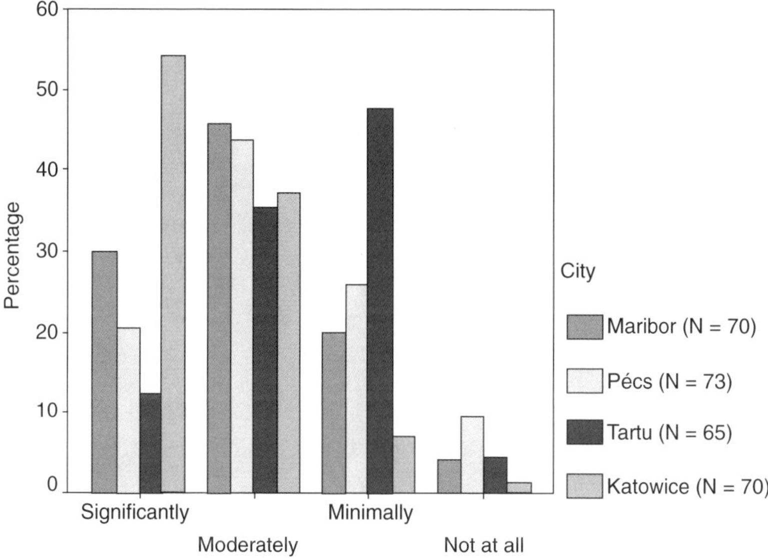

Respondents were asked: How much do you think EU enlargement has benefited your city?

Figure 6.4 Elite opinions of the benefit of EU enlargement to the city

beneficiary from the relationship with the EU (Figure 6.6). Even in Tartu, notwithstanding the fact that Estonia has consistently been among the most Eurosceptic of candidate countries and the local elite in Tartu remain ambivalent about the potential benefits at the local level, 89 per cent of our respondents were of the opinion that their country was the key beneficiary in its relationship with the EU. The evidence suggests that the sub-national elites are far from hostile to the EU or opposed to their countries' impending accession. Rather they have been excluded from the enlargement process and, consequently, are poorly informed about the process and its implications. Despite their lack of knowledge of the EU, and their failure to understand its relevance for their level of governance, they are in general pragmatically and positively predisposed to the economic benefits of membership of the EU at the macro-level.

These elites are pragmatic rather than actively Eurosceptic and therefore are potentially open to a greater level of engagement and connectedness with the EU in the future. The elites generally see the future of their country closely tied to the EU. in Tartu 71 per cent of respondents saw their country's future most closely tied to the EU (with a

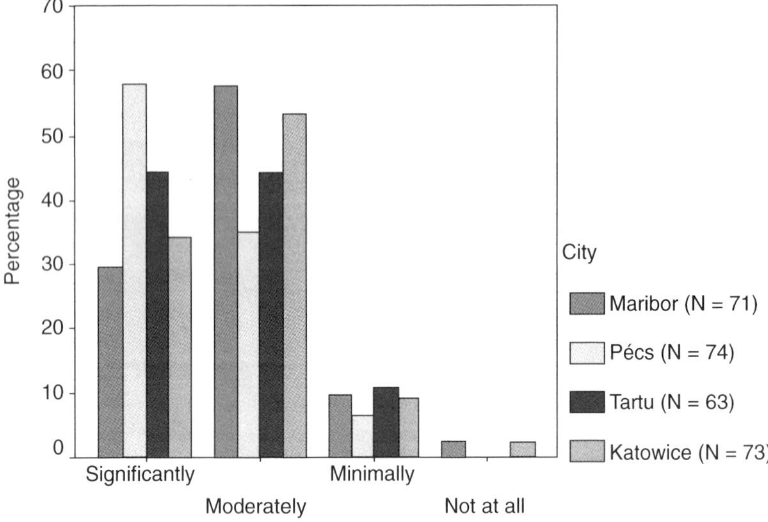

Respondents were asked: How much do you think your country benefits from its relationship with the EU?

Figure 6.5 Elite opinions of the benefit of EU enlargement to the country

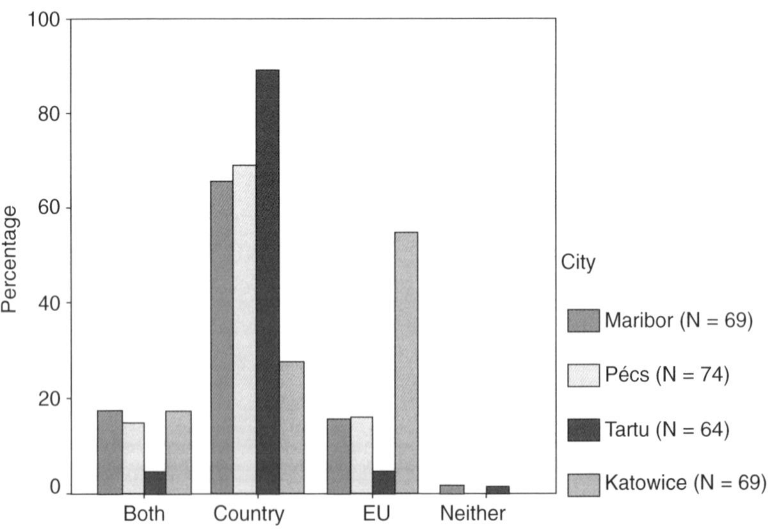

Respondents were asked: Who do you think benefits most out of the relationship between your country and the European Union?

Figure 6.6 Elite opinions of who benefits most from EU enlargement

further 22 per cent citing Scandinavia and Germany). In the cases of Pécs, Maribor and Katowice, 82 per cent of respondents saw their country's future most closely tied to the EU (with a further 5, 7 and 9 per cent respectively specifically highlighting Germany). This indicates that the sub-national elites have consolidated views about the future external orientation of their economic and security relations.

The elites are also receptive to policy changes emanating from EU pressures if they will promote accession, even such intrusive proposals as the reform of internal territorial administrative boundaries (Figure 6.7). Resistance to this idea came only in those cases where it might result in an empowerment of territorialized ethnic minorities (as in Tartu). In Pécs, just under 81 per cent were prepared to accept the redrawing of administrative boundaries in compliance with EU funding criteria and a further 5.6 per cent would accept it 'in some places'. In the case of Maribor, an equally high number (79 per cent) was prepared to accept the redrawing of administrative boundaries, and a further 11 per cent were prepared to countenance such changes 'in some places'. These results indicate a receptiveness to territorial administrative changes that will accommodate EU accession. A greater

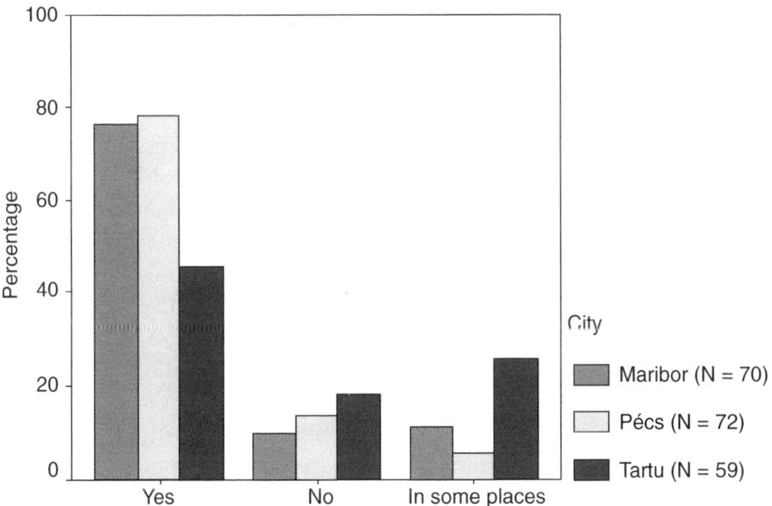

Respondents were asked: Do you agree with the proposition that traditional administrative boundaries should be redrawn, if necessary, to comply with EU funding criteria?

Figure 6.7 Elite opinions on the redrawing of administrative boundaries

resistance to this idea was apparent in the city of Tartu, which although it does not have a large ethnic Russian population reflects the general apprehension among ethnic Estonians about Russian ethnic empowerment in the country. Here only 51 per cent would agree with internal boundary changes, while just over 20 per cent disagreed outright with the proposition, and 29 per cent would agree to such changes only 'in some places'.

Responses to this question may also have contained an implicit aspiration on the part of the sub-national elite members for greater involvement in the EU enlargement process. Such a perception is confirmed by other data. A public opinion survey conducted in 2000 by CEORG revealed a significant perception of a need for greater involvement of the sub-national level in the enlargement process. When asked at which level of administration EU financial resources should be distributed in the first instance, only 13 per cent of those asked in the Czech Republic, 8 per cent in Poland and 26 per cent in Hungary thought funds should be distributed centrally. Whereas 39 per cent in the Czech Republic, 49 per cent in Poland and 44 per cent in Hungary thought funds should be primarily distributed locally or regionally. A further 31 per cent in the Czech Republic, 32 per cent in Poland and 19 per cent in Hungary supported a more or less equal distribution between the two levels.[17]

Given that Poland's regionalization reform had already been completed by the time of our interviews in 2000, the elite respondents in Katowice were asked a different question in an attempt to gauge their perceptions of the influence of the EU on the process of regional reform. As we discussed in Chapter 5 the Polish regional reforms of 1999 were driven primarily by endogenous political dynamics, and EU influence was subordinate to domestic pressures. Nevertheless, our findings in Katowice show that a significant majority, 64 per cent, of the elite in the city still felt that the 'design' of the reform was influenced by EU conditionality or a least a combination of Polish priorities and EU conditionality. At the same time, the elites recognized that the role of the EU was considerably less important for the outcome of the reform, with a large number (39 per cent) concluding that the reform overwhelmingly reflected Polish priorities (Figure 6.8).

Elite identity

The study of European identity is quite properly focused on the issue of 'who belongs?' One of the key schisms in the legal, sociological and

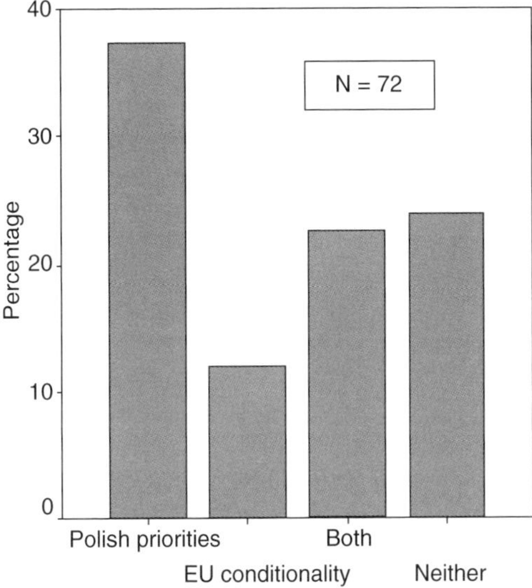

Respondents were asked: Do you think that the reform of regional and district governance structures in Poland in 1999 was on the whole the result of 1. Polish priorities, 2. EU conditions, 3. both, 4. neither?

Figure 6.8 Katowice elites' opinions on EU influence on Polish regional reform

political science debates over the construction of a European identity is between the notion of a mass or 'demos' identity, and the question of the role of the elites.[18] Soysal categorizes the analyses of European identity construction as falling into three modes: the 'cultural collectivity' of a shared European cultural heritage, an 'individual subjectivity' reflected in distinct 'European sensibility of self', and 'institutional unity' which forges and communicates the bonds of the 'we-community'.[19] Studies of Europeanization by political scientists tend to focus on the third mode and, specifically, how the elites that dominate public life at all levels of society are one of the most critical components for identity construction, and among the most active engineers of the process. Other studies have demonstrated the steady increase in the time and effort invested by the EU to contrive policy discourses and activities which confer legitimacy on 'Europeanness', although the EU itself has employed shifting notions of what 'European identity' means from the Copenhagen EC Summit in December 1973 when the concept was first designed at an official level.[20] The theories of European identity construction and of Europeanization intersect at the point of the 'compliance puzzle'. Why do actors or elites at the state level comply with EU norms? The literature on Europeanization, as we discussed in Chapter 1, suggests that greater transnational social interaction by agents (actors and elites) through institutionalized connectedness to EU activities promotes social learning and norm acculturation, and is power-enhancing, and thus shifts and consolidates preferences. Elites also play an important role in the process of norm diffusion in the wider societal levels as they transmit European identity to the 'demos'. What is less clear is whether this is all merely a coincidence or is there some causative effect at work. Is it that elites which self-identify with being 'European' are more predisposed to assimilate Europeanized norms and values? Or is it that those elites which engage in EU activities become 'Europeanized' as an effect of participation itself?

To measure the level of identification with Europe among the sub-national elites in the CEECs, our elite respondents were asked to select and rank their identity from a list of options. They were offered a range of options with some variations to take account of country and local particularities. In general, all elites were offered preferences including Europe, Central Europe, their country, the region, and the city. The results reveal a wide variation across countries (Figure 6.9). The 'European' identity is primary, that is, had most first preferences, only in Pécs. It was the secondary identity, after country, in Maribor, and was tertiary in Katowice and Tartu, after country and region/city. This 27 per cent of respondents in Pécs opted for 'European' as their primary identity compared to 21 per cent in Maribor, 17.6 per cent in Katowice and a mere 9 per cent in Tartu. The results reveal a low level of identification of the sub-national elites with 'Europe'. Regional and local identities are also strong in some cases. Given the salience of the 'thousand year history' of the county level in Hungary in domestic debates over reform, it is at first sight surprising that the city identity is much more significant in Pécs than the county identity. Only 8 per cent of respondents chose Baranya county as their primary identity, whereas 24.3 per cent chose the city. We should note, however, that the city (municipality) is the bedrock of local power in the Hungarian system and county power structures are often located in the main city of the county. We can infer that this institutional concentration at the city level is what accounts for the stronger city identity. Moreover, the Pécs elite was exceptional in that it was the only case where the 'European' identity was ranked first (27 per cent), Central European was the second most preferred option (21.6 per cent), and the national identity came in third place (18.9 per cent). In the other three cases the national identity was the first preference for the primary identity by far. In the small centralized countries such as Slovenia and Estonia, where the capital city and the national level is so predominant, it is to be expected that the country identity scores highly. In the case of Estonia, the city level also scored significantly and regional identity is nonexistent. In Katowice, where the elites are among the most positively predisposed towards the EU, regional identity was the second most preferred primary identity after the national identity. The case of Katowice suggests that a combination of democratized regional government to some extent recaptures and reinforces 'historic' regional identity, and may contribute to a strengthening of positive attitudes to the EU. Just over 27 per cent of respondents in Katowice chose the locale (primarily the region – 20.3 per cent – and to a much lesser extent also including the city) as their primary identity. This high degree of regional identity in Katowice was paralleled only by the equally

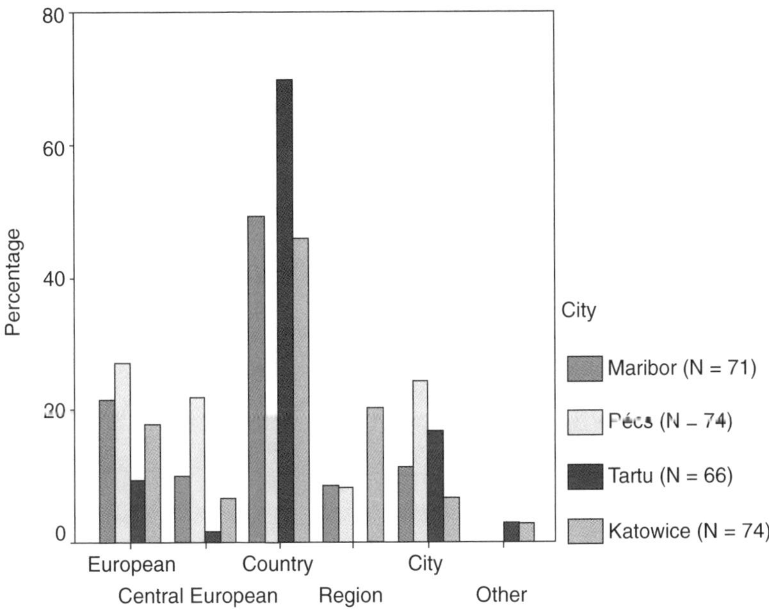

Respondents were asked: In your opinion, which of the following words best describes you (in order of preference)?

Figure 6.9 Sub-national elite identity

strongly held identity in Pécs. Consequently, while three of the four cities exhibit a strong national identity among the elites, and only one revealed a strong European identity, there are also a range of relatively strongly held sub-national identities (either regional or city).

Conclusion

If being bonded to a European identity-in-the-making and Euopeanization are, in essence, about 'ways of doing things', the evidence reviewed here demonstrates the fragility and shallowness of these processes in the CEECs. During the latter phase of the accession process the engineers of these processes, the elites, still exhibited low levels of knowledge and poor understanding of the EU and its activities, and weakly identify with Europeanness. Rather they are more strongly connected with domestic-level issues of transition and localized (or regional) identities. The disconnection of the sub-national elites from the EU partly reflects their structural exclusion from the accession negotiations as this was an important mechanism for the acculturation of norms and discourse, and policy learning. Accession to the EU, consequently, is generally perceived by the sub-national elites as a national elite or EU 'benefit'. Given that the sub-national elites are expected to play a pivotal role in the management and implementation of key enlargement policy objectives – particularly in the areas of regional policy and structural funds, agriculture and the environment – their weak cognitive and normative connectedness to the EU project may well undermine compliance and hinder implementation of policy in the short term.

The evidence presented above shows that the decisional calculus of sub-national elites in accession states has been dominated by their focus on managing the immediate problems of transition, and thus it has been difficult for them to connect to the strategic political vision of European integration. The 'normative gap' in 'Europeanization' at the sub-national level identified here may well have been a significant factor in the low turnouts in many of he referenda on EU accession such as Hungary (45.5 per cent), Slovakia (52 per cent), Czech Republic (55 per cent), and Poland (58.8 per cent).[21] Equally, it must have an impact on the implementation of 'deep integration'. These elites are weakly 'Europeanized' but this weakness is compounded by their positional and functional power in key policy areas. Consequently, sub-national elites who are disengaged from the enlargement process and fail to see the benefits for them, are the bedrock of a potential crisis of implementation in the post-enlargement period.

It is striking that the one case where the evidence for the normative gap was consistently narrower was among the elites in Katowice. It appears that a democratizing regionalization that involves significant regional self-government, may *inter alia* foster a higher level of norm connectedness of elites with the EU and have positive consequences in promoting cognitive change to a higher level of commitment and compliance with a further deepening of he process of EU integration. The institutional framework shapes the perceptions and actions of the elites functioning within the institutional space. This suggests that the process of European integration in CEECs should be as concerned with the promotion of democratic governance at all levels as it is with the 'administrative capacity' for policy implementation.

If we assume that the accession negotiations were a powerful 'Europeanizing' influence on national elite norms and behaviour we can infer that the structural exclusion of the sub-national elites from the enlargement process contributed to their weaker levels of 'Europeanization'. This exclusion reinforced a scissors effect in the norms and attitudes of the CEEC elites, with a disjuncture between the more 'Europeanized' values into which the national elites were assimilated and the knowledge gap about the EU and the greater resistance levels to the infiltration of EU norms among sub-national elites. A significant normative fissure between national and sub-national elites is obviously not conducive to policy coherence, administrative consistency and good governance. Indeed, it may lead to dysfunctional governance, particularly where the sub-national elites play a key role in policy implementation. Such bifurcated 'Europeanization' in the domestic setting may result in 'differential empowerment' in domestic politics, although, as noted earlier, this is a factor that will take time to develop. Of more immediate concern is whether it will generate compliance and commitment problems in the implementation of policy in the short term.

Conclusion

The two most widely employed concepts in the framing of the debates about EU enlargement and European integration are 'Europeanization' and 'conditionality'. Yet, both concepts are employed rather nebulously and lack coherent explanatory frameworks. The term 'Europeanization' has been stretched to encapsulate phenomena beyond its original locus in the framework of EU policy-making to emphasize how European norms, structures and policies filter into domestic politics. The evidence with regard to the resulting systemic convergence remains, however, inconclusive. The concept suggests that greater connectedness to EU activities not only provides incentives and advantages in domestic level political games by promoting 'differential empowerment' but also progresses normative assimilation and the collective embrace of a 'European' identity. In the context of EU enlargement, both policy-makers and policy analysts generally view conditionality as the primary mechanism of Europeanization. Broadly, the use of the term 'EU conditionality' assumes that there is a power asymmetry between the actor setting and enforcing the conditions and the actor that must comply. The term 'conditionality' implies a consensus on rules and their transmission mechanisms within the EU, with clear-cut benchmarks, and consistency and continuity in the transfer of rules over time. Inherent in the assumption that a power asymmetry characterizes EU enlargement conditionality is the implication that it drives policy change and institution-building in the CEECs, while also facilitating greater convergence than is evident in the member states. Much less is said about the dislocating effects on the candidate states' 'ownership' of such changes and the implications that this might have for implementation. This book has critically engaged with both of these key concepts. In particular, rather than assuming a powerful linkage between conditionality and Europeanization, we have empirically tested for the 'Europeanizing' effects of enlargement conditionality in the CEECs by examining the process of regionalization, the construction of the institutional architecture for regional policy, and the normative capacity of the elites at a level that will be critical for the implementation of post-enlargement policies.

Much of the discussion about Europeanization and conditionality tends to focus on the bilateral negotiations between the Commission and the governments of the CEECs over the adoption into national legislation of the 80,000 plus pages of the *acquis*. It is important to distinguish, however, between the formal rush by candidate states to adopt the *acquis* into domestic law and their 'capacity' to effectively and meaningfully implement its provisions. In practice, the adoption of the *acquis* by formal legislative engineering in the CEECs has to be accompanied by a more informal process of normative adaptation and policy learning if the former is to be effective. One of the policy areas where the contrast between formal adoption, capacity, and implementation issues is most evident is in regional policy (Chapter 21 of the negotiations on the *acquis*). Regional policy has been one of the most controversial issues in the accession negotiations, as evidenced by the fact that it was one of the last chapters to be closed by the candidates before the Copenhagen Council in December 2002 took the decision on the date for enlargement. The reasons for this are twofold. Firstly, it is of immense financial significance in the enlargement process, with over half of the EU assistance to the new members being allocated for 'structural actions'. Secondly, the EU's attempt to shape the institutional template for the delivery of regional policy in the CEECs caused friction with one of the most politically sensitive core issues of sovereignty over state-territorial organization. Furthermore, the EU's interference occurred at a time when most of the CEECs had already embarked on the process of reforming their state-territorial organization as part of their own transition processes. Thus, in some cases, the parameters of the debate had already been well-defined, or constitutional constraints on outcomes had already been imposed by the early phase of the transition process and were thus *prior* to accession.

EU conditionality fits within a historical Western pattern of aid conditionality. The objectives of EU conditionality are consistent with traditional Western objectives of aid, principally, the economic and security interests of the 'donor' state(s). This linkage between economic and political conditionality and financial aid in EC and EU policy toward Eastern Europe is critical for understanding the process of enlargement. The evidence discussed in this book suggests that the prospect of EU membership helped to reinforce processes of democratization that were already well under way in most of the CEECs. EU conditionality for membership, on the other hand, was in practice so generic and had such diffused institutional and attitudinal impact in the policy area analysed here during enlargement, that it fits well within the definition of international conditionality more broadly as being in essence 'declaratory policy'. Certainly the EC and then EU paid serious attention to conditionality as a rhetorical device during enlargement but not to its substantive and credible application.

The EU's conditionality underwent several transformations as enlargement progressed. EU conditionality initially emphasized the vague normative statement of the 'Copenhagen criteria' of December 1993. This normative dimension was certainly most important as a factor in the early decisional phase about enlargement and thereby shaped the general outlook of transition in the CEECs. This normative point of reference remained an important structuring device for the EU's monitoring of the candidates during the actual accession process from 1997 onwards. The shift to a concentration on the *acquis* and 'capacity' issues came at the Madrid Council in December 1995, was consolidated in the Commission's Opinions on individual candidates in 1997, and became the main focus for the Commission's Regular Reports in 1998– 2002. The fundamental problem with both of these normative and technocratic variants of conditionality is that the Commission has generally lacked agreed benchmarks for the CEECs to adhere to. The domain of regional policy illustrates well many of the difficulties arising from the lack of standards and benchmarks for evaluating progress on complying with the conditionality. It also exemplifies the tension within the EU's own complex institutional framework for regional policy-making where the Commission has a limited remit regarding the design of the wider political institutional environment in which the policy is delivered.

When we examined how the EU has addressed the issue of regional policy during the enlargement process we focused on the role of the Commission as the key locomotive pulling the enlargement process along. The Commission's approach to regionalization has been characterized by confusion and poor communication of policy recommendations to the candidates as regards what institutional requisites were entailed in the conditionality for regional policy and what kind of capacity was necessary. The weakness of conditionality in this policy area was largely due to the fact that there is no standard model of regionalization within the existing member states and the management of structural funds is a matter for member states' 'own rules'. Some areas of the *acquis* are 'thicker' and others are 'thinner' on regulatory content. Thus, the *acquis* itself is a structural impediment to a uniform and consistent EU conditionality. Regional policy is a thin, if not the thinnest area of the *acquis* despite its budgetary implications. Consequently, the performance tasks set for the CEECs by the Commission in this policy area have not been easily devised, evaluated or benchmarked. The policy tracking method employed in this book reveals the tensions within the Commission, and between it and candidate countries over the form and institutional environment of regional policy in the CEECs. The evidence presented here suggests that there were two opposite trends in the Commission's approach. During the initial phase of the enlargement process key actors within the Commission who were involved in accession preferred a particular 'model' of politically decentralized regional self-government and were proactive in applying their power to achieve this through 'informal conditionality'. Subsequently, conflicting signals and competing visions within the Commission (and these divisions cross-cut DGs and sections within DGs) as to what constituted the ideal institutional architecture for managing regional policy became more apparent.

The Commission's institutional preferences were initially less shaped by fiscal concerns and more by the normative impetus to find an institutional reconfiguration of the territorial dimension of governance that would further democratization and deliver 'multi-level governance' and 'partnership' in regional policy. Over time in the post-Agenda 2000 period, however, the Commission's preferences consolidated around a particular kind of functionalist and technocratic model that stressed elements such as centralized management and control of structural funds that were more in line with the technical provisions of the *acquis*. Thus in the period from 1996–99 through its Regular Reports on the candidate countries and PHARE-sponsored regional programmes as well as numerous interactions between the candidates' representatives and Commission officials in Brussels and the delegations in the candidate countries themselves, the Commission sought directly or indirectly to shape the process of regionalization in the candidate countries. The pressure from the Commission created a strong perception among the negotiating elites in the CEECs that the Commission favoured regional self-government. That perception only began to shift in 2000–01, as the deadline for enlargement drew closer, when the Commission put more emphasis on a centralized approach to regional policy and the management of regional funds, while raising concerns about insufficent capacity at the local and regional level and the lack of coordination between the national, regional and local level institutions.

Joining the NUTS statistical classification system, an element of the EU's Structural Funds Regulations, has been an informal condition of the pre-accession phase but it was made a formal membership criterion for the EU as a whole only in 2003. Within the EU the NUTS II regions were configured by the member states and subsequently were approved pro forma by Brussels. In contrast, the Commission (via Eurostat) has been deeply involved in the designation of NUTS regions in the CEECs. The Commission's Regular Reports on candidates have commended reforms that aligned new regional political or administrative structures with NUTS II regions. Both Hungary's administrative-statistical variant of regional reform of 1996 and Poland's regional self-government variant of reform of 1999 fit the NUTS II criteria and were initially praised by the Commission. The emphasis on technocratic criteria and standardization, and the pressure for regionalization despite size, historical tradition and political sensitivities concerning ethnic minorities and potential territorial challenges, has caused friction between the Commission and some CEECs, such as Romania, Slovakia and Estonia. The Commission's push for regionalization in Romania, for example, led to fears that it was encouraging nascent federalism and the potential separatist aspirations of the Hungarian minority in Transylvania.

The enlargement process involved a learning curve for the Commission and its key agencies in the CEECs such as PHARE. The confusion within the Commission reflected the different remits and interests of the various actors in the Commission, in particular competing logics between normative and functional regions and the tension between 'partnership' and 'control' in the delivery of regional policy. Furthermore, the Commission's own monitoring and evaluation mechanism for its conditionality, the Regular Reports, were vague and inconsistent. Moreover, a fully-fledged elaboration of the technical requirements for the management of regional funds was only given by the Commission in its communiqué of July 2003 – after the date for enlargement to proceed had been agreed.

The power asymmetry in favour of the Commission in the negotiations has meant that the CEECs have felt pressured to react even to under-defined signals emanating from the Commission. The diverging outcomes in the CEECs in this policy area demonstrate, however, that EU conditionality was much weaker than might have been expected given the assumptions regarding symmetric outcomes suggested by the conditionality and Europeanization approaches. Since 1996 there have been two main trends in regionalization in the CEECs. First, the democratized and decentralized variant of regional self-government that included the establishment of elected regional councils with significant powers over regional development such as in Poland, the Czech Republic and to a lesser extent Slovakia (in Poland these overlapped with NUTS II regions). Second, the administrative-statistical variant, where NUTS II regions were demarcated and regional development councils were established as centrally appointed quangos, with largely advisory functions (Hungary), or where most powers over regional development and funding were retained in central ministries (for example, Baltic states and Slovenia).

The outcome of the interactions over these policy areas appears to have been more strongly affected by path-dependent factors in the domestic political settings in the CEECs than the explicit/formal or implicit/informal conditionality emanating from the Commission. Some governments, for example, have chosen to build on pre-existing regional identities. Where such identities are weak or nonexistent, this option is less viable. Moreover, in some countries regional identities are closely linked to ethnic identities and contested boundaries, a reality that governments are reluctant to enhance through regionalization (for example, in Romania and Slovakia where there are significant territorialized Hungarian minority populations). The Commission's initial drive for Europeanization through regionalization thus collided with the interests of national elites who were concerned about the awakening and empowering of regional and local identities in the CEECs, some of which had been long dormant. Some countries have looked both to their pre-1945 past and to the systems of local government in Western Europe and the model promoted by the EU. States that were formerly part of the Austro-Hungarian empire had the experience of a system of state administrative and self-governing territorial administration dating from the mid-nineteenth century and enduring in most cases until 1945. Regionalization in Poland was driven by an overarching domestic consensus to decentralize, although without adopting full-blown federalism. In the Czech Republic, despite an early constitutional commitment to regional government, the reform was delayed by an ideological polarization in the domestic politics of transition which was territorialized in a centre-regional cleavage. While the need to respond to EU pressures for democratization was a factor in the regionalization of Slovakia, its form was strongly shaped by domestic political pressures to minimize the role of the Hungarian minority in regional government. In response to the functional logic underlying the pressures emerging from the European Commission to establish administrative capacity at the regional level, policy-makers in some CEECs have also revived communist-era planning regions as models for new regional development agencies (for example in Hungary). Finally, small countries such as Slovenia and the Baltic states, with weak historical traditions of regional governance and little functional need for it, and a large territorialized Russian minority in Latvia and Estonia, have chosen to retain their centralized systems of governance. On balance, the evidence suggests that path dependency in the form of domestic political considerations, informed by historical legacies, played a more salient role in regionalization than a clear causative effect of 'real' or perceived EU conditionality.

To assess the relative importance of the domestic factors shaping policy during the enlargement process we have provided detailed case studies of the processes of regionalization in Poland and Hungary. Poland and Hungary illustrate the alternate variants of regionalization. Poland carried out the first democratizing regionalization in the CEECs, but it would be erroneous to link this development causally with enlargement or EU conditionality. The Polish regional reform was initiated as part of the country's democratic transition from communism in 1989–90. The main reason why Poland's regional self-government structures did not become operational until 1999 was largely due to domestic political opposition from the socialist and agrarian parties and transitional political cycles. The replacement of the liberal Suchocka government by a socialist-agrarian coalition in 1993 scuppered an early attempt at reform, and it only returned to the political agenda when the new AWS coalition government came to power in 1997. The final designation of the Polish regions dovetailed with EU requirements, in particular the NUTS II criteria, but the reform was driven overwhelmingly by domestic political conditions rather than EU accession. Indeed, the Polish self-governing regions were installed at a time when the Commission had turned against this kind of development and was instead pushing for centralization. Accordingly, subsequent Regular Reports contained criticism of the reforms for not making sufficient contributions to the required administrative capacity and centralized management.

Hungary is the candidate country where the Commission was most proactive in shaping regionalization. As early as 1992, PHARE sponsored programmes in Hungary to facilitate government strategies on regional development and decentralize the formulation and implementation of regional policy. The administrative model changed repeatedly in reaction to Commission evaluations. Praise of Hungary's 1996 reform in the Commission's Opinions of 1997 was followed by overt criticisms in subsequent reports. As with Poland, the issue of regionalization in Hungary was driven more by domestic transition politics than the external pressures from the Commission. The issue was politically divisive, though more cross-cutting of the ideological spectrum than was the case in Poland. Most importantly, in Hungary there were major structural constraints on regionalization which had been set in place by the transition. A reform to introduce regional self-government required a constitutional amendment which in turn required a two-thirds parliamentary majority – something that was very difficult to achieve given the political divisiveness of the issue. Moreover, the local government act of 1990 had concentrated power to municipal and local governments whose elites were reluctant to lose power to new regional self-governments.

Enlargement has involved not only the export of a menu of institutional and regulatory templates to the CEECs, but also an attempt to diffuse 'Europeanizing' norms and practices. Despite the critical importance of regional policy, the sub-national elites were structurally disengaged from the enlargement process. Even when regionalization began to be deliberated as part of the adoption of Chapter 21 of the *acquis*, the process remained in essence a bilateral exchange between central governments and the Commission. Furthermore, the formulaic critiques of the weak 'capacity' at the regional level was understood by the Commission as meaning in the first instance weak organizational structures and administrative understaffing that might pose serious constraints on the future ability to extract and efficiently use the EU funds. The Commission did not, however, concern itself with the normative content of 'capacity'. This structural disengagement of the sub-national elites from the enlargement process has dislocated these elites from a key mechanism for their normative acculturation into the EU. While there are indications of growing horizontal integration based on Europe-wide networks, during the accession process sub-national elites in the CEECs were poorly informed about EU activities, tended not to recognize the potential tangible benefits of the EU for this level of government, and held at best pragmatic understandings of what the EU stands for. For this level of the elite in the CEECs, EU membership entails economic integration as opposed to political integration. EU enlargement was, moreover, widely perceived to be a national project by and for national governments and elites. This gap in engagement is likely to persist until the divergence between national and regional elite perceptions is addressed. This requires a more active communicative strategy that goes beyond the Commission's tendency to focus on funding symbolic and decorative transmissions of Europeanness in the new member states, as for example during the build-up to the one-off referenda campaigns in the CEECs. Most importantly, it requires a strategy to structurally engage and promote the wider assimilation of the sub-national elites into policy-making and norms.

It is one of the many paradoxes of enlargement that the Commission's concern with 'regional capacity' was paralleled by the exclusion of the sub-national elites. It is not altogether surprising, therefore, that the Commission's Regular Reports record a lack of sub-national implementation and enforcement of EU rules and policies that have been formally agreed in bilateral negotiations with national governments. This divergence between 'state-level' compliance with EU accession conditionality and the weak implementation capacity identified by the EU reports, and the poor normative assimilation at the sub-national level confirmed in this book, raises important questions about the commitment and compliance dilemmas that an enlarged EU will face. The sub-national elites may become more institutionally connected and normatively secured to the EU in the post-enlargement period by their involvement in EU policy implementation. This assumes, however, that those EU policies that will be pivotal for the sub-national level, such as structural funds, will be managed in the CEECs in a manner that promotes wider cognitive and normative change through greater sub-national elite participation. As we know from the experience of the existing EU member states, structural funds are managed in a variety of ways from the highly centralized to highly decentralized. Furthermore, the Commission has forced the adoption of a centralized managerial approach to structural funds in the latter stages of the accession process precisely because the sub-national elites and institutions are not in a position to fully utilize the financial transfers that will come from the EU, in particular regional funds. Thus, ultimately, the extent to which 'Europeanization' proceeds to close the gap between the attitudes of national and sub-national elites in the CEECs depends immensely on whether the institutional and organizational structures for the management of structural funds become inclusive and deliver the EU's own principle of 'partnership'. Such institution-building requires the new member states to invest more of their sparse resources in building more capacity, both organizational and normative, at the sub-national level of governance, and given their financial constraints, this will take time. Our data do not contradict the 'differential empowerment' thesis, but rather refine it to demonstrate the great variations which qualify its effects. These effects can only evolve and be measured over time, and may vary depending on the domestic and international influences on a particular country.

The question of whether the wider Europe will become 'deeper' remains an open one. Sub-national elites are one of the key channels for communicating national and international values throughout society. This kind of local power is all the more accentuated in the CEECs given that the penetrative power of the state has been weakened by transition. A crucial mechanism for the transmission of norms and mobilization of voters, political parties, are still weakly institutionalized at the local level in the CEECs. Consequently, sub-national elites retain a significant impact on the mobilization of voters and on the shaping of voter preferences. Their disengagement from the EU must have been a factor in the low turnouts in the referenda in some of the key accession states.

The regional developments in the CEECs are more similar to the trends in Western Europe than the structure of the enlargement process might have led us to expect. In Western Europe regions have developed in the main either as a product of technocratic manipulation, or as a product of regionalism and mobilization 'from below' and 'from within' that acted as an anvil against which the drive for EU integration hammered the nation-state. The asymmetrical form of regionalization in the CEECs is, in fact, a convergence with the diversity of regional government in the member states. The key difference is that in the case of the CEECs regionalization is largely proceeding domestically 'from above' in the absence of regionalist mobilization. Thus, in contrast to Western Europe, regional institutions are being created in most CEECs in the context of transition and EU enlargement prior to regionalist mobilizations, though we may infer that regionally-based institutions may well provide a platform for future regionalist mobilizations.

EU enlargement conditionality is more usefully analysed as an interactive and dynamic process rather than one that should be examined only in terms of clear causative effects within a narrowly positivist framework. By investigating how EU conditionality operated in a key policy area during enlargement we have demonstrated the dynamic and fluid nature of both the concept and its impact on the candidates. Although formal conditionality was weak due to the thinness of the *acquis* in regional policy and the lack of an EU model on how to

'Europeanize' regional policy, the Commission applied informal pressures to shape regionalization in the CEECs in an ad hoc and erratic manner, initially promoting decentralization and latterly centralization. Despite the pressures, the diverse institutional outcomes in the regionalization of the CEECs have been overwhelmingly driven by domestic political factors arising out of their transitions from communism rather than by EU conditionality pressures. This finding focuses our attention on the need to better conceptualize the relationship between transition and enlargement.

We can conclude that the lack of detailed explicit conditionality embedded in the *acquis* was only partly and inconsistently compensated for by 'soft' or more informal conditionality, such as the recommendations in the Regular Reports or direct contacts with Commission officials. The widespread notion of conditionality, which informs much of the political and scholarly debate about EU enlargement, portrays EU enlargement conditionality as a 'catch-all' instrument of Europeanization in the CEECs. This 'myth of conditionality' is not sustainable once we take account of those key policy areas where there is a 'conditionality gap' and where the resistance levels to Europeanization are based on domestic political transition constraints. The transition was an active interface with enlargement which generated preferences that often overrode external incentives and pressures. Thus, the concept of conditionality should be seen less as a generic instrument for applying pressures for rule adoption on the candidates. Instead of one coherent variable it is better understood as a process which involves a tool bag of differentiated and shifting instruments, including prescriptive norms, institutional formats, and preferences for delivering legislative and policy compliance. Where formal conditionality was weak, the use of informal conditionality reflected the debates and preferences of the key relevant actors in the Commission at any given time. Consequently, the application of conditionality must be analysed on a case-by-case basis with regard to policy domain and country, paying attention to the multi-level actors involved both on the side of the EU and the candidate countries, their perceptions, the signalling of different rewards and sanctions, the interactions over compliance, and how as a process it develops over time.

Notes

Introduction

1. Speech to the European Parliament, 9 October 2002: http://europa.eu.int/comm/commissioners/verheugen/speeches_en.htm.
2. See Graham Avery (forthcoming 2004) 'The Enlargement Negotiations', in Fraser Cameron (ed.), *The Future of Europe: Enlargement and Integration*, London: Routledge.
3. Authors' interview with a senior official in the Estonian Mission to the EU, Brussels, 11 December 2000.
4. http://edition.cnn.com/2003/WORLD/europe/06/15/czech.euvote/index.html.
5. Within a positivist framework conditionality is best conceived of as an intervening variable, while 'EU norm adoption', including elements like the 'density of the *acquis*' and 'clarity of rules', represents the dependent variable. See Frank Schimmelfennig and Ulrich Sedelmeier (2003), 'The Europeanization of Eastern Europe: Evaluating the Conditionality Model', European University Institute Workshop, Florence, 4–5 July. This type of framework may be apt to generate 'tidier' results with regard to formalized hypotheses, but the research focus moves away from the phenomenon of conditionality as such, which remains an *a priori* and under-conceptualized category.
6. Michael Keating (1998) 'The New Regionalism', in Michael Keating, *The New Regionalism in Western Europe: Territorial Restructuring and Political Change*, Cheltenham: Edward Elgar, 72–111.
7. See European Council (2002) *Presidency Conclusions. Annex I*, Copenhagen European Council, 12–13 December 2002: http://ue.eu.int/newsroom/councilHomePage.asp?LANG=1.
8. Alan Mayhew (1998) *Recreating Europe: the European Union's Policy towards Central and Eastern Europe*, Cambridge: Cambridge University Press; Susan S. Nello and Karen Smith (1998) *The European Union and Central and Eastern Europe: the Implications of Enlargement in Stages*, Aldershot: Ashgate; Helen Tang (ed.) (2000) *Winners and Losers of EU Integration: Policy Issues for Central and Eastern Europe*, Washington, DC: World Bank.
9. For a similar approach in the field of administrative reforms see Klaus H. Goetz (2000) 'European Integration and National Executives: a Cause in Search of an Effect?', *West European Politics*, 23 (4), 211–31; Antoaneta Dimitrova (2002), 'Enlargement, Institution-Building and the EU's Administrative Capacity Requirement', *West European Politics*, 25 (4), 171–90.
10. Our analysis of the role of the Commission is based on thirty-two interviews conducted with officials in DG Enlargement, DG Regio, PHARE, the Forward Planning Unit, and candidate country delegations in Brussels, mainly in 2000–01, with a few additional follow-up interviews at the end of 2003–04. For previous studies of the impact of EU enlargement on the attitudes and norms of elites at the sub-national level in the CEECs see James

Hughes, Gwendolyn Sasse and Claire Gordon (2001) 'The Regional Deficit in Eastward Enlargement of the European Union: Top Down Policies and Bottom Up Reactions', ESRC 'One Europe or Several?' Working Paper 29/01, Brighton: Sussex University; James Hughes, Gwendolyn Sasse and Claire Gordon (2002) 'Saying "Maybe" to the "Return to Europe": Elites and the Political Space for Euroscepticism in Central and Eastern Europe', *European Union Politics*, 3 (3), 327–55.

11. For classic works on transition see Adam Przeworski (1991) *Democracy and the Market: Political and Economic Reforms in Eastern Europe and Latin America*, Cambridge: Cambridge University Press; Juan J. Linz and Alfred Stepan (1996) *Problems of Democratic Transition and Consolidation: Southern Europe, South America and Post-Communist Europe*, London: Johns Hopkins University Press; Guillermo O'Donnell and Philippe Schmitter (1986) *Transitions from Authoritarian Rule. Tentative Conclusions about Uncertain Democracies*, Baltimore: Johns Hopkins University Press. For an excellent overview of the enlargement process in the 1990s see Helen Wallace and Ulrich Sedelmeier (2000) 'Eastern Enlargement', in Helen Wallace and William Wallace (eds), *Policy-making in the European Union*, 4th edition, Oxford: Oxford University Press.

1. The logic of enlargement conditionality and Europeanization

1. Heather Grabbe (2001) 'How Does Europeanisation Affect CEE Governance? Conditionality, Diffusion and Diversity', *Journal of European Public Policy*, 8 (6), 1013–31 and Heather Grabbe (2002) 'European Union Conditionality and the *Acquis Communautaire*', *International Political Science Review*, 23 (3), 252.
2. Karen Smith (1998) *The Making of EU Foreign Policy: the Case of Eastern Europe*, New York: St Martin's Press.
3. Grabbe (2002: 262). She identifies five levers of EU conditionality: 1. access to negotiations and further stages in the accession process, 2. provision of legislative and institutional templates, 3. aid and technical assistance, 4. policy advice and twinning projects, 5. monitoring, *demarches*, and public criticism.
4. Grabbe (2002: 264).
5. Frank Schimmelfennig, Stefan Egert and Heiko Knobel (2001), 'Costs, Commitment and Compliance: the Impact of EU Democratic Conditionality on Latvia, Slovakia and Turkey', *Journal of Common Market Studies*, 41 (3), 495–518.
6. For a study of the use of conditionality in the adoption of the *acquis* by the CEECs see Grabbe (2001). For the role of EU conditionality in 'democracy promotion' see Smith (1998); Karen E. Smith (2001a) 'Western Actors and the Promotion of Democracy', in Jan Zielonka and Alex Pravda (eds), *Democratic Consolidation in Eastern Europe*, vol. 2, *International and Transnational Factors*, Oxford: Oxford University Press, 31; Karen E. Smith (2001b) 'The EU, Human Rights and Relations with Third Countries: "Foreign Policy" with an Ethical Dimension?', in Karen E. Smith and

Margot Light (2001) *Ethics and Foreign Policy*, New York: Cambridge University Press, 185–204; Jan Zielonka (2001) 'Conclusions: Foreign Made Democracy', in Jan Zielonka and Alex Pravda (eds), *Democratic Consolidation in Eastern Europe, Vol. 2*, Oxford: Oxford University Press, 511.

7. For more recent work in this area, see the papers presented at the ECPR Joint Sessions, Turin, 2002, Workshop: Enlargement and European Governance: (http://www.essex.ac.uk/ecpr/events/jointsessions/paperarchive/turin.asp?section=4) and at the RSCAS Workshop 'The Europeanization of Eastern Europe: Evaluating the Conditionality Model', EUI Florence, 4–5 July 2003.
8. Phillippe E. Schmitter (1996) 'The Influence of the International Context upon the Choice of National Institutions and Policies', in Lawrence Whitehead (ed.), *The International Dimensions of Democratization*, Oxford: Oxford University Press, 30.
9. President of the Commission Romano Prodi has consistently used the enlargement process as a rationale for increasing the EU budget and rejecting budgetary tightening. As he put it in a speech at LSE on 19 January 2004: 'the eve of the biggest enlargement in the EU's history ... is an odd moment to propose lowering the ceiling on resources'. In the debate on the EU budget ceiling in 2003–04 the Commission favours a cap on spending of 1.24 per cent of GDP while member states such as Britain and Germany favour a cap of 1 per cent. The difference amounts to some £30 billion per year.
10. For a critique of the role of Western policy advisers and consultants in the CEEC transitions see Janine Wedel (1998) *Collision and Collusion: the Strange Case of Western Aid to Eastern Europe, 1989–1998*, New York: St Martin's Press.
11. For studies of PHARE see Alan Mayhew (1998) *Recreating Europe: the European Union's Policy towards Central and Eastern Europe*, Cambridge: Cambridge University Press; Peter Heil (2000) *PHARE in Hungary: the Anatomy of a Pre-accession Aid Programme, 1990–1999*, Unpublished PhD Thesis, Budapest. PHARE was tasked to the Commission apparently at the suggestion of US President George Bush, see Helen Wallace and Ulrich Sedelmeier (2000) 'Eastern Enlargement', in Helen Wallace and William Wallace (eds), *Policy-making in the European Union*, 4th edition, Oxford: Oxford University Press, 427–60 (433).
12. This argument is developed by Frank Schimmelfennig (2001) 'The Community Trap: Liberal Norms, Rhetorical Action, and the Eastern Enlargement of the European Union', *International Organization*, 55 (1), 47–80.
13. See Andrew Moravcik and Milada Vachudova (2003), 'National Interests, State Power and EU Enlargement', *East European Politics and Societies*, 17 (1), 42–57.
14. For studies of aid conditionality generally see: Olav Stokke (1995), *Aid and Political Conditionality*, London: Frank Cass; Tony Killick (1998), *Aid and the Political Economy of Policy Change*, London: Routledge; Gordon Crawford (2001), *Foreign Aid and Political Reform: a Comparative Analysis of Democracy Assistance and Political Conditionality*, Basingstoke: Palgrave. The EU's role in Central and Eastern Europe is not discussed in Stokke's work, while Crawford provides a two-page summary of the EU instruments for aid to

the CEECs, but without integrating them into his overall analysis of aid conditionality.

15. Stokke (1995: 3).
16. The UN's Expanded Programme of Technical Assistance (EPTA) was created in 1949. In 1950 it was transformed into the UN Development Programme (UNDP).
17. John Killick (1997) *The United States and the European Reconstruction, 1945–1960*, Edinburgh: Keele University Press; Alan Milward (2000) *The European Rescue of the Nation State*, 2nd edition, London: Routledge.
18. Stokke (1995: 1–2). As George Schultz, Reagan's Secretary of State explained in a speech to Congress in 1984, foreign aid was 'in effect, the foreign policy budget of the United States ... which directly protects and furthers US national interests abroad' (cited in Stokke, 1995: 2, n. 1).
19. John Walton and David Seddon (1994) *Free Markets and Food Riots: the Politics of Global Adjustment*, Oxford: Blackwell, 333.
20. Georg Sorensen (1993) *Democracy and Democratization: Dilemmas in World Politics*, Boulder, CO: Westview Press Inc.; Gordon Crawford (2003) 'Promoting Democracy from Without – Learning from Within (Part I)', *Democratization*, 10 (1), 77–98; Gordon Crawford (2003) 'Promoting Democracy from Without – Learning from Within (Part II)', *Democratization*, 10 (2), 1–20.
21. Susan S. Nello (2001) 'The Impact of External Economic Factors: the Role of the IMF', in Jan Zielonka and Alex Pravda (eds), *Democratic Consolidation in Eastern Europe, Vol. 2*, Oxford: Oxford University Press, 79.
22. For the classic statement of this position see Seymour Martin Lipset (1959) 'Some Social Requisites of Democracy', *American Political Science Review*, 53, 69–105.
23. Walton and Seddon (1994: 335).
24. Randall W. Stone (2002), *Lending Credibility, the International Monetary Fund and the Post-Communist Transition*, Princeton: Princeton University Press.
25. Smith (2001a: 31). Other key actors, apart from the EU, involved in the project included individual states and multilateral organizations such as the CSCE/OSCE, the Council of Europe, NATO, IMF, World Bank, and EBRD.
26. Stokke (1995: 22–3).
27. In theory, EBRD loans are to be made only to states committed to 'multi-party democracy, pluralism, and market economics'. In practice loans have been made to dynastic and quasi-totalitarian but resource-rich regimes such as those of Azerbaijan and Central Asia.
28. Crawford (2001: 4, 59–60).
29. Stokke (1995: 22, n. 16); Peter Burnell (1994) 'Good Government and Democratization: a Sideways Look at Aid and Political Conditionality', *Democratization*, 1 (3), 485–503.
30. Previously, the EC had employed a conditional human rights protection statement in the Preamble of Lomé III (1985–89), and continued this in the ACP/EU Cotonou Partnership Agreement 2000, that is to say, in the non-legally binding part of the Convention. This condition had never been activated, even into the 1990s, with the sole exception of sanctions against Togoland – though the military regime there had been in power since 1963.

31. European Council (1991), *Presidency Conclusions*, Luxembourg European Council, 28–29 June 1991, annex, Luxembourg: Office for Official Publications of the European Communities: http://www.europarl.eu.int/summits/luxembourg/lu2_en.pdf.
32. European Council Resolution (1991) *Resolution on Human Rights, Democracy and Development*, 28 November 1991, Luxembourg: Office for Official Publications of the European Union: http://europa.eu.int/comm/external_relations/human_rights/doc/cr28_11_91_en.htm.
33. European Union (1992) *Treaty on European Union*, 7 February 1992, Luxembourg: Office for Official Publications of the European Communities: http://europa.eu.int/abc/obj/treaties/en/entoc01.htm.
34. European Union (1997) *Treaty of Amsterdam Amending the Treaty on European Union, The Treaties Establishing the European Communities and Related Acts*, Official Journal C 340, 10 November 1997, Luxembourg: Office for Official Publications of the European Communities: http://europa.eu.int/eur-lex/en/treaties/dat/amsterdam.html.
35. For example, at the height of the new rhetoric, Hurd made the decision to release UK tied aid to Malaysia for the highly controversial Pergau Dam project in 1991, in the face of not only clear evidence of that country's poor progress on democracy and its abysmal human rights record, but also of the serious environmental damage that the project would cause, and in clear breach of the UK's own legislation on aid. Under the UK's 1980 Overseas Development and Co-operation Act, aid can only be used for 'promoting the development or maintaining the economy of a country ... or the welfare of its people'. The World Development Movement won a High Court Judicial Review on the case and the aid was cancelled in 1994.
36. See Crawford (2001: 211–27).
37. Stokke (1995: 46).
38. Smith (2001a: 33).
39. Germany and the UK support enlargement largely for security reasons and the potential new markets, France and Italy are concerned with the implications for the CAP and the diminishing of their authority within EU decision-making, Spain, Ireland, Portugal and Greece are concerned about losing structural funds (Schimmelfennig, 2001). These traditional divisions have been further fragmented by divisions in early 2003 over the war against Iraq.
40. See European Council (1993): http://www.europarl.eu.int/enlargement_new/europeancouncil/pdf/cop_en.pdf.
41. Thomas Carothers (1999) *Aiding Democracy Abroad: the Learning Curve*, Carnegie Endowment for International Peace, Washington, DC.
42. For the weak credibility of aid conditionality toward Eastern Europe see Wedel (1998); Stone (2002). For aid towards Russia and the FSU see Joseph Stiglitz (2002) 'Who Lost Russia', in *Globalization and its Discontents*, Harmondsworth: Penguin; Stone (2002); Peter Reddaway and Dmitri Glinski (2001) *The Tragedy of Russia's Reforms: Market Bolshevism against Democracy*, Washington: United States Institute of Peace.
43. The CEEC group included six of the former 'Soviet bloc' states in the region (Poland, Hungary, Czech and Slovak Republics, Romania, Bulgaria), to which were added the three former 'Baltic republics' of the USSR (Estonia, Latvia

and Lithuania), and one former republic of Yugoslavia (Slovenia). It excluded all the other post-communist states of the FSU/CIS and the Balkans.

44. The FSU/CIS zone was, in practice, also sub-divided, with the EU focusing its economic cooperation and aid on the Russian Federation and Ukraine, which have received the bulk of Tacis disbursements, overwhelmingly for infrastructural and environmental projects. Less than 5 per cent of total cumulative aid disbursed in 1991–99 went into 'democracy promotion'. Tacis was set up in 1991 as a technical assistance programme to promote economic transition in twelve Eastern European countries not covered by PHARE. In the current budget cycle (2000–06) its mandate has been reoriented more closely towards the promotion of democratization and the rule of law in Eastern Europe and Central Asia. See http://europa.eu.int/comm/external_relations/ceeca/tacis/. To some extent the EU's new 'Neighbourhood' Policy (2004) formalizes this subdivision of the CIS zone.
45. Mayhew (1998).
46. Mayhew (1998). According to a personal communication from Alan Mayhew to the authors, the division of the available PHARE commitment appropriations was made according to the following criteria while he worked there up to 1995: population, demonstrated absorption capacity, expressed priorities (for example, on the importance of environmental funds or on the division of funds between Slovakia and the Czech Republic after their separation), recommendations of the PHARE management committee (for example, on the use of PHARE funds for investment, which then had an impact on country allocations), the continued funding needs of successful programmes. Clearly, these are exclusively economic criteria.
47. The PHARE Programme was funded to the amount of 10.5 billion ecus (as they were then) for the period 2000–06 and was to focus essentially on priorities linked to the adoption of the *acquis communautaire* by candidates, especially in regard to administrative and judicial capacity-building and attracting investment into the applicant countries.
48. See Hughes and Sasse (2003) 'Monitoring the Monitors: EU Enlargement Conditionality and Minority Protection in the CEECs', *Journal of Ethnopolitics and Minority Issues in Europe*, 1, 1–28. If we compare the Europe Agreements, the 'Copenhagen criteria' and the TEU, a softening of the normative content of the EU's political conditionality is evident over time. This is most obvious in the 'common values' of member states declared in the TEU, which draw selectively from the values set out by the EU in the first Copenhagen criterion (see Table 1.2). Article 6 (1) TEU defines the 'common values' as 'liberty, democracy, respect for human rights and fundamental freedoms and the rule of law', but expressly excluded the normative commitment of 'respect for and protection of minorities' included in the Copenhagen criteria. That Article 6 (1) draws on the Copenhagen criteria is specifically alluded to in Article 49, which specifies that the principles laid out in Article 6 (1) are preconditions for any state applying for EU membership. There is a clear contradiction between the TEU and the first Copenhagen criterion, but the TEU is legally binding and, therefore, clarifies that the EU has abandoned the minority protection provision of the conditionality for membership. The exclusion of an explicit minority protection requirement is also consolidated by the Draft Constitution for

Europe (2003). The EU legal terminology suggests that at the very least a shifting standard, if not a double standard, is at work. The protection of minorities appears to be understood by the EU in 1993 as a norm that should be implemented by candidates for membership but not by member states. By the time of the TEU in 1997, however, this norm had been abandoned in law for future candidates, though it retained its rhetorical prominence in the enlargement process and especially in the Regular Reports.

49. Johan P. Olsen (2001) 'The Many Faces of Europeanization', ARENA Working Papers, WP 1/2, 10.
50. Olsen (2001: 21–2).
51. See Wade Jacoby (2004) *The Enlargement of the European Union and NATO: Ordering from the Menu in Central Europe*, Cambridge: Cambridge University Press (2004).
52. Beate Kohler-Koch (2002) 'European Networks and Ideas: Changing National Policies?' *European Integration On-line Papers*, 6 (6): http://eiop.or.at/eiop/texte/2002–006a.htm.
53. The original conception of 'Europeanization' as a 'top-down' process was elaborated by Robert Ladrech (1994) 'Europeanization of Domestic Politics and Institutions: the Case of France', *Journal of Common Market Studies*, 32 (1), 69–88. For more recent studies see Kevin Featherstone (2003), 'Introduction: in the Name of Europe', in Claudio Radaelli and Kevin Featherstone (eds), *The Politics of Europeanization*, Oxford: Oxford University Press, 3–26; Claudio M. Radaelli (2000), 'Whither Europeanization: Concept Stretching and Substantive Change', *European Integration On-line Papers*, 4 (8), 1–27: http://eiop.or.at/eiop/texte/2000-008a.htm; Tanja A. Börzel and Thomas Risse (2000) 'When Europe Hits Home: Europeanization and Domestic Change', *European Integration On-line Papers*, 4(15), 1–13: http://eiop.or.at/eiop/texte/2000-015a.htm); Beate Kohler-Koch and Rainer Eising (eds) (1999) *The Transformation of Governance in the European Union*, London: Routledge, 268–70; Alastair I. Johnston, 'Treating International Institutions as Social Environments', *International Studies Quarterly*, 45, 487–515.
54. Featherstone (2003: 7).
55. Olsen (2001: 3). Olsen subsumes five extremely wide-ranging phenomena under the label Europeanization: changes in external territorial boundaries; the development of institutions at the European level; the penetration of national and sub-national systems of governance by a European political centre and European-wide norms; the export of forms of distinct political organization and governance beyond European territory; and the wider political project aiming at a unified and politically stronger Europe.
56. Christos J. Paraskevopoulos (2001) *Interpreting Convergence in the European Union. Patterns of Collective Action, Social Learning and Europeanization*, Basingstoke: Palgrave, xxi.
57. Radaelli (2003: 3).
58. C. Knill and D. Lehmkuhl (1999) 'How Europe Matters. Different Mechanisms of Europeanization', *European Integration On-line Papers*, 3 (7), 1–11: http://eiop.or.at/eiop.
59. Börzel and Risse (2000: 1–3).
60. Olsen (2001: 14); Radaelli (2000: 19).

61. Featherstone (2003: 4).
62. Knill and Lehmkuhl (1999: 1–2).
63. K.H. Goetz (2000), 'European Integration and National Executives: a Cause in Search of an Effect?', *West European Politics*, 23 (4), 211–31.
64. Schimmelfennig et al. (2001). See also introduction n. 5.

2. Communist legacies and regionalization

1. See Juan Linz and Alfred Stepan (1996) *Problems of Democratic Transition and Consolidation: Southern Europe, South America and Post-Communist Europe*, Washington, DC: Johns Hopkins University Press.
2. On path dependency and initial starting conditions, see Adam Przeworski (1991) *Democracy and the Market – Political and Economic Reforms in Eastern Europe and Latin America*, Cambridge: Cambridge University Press, and David Stark (1992) 'Path Dependence and Privatization Strategies in East Central Europe', *East European Politics and Societies*, 6 (1), 17–51.
3. For studies of transition which stress the role of elites see Dankwart Rustow (1970) 'Transitions to Democracy: Towards a Dynamic Model', *Comparative Politics*, 2 (3), 337–63; John Higley and Michael Burton (1989) 'The Elite Variable in Democratic Transitions and Breakdowns', *American Sociological Review*, 54, 17–32; Przeworksi (1991).
4. For a discussion of the issue of legacies see Beverly Crawford and Arend Lijphart (1995) 'Explaining Political and Economic Change in Post-Communist Eastern Europe: Old Legacies, New Institutions, Hegemonic Norms and International Pressures', *Comparative Political Studies*, 28 (2), 171–99.
5. See Judy Batt (2002) 'Introduction: Regions, State and Identity in Central and Eastern Europe', *Regional and Federal Studies*, 12 (2), 1–14.
6. Katarzyna Wolczuk (2002) 'Conclusion: Identities, Regions and Europe', *Regional and Federal Studies*, 12 (2), 207.
7. Michal Illner (1998) 'Territorial Decentralization: an Obstacle to Democratic Reform in Central and Eastern Europe', in Jonathan D. Kimball (ed.), *The Transfer of Power: Decentralization in Central and Eastern Europe*, Budapest: Local Government and Public Service Reform Initiative, 14.
8. Two excellent studies of the establishment and consolidation of communist power are Paul Lewis (1994) *Central Europe Since 1945*, London: Longman; George Schöpflin (1993) *Politics in Eastern Europe 1945–1992*, Oxford: Blackwell.
9. For the interaction between European integration and the development of local government in Western Europe see Michael J.F. Goldsmith and Klaus K. Klausen (eds) (1997) *European Integration and Local Government*, Northampton, MA and Cheltenham, UK: Edward Elgar; Ed Page (1995) 'Patterns and Diversity in European State Development', in Jack Hayward and Ed Page (eds), *Governing the New Europe*, London: Sage.
10. Marie-Claude Maurel (1989) 'Administrative Reforms in Eastern Europe: an Overview', in Richard Bennett (ed.), *Territory and Administration in Europe*, London: Pinter, 111–23 (116).
11. Janos Kornai (1992) *The Socialist System: the Political Economy of Communism*, Oxford: Clarendon Press, 35; Michael Waller (1981) *Democratic Centralism: an Historical Commentary*, Manchester: Manchester University Press.

12. Jaroslaw Piekalwicz (1980) 'Polish Local Politics in Flux', in Daniel Nelson (ed.), *Local Politics in Communist Countries*, Lexington: The University Press of Kentucky. For the role of party secretaries see Paul Lewis (1989) *Political Authority and Party Secretaries in Poland, 1975–1986*, Cambridge: Cambridge University Press.
13. Ingemar Elander and Mattias Gustafsson (1993) 'The Re-emergence of Local Self-Government in Central Europe: Some Notes on the First Experience', *European Journal of Political Research*, 23 (3), 305.
14. See Lewis (1994); Schöpflin (1993). For a general history see Richard J. Crampton (1994) *Eastern Europe in the Twentieth Century and After*, London: Routledge. For a specific case study see Bennett Kovrig (1979) *Communism in Hungary: From Kun to Kádár*, Stanford, CA: Hoover Institution.
15. For example, in the case of Hungary, six economic-planning regions were delimited, while the administrative counties were left unchanged. See Tivadar Bernat (ed.) (1985) *An Economic Geography of Hungary*, Budapest: Akademiai Kiado, 335.
16. Ed Hewett (1988) *Reforming the Soviet Economy: Equality vs. Efficiency*, Washington, DC: Brookings Institution.
17. W. Surazska, J. Bucek, L. Malikova and P. Danek (1996) 'Towards Regional Government in Central Europe: Territorial Restructuring of Postcommunist Regimes', *Environment and Planning C: Government and Policy*, 15, 441–2.
18. For subsidiarity see *Treaty on European Union*, 1992, Title II, Article G, 5. http://europa.eu.int/abc/obj/treaties/en/entoc01.htm.
19. See Kovrig (1979).
20. Surazska et al. (1997: 441–4).
21. For details on administrative reforms see Denis J. Galligan and Daniel M. Smilov (1999) *Administrative Law in Central and Eastern Europe*, Budapest: CEU Press.
22. Joachim Jens Hesse (1998) 'Rebuilding the State: Administrative Reform in Central and Eastern Europe', in Joachim Jens Hesse (ed.), *Preparing Public Administrations for the European Administrative Space*, Sigma Paper no. 23, Paris: OECD.
23. These amendments made provision for the strengthening of self-governing institutions at the county level. See Ilona Palne Kovács (1999) 'Regional Development and Local Government in Hungary', in Zoltan Hajdú (ed.), *Regional Processes and Spatial Structures in Hungary in the 1990s*, Pécs: Centre for Regional Studies, 65–7.
24. Helmut Wollmann (1997) 'Institution Building and Decentralization in Formerly Socialist Countries: the Cases of Poland, Hungary and East Germany', *Environment and Planning C: Government and Policy*, 15, 467; Adrian Campbell (1995) 'Local Government in Romania', in Andrew Coulson (ed.), *Local Government in Eastern Europe*, Northampton, MA and Cheltenham, UK: Edward Elgar, 76–101; Joanna Regulska (1997) 'Decentralization or (Re)centralization: Struggle for Political Power in Poland', *Environment and Planning C: Government and Policy*, 15 (2), 187–208.
25. Kenneth Davey (1995) 'Local Government in Hungary', in Andrew Coulson (ed.), *Local Government in Eastern Europe*, Northampton, MA and Cheltenham, UK: Edward Elgar, 69–70.

26. Richard J. Bennett (1997) *Local Government in Post-Socialist Cities*, Budapest: Open Society Institute.
27. James Hughes, Gwendolyn Sasse, Claire Gordon and Tatiana Majcherkiewicz (2004) 'Silesia and the Politics of Regionalisation in Poland' and Tomasz Zarycki 'The Regional Dimension of the Polish Political Scene', in Tomasz Zarycki and George Kolankiewicz (eds), *Regional Issues in Polish Politics*, London: School of Slavonic and East European Studies, University College London, 90 and 249–50.
28. See the discussion in Kenneth Davey (2002) 'Decentralization in CEE Countries: Obstacles and Opportunities' and A.J.G. Verheijen (2002) 'Removing Obstacles to Effective Decentralization: Reflecting on the Role of the Central State', in Gábor Péteri (ed.), *Mastering Decentralization and Public Administration Reforms in Central and Eastern Europe*, Budapest: OSI/LGI, 33–42 and 45–54.
29. Campbell (1995: 76). See also Sulev Mäeltsemees (2000) 'Local Government in Estonia', in Tamas Horvath (ed.), *Decentralization, Experiments and Reform*, Budapest: LGI Books, 61–114.
30. See, for example, the study of Czech and Slovak reforms in this field by Martin Brusis (2003) 'Regionalisation in the Czech and Slovak Republics: Comparing the Influences of the European Union', in Michael Keating and James Hughes (eds), *The Regional Challenge in Central and Eastern Europe: Territorial Restructuring and European Integration*, Paris: P.I.E.-Peter Lang, 89–106.
31. Peter Heil (2000) 'PHARE in Hungary: the Anatomy of a Pre-Accession Aid Programme, 1990–1999', unpublished PhD thesis, Budapest.
32. Karel Lacina and Zdena Vajdova (2000) 'Local Government in the Czech Republic', in Tamas Horvath (ed.), *Decentralization: Experiments and Reform*, Budapest: LGI Publications, 255–96 especially at 258.
33. Surazska et al. (1997: 440).
34. For analyses of Czechoslovakian federalism see Carol Skalnik-Leff (1988) *National Conflict in Czechoslovakia, the Making and Remaking of a Nation-State, 1918–1987*, Princeton, NJ: Princeton University Press; Abby Innes (2001) *Czechoslovakia: the Short Goodbye*, New Haven: Yale University Press; Stanislav Kirschbaum (2003) 'Czechoslovakia: the Creation, Federalisation and Dissolution of a Nation-State', in John Coakley (ed.), *The Territorial Management of Ethnic Conflict*, London, Frank Cass, 2nd edition, 229–63.
35. Martin Brusis (1999) 'Re-Creating the Regional Level in Central and Eastern Europe: an Analysis of Administrative Reforms in Six Countries', in Eric von Breska and Martin Brusis (eds), *Central and Eastern Europe on the Way to the European Union: Reforms of Regional Administration in Bulgaria, the Czech Republic, Estonia, Hungary, Poland and Slovakia*, Munich: Centre for Applied Policy, Geschwister-Scholl-Institute for Political Science, University of Munich, 99; Michal Illner (1997) 'The Territorial Dimension of Public Administration Reforms in East Central Europe', Prague: Institute of Sociology, Academy of Sciences of the Czech Republic, Working Paper no. 7, 40.
36. Lacina and Vajdova (2000: 261); Richard J. Bennett (1993) (ed.) *Local Government in the New Europe*, London: Belhaven Press, 10.
37. Illner (1998).
38. See table of 'State Administrative Organs Operating at the District and Regional Levels in the Czech Republic' in Lacina and Vjadova (2000: 263).

39. Galligan and Smilov (1999: 50).
40. Surazska et al. (1997: 455).
41. Vit Novotny (1998) 'Regional Government in the Czech Republic: the Process of its Creation in the Constitutional Context', Paper presented at the Annual Conference of the Political Studies Association Specialist Group on Communist and Post-Communist Politics.
42. Elander and Gustafsson (1993: 305).
43. Amendments to the Local Government Act in 1994 gave both local and county-level self-governments independent tax-raising powers.
44. Palne Kovács (1999: 55).
45. Gabor Bende-Szabo (1999) 'The Intermediate Administrative Level in Hungary', in Eric von Breska and Martin Brusis (eds), *Central and Eastern Europe on the Way to the European Union: Reforms of Regional Administration in Bulgaria, the Czech Republic, Estonia, Hungary, Poland and Slovakia*, Munich: Centre for Applied Policy, Geschwister-Scholl-Institute for Political Science, University of Munich; http://www.oecd.org/puma/sigmaweb.
46. Gyula Horváth (1996) 'Transition and Regionalism in East Central Europe', Occasional Paper no. 7, Tubingen: Europaisches Zentrum fur Foderalismus-Forschung, 34.
47. Brigid Fowler (2001) 'Debating Sub-state Reform on Hungary's "Road to Europe"', One Europe or Several? Working Paper 21/01, Brighton: University of Sussex.
48. Brigid Fowler (2002) 'Hungary: Patterns of Political Conflict over Territorial-Administrative Reform', *Regional and Federal Studies*, 12 (2), 15–40.
49. Kristan Gerner (1999) 'Regions in Central Europe under Communism: a Palimpsest', in Sven Tagil (ed.), *Regions in Central Europe: the Legacy of History*, London: Hurst & Company, 188; and Daniele Caramani (2003) 'State Administration and Regional Construction in Central Europe: a Comparative-Historical Perspective', in Michael Keating and James Hughes (eds), *The Regional Challenge in Central and Eastern Europe: Territorial Restructuring and European Integration*, Paris: P.I.E.-Peter Lang, 25–6 and 33.
50. Surazska et al. (1997).
51. Surazska et al. (1997: 443).
52. Jerzy Regulski (1993) 'Rebuilding Local Government in Poland', in Richard J. Bennett (ed.), *Local Government in the New Europe*, London: Belhaven Press, 197–207; Jerzy Regulski (1999) 'Building Democracy in Poland, the State Reform of 1998', Discussion papers, No. 9, Budapest: the Local Government and Public Services Reform Initiative, Open Society: http://lgi.osi.hu/news/2001/20010202.htm.
53. See Regulski (1993: 200) for further details of discussions.
54. Regulski (1999).
55. Wiktor Glowacki (2002) 'Regionalization in Poland', in Gerard Marcou (ed.), *Regionalization for Development and Accession to the EU: a Comparative Perspective*, LGI Studies, Budapest: Open Society Institute, 105.
56. Andrzej Kowalczyk (2000) 'Local Government in Poland', in Tamas Horvath (ed.), *Decentralization: Experiments and Reform*, Budapest: LGI Publications, 221. For discussion on different party positions on Poland's regional reforms, see Glowacki (2002: 110–11).

57. Grzegorz Gorzelak (1998) *Regional and Local Potential for Transformation in Poland*, Regional and Local Studies Series No. 14, Warsaw: European Institute for Regional and Local Development, 16–17.
58. See Brusis (2003); Alexandra Bitušiková (2002), 'Slovakia: an Anthropological Perspective on Identity and Regional Reform', *Regional and Federal Studies*, 12 (2), 41–64.
59. See James Hughes and Gwendolyn Sasse (2003) 'Monitoring the Monitors: EU Enlargement Conditionality and Minority Protection in the CEECs', *Journal of Ethnopolitics and Minority Issues in Europe*, 1, 1–28.
60. The Hungarian Coalition Party had even put forward the idea of a thirteen-region solution, demanding a region around Komarno where the Hungarian majority is concentrated. See Hughes and Sasse (2003).
61. Eva Perger (1989) 'An Overview of East European Developments', in Richard Bennett (ed.), *Territory and Administration in Europe*, London: Pinter, 103–4.
62. Perger (1989: 103–4).
63. Mirko Vintar (1999) 'Re-engineering Administrative Districts in Slovenia', Discussion Paper No. 11, Local Government and Public Service Reform Initiative, Budapest: LGI Publications.
64. Stanka Setnikar-Canka, Stane Vlaj and Maja Klun (2000) 'Local Government in Slovenia', in Tamas Horvath (ed.), *Decentralization, Experiments and Reform*, Budapest: LGI Books, 390.
65. Anatol Lieven (1993) *The Baltic Revolution: Latvia, Lithuania, Estonia and the Path to Independence*, New Haven: Yale University Press; Graham Smith (1994) *The Baltic States: the National Self-Determination of Estonia, Latvia and Lithuania*, London: Macmillan; Jan Arveds Trapans (1991) *Toward Independence: the Baltic Popular Movements*, Boulder: Westview.
66. Mäeltsemees (2000: 66).
67. For details of recent changes in the administrative divisions, see http://www.stat.vil.ee/pks/indexi.htmlv.
68. See David J. Smith (2002) 'Narva Region within the Estonian Republic: from Autonomism to Accommodation?', *Regional and Federal Studies*, 12 (2), 89–110.
69. Perger (1989: 102–3).
70. Glen Wright (2002) 'Assessment of Progress towards Local Democratic Systems', in Gábor Soós, Gábor Tóka and Glen Wright (eds), *State of Local Democracy in Central Europe*, Budapest: Local Government and Public Reform Initiative, 378.
71. Campbell (1995: 81).
72. Eniko Baga (2004) 'Romania's Western Connection: Timisoara and Timis County', in Melanie Tatur (ed.) *The Making of Regions in Post-Socialist Europe: the Impact of Culture, Economic Structure, and Institutions*, Opladen: Leske+Budrich.
73. See Hughes and Sasse (2003).

3. The Commission, conditionality and regional policy

1. European Council (1993) *Presidency Conclusions*, Copenhagen European Council, 21–22 June 1993.
2. Heather Grabbe and Kirsty Hughes (1997) 'Redefining the European Union: Eastward Enlargement', RIIA Briefing paper 36, London: Royal Institute for

International Affairs; Karen Henderson (ed.), (1999) *Back to Europe: Central and Eastern Europe and the European Union*, London: UCL Press.

3. European Council (1994) *Presidency Conclusions*, Essen European Council, 9–10 December 1994; and European Council (1995) *Presidency Conclusions*, Madrid European Council, 15–16 December 1995: http://europa.eu.int/european_council/conclusions/index_en.htm.
4. James Hughes, Gwendolyn Sasse and Claire Gordon (2003) 'EU Enlargement, Europeanisation and the Dynamics of Regionalisation in the CEECs', in Micheal Keating and James Hughes (eds), *The Regional Challenge in Central and Eastern Europe: Territorial Restructuring and European Integration*, Paris: P.I.E.- Peter Lang, 69–88.
5. European Council (1995) *Presidency Conclusions*, Madrid European Council.
6. European Commission (ed.) (1997) *Agenda 2000 – Vol. 1 For a Stronger and Wider Union*, COM/97/2000 final, Luxembourg: Office for Official Publications of the European Communities; European Commission (ed.) (1997) *Agenda 2000 – Commission Opinions on the Application for Membership of the European Union*, Luxembourg: Office for Official Publications of the European Communities.
7. European Council (1997) *Presidency Conclusions*, Luxembourg European Council, 12–13 December. See also the information on the negotiations process on the EU's enlargement website: http://europa.eu.int/comm/enlargement.
8. European Council Regulation (1999) No. 1260/1999 of 21 June 1999 laying down general provisions on the Structural Funds, Official Journal L161, Luxembourg: Office for Official Publications of the European Union, chapter I, article 1; chapter II, article 3 (1), article 7 (1), article 7 (2) and annex.
9. The conclusion of the accession negotiations has left only the capital city areas of Prague (Czech Republic) and Bratislava (Slovakia) excluded from Objective 1 funding, though they will qualify for Objective 3 support. Both Kozep Magyarorszag (the Budapest region in Hungary) and Slovenia will most likely be the only other regions to exceed the threshold in the near term: http://www.europa.eu.int/comm/enlargement/negotiations/pdf/negotiations_report_to_ep.pdf.
10. European Commission (ed.) (2001), *Enlargement of the European Union: an Historic Opportunity*, Luxembourg: Office for Official Publications of the European Communities, 46.
11. European Commission (ed.) (2002) Directorate General Enlargement, *Enlargement of the European Union, Guide to the Negotiations, Chapter by Chapter*, April 2002, Luxembourg: Office for Official Publications of the European Communities, Sec 102 Final, 2: http://europa.eu.int/comm/enlargement/negotiations.
12. European Council (2002), *Presidency Conclusions*, Copenhagen European Council, 12 and 13 December 2002.
13. Fritz Breuss (2001) 'Macroeconomic Effects of Enlargement for Old and New Members', WIFO Working Paper 143, March, Vienna, 2, 14.
14. Wim Kok (2003) 'Enlarging the European Union: Achievement and Challenges', Report of Wim Kok to the European Commission, RSCAS, European University Institute, 26.
15. Breuss (2001: 12).
16. European Council Regulation (1999) chapter III, article, 7 (8).

17. See John Bachtler, Fiona Wishlade and Douglas Yuill (2001) 'Regional Policy in Europe after Enlargement', Regional and Industrial Policy Research Paper no. 44, European Policies Research Centre, University of Strathclyde, 1–39.
18. The Commission's Enlargement Strategy Paper, approved at the European Council at Nice in December 2000, singled out Chapter 21 – as well as Chapter 7 (Agriculture) and Chapter 26 (Financial and Budgetary Provisions) – as the priority for the negotiations in 2002. European Commission (ed.) (2000) *Enlargement Strategy Paper: Report on Progress towards Accession by each of the Candidate Countries*, Luxembourg: Office for Official Publications of the European Communities. Among the CEECs the Czech Republic was first to provisionally close Chapter 21 in April 2002. Estonia, Latvia and Lithuania followed in June 2002; Hungary, Slovakia and Slovenia in July 2002; and Poland in October 2002.
19. Michael Keating and Lisbeth Hooghe (1996) 'By-Passing the Nation-State? Regions and the EU Policy Process', in Jeremy John Richardson (ed.), *European Union, Power and Policy-Making*, London: Routledge, 224–6; Ian Bache (1998) *The Politics of European Union Regional Policy. Multi-Level Governance or Flexible Gatekeeping?*, Sheffield: Sheffield Academic Press; European Council Regulation (1999).
20. In some states structural funds are controlled by central finance ministries (as in the UK, Ireland and France). For a criticism of the 'fairy-tale character' of the structural funds which are often treated as a reimbursement for national spending rather than a genuine instrument of regional development policy see Michael Keating (1993) *The Politics of Modern Europe*, Aldershot: Edward Elgar, 299–300.
21. Keating (1993: 302–7); Lisbeth Hooghe (1995) 'Subnational Mobilization in the European Union', *West European Politics*, 18 (4), 175–98; Charlie Jeffery (2000) 'Sub-National Mobilization and European Integration: Does it Make Any Difference?', *Journal of Common Market Studies*, 38 (1), 20; Beate Kohler-Koch (2002) 'European Networks and Ideas: Changing National Policies?', *European Integration On-line Papers*, 6 (6): http://eiop.or.at/eiop/texte/2002-006a.htm.
22. Lisbeth Hooghe and Gary Marks (2001) *Multi-level Governance and European Integration*, New York: Rowman & Littlefield Publishers, 85.
23. Hooghe and Marks (2001: 85–6). To illustrate the point Hooghe and Marks cite the following Commission statement of 1999: 'the delivery system developed for the structural funds is characterized by multi-level governance'.
24. European Council Regulation (1999) article 8.
25. The number of such offices grew from 100 by 1995 to 150 by 1999 (Hooghe and Marks, 2001: 86).
26. Authors' interview with PHARE official, 14 December 2000.
27. See European Council (1993): http://www.europarl.eu.int/enlargement_new/europeancouncil/pdf/cop_fr.pdf.
28. James Hughes, Gwendolyn Sasse and Claire Gordon (2001) 'The Regional Deficit in Eastward Enlargement of the European Union: Top Down Policies and Bottom Up Reactions', ESRC 'One Europe or Several?' Working Paper 29/01, Brighton: Sussex University, 1–57. See also Antoaneta L. Dimitrova (2002), 'Enlargement, Institution-Building and the EU's Administrative Capacity Requirement', *West European Politics*, 25 (4), 171–90.

29. European Union Committee of the Regions (1999) *Resolution of the Committee of the Regions on 'The Ongoing EU Enlargement Process'*, Brussels, 24 November 1999; European Union Committee of the Regions (2001) *Opinion of the Committee of the Regions on 'Supporting the Development of Institutional Structures at Local and Regional Level in the Applicant Countries'*, Brussels, 14 November 2001.
30. European Commission (ed.) (1997) *Agenda 2000 – Commission Opinion on the Czech Republic's Application for Membership of the European Union*, Doc. 97/17, Luxembourg: Office for Official Publications of the European Communities; European Commission (ed.) (1997) *Agenda 2000 – Commission Opinion on Estonia's Application for Membership of the European Union*, Doc. 97/12, Luxembourg: Office for Official Publications of the European Communities; European Commission (ed.) (1997) *Agenda 2000 – Commission Opinion on Hungary's Application for Membership of the European Union*, Doc. 97/13, Luxembourg: Office for Official Publications of the European Communities; European Commission (ed.) (1997) *Agenda 2000 – Commission Opinion on Poland's Application for Membership of the European Union*, Doc. 97/16, Luxembourg: Office for Official Publications of the European Communities; European Commission (ed.) (1997) *Agenda 2000 – Commission Opinion on Slovenia's Application for Membership of the European Union*, Doc. 97/19, Luxembourg: Office for Official Publications of the European Communities.
31. European Commission (2002), Directorate General Enlargement, *Enlargement of the European Union, Guide to the Negotiations, Chapter by Chapter*, April 2002, Luxembourg: Office for Official Publications of the European Communities: http://europa.eu.int/comm/enlargement/negotiations.
32. European Council Regulation (1999).
33. For details of PHARE see European Commission (ed.) (2000) *PHARE 2000 Review, Strengthening Preparations for Membership*, COM (2000) 3103/2, Luxembourg: Office for Official Publications of the European Communities. For a discussion of problems with 'Twinning' see Hughes, Sasse and Gordon (2001: 51–3).
34. Attila Agh (2002) 'The Reform of State Administration in Hungary: the Capacity of Core Ministries to Manage Europeanization', Budapest Papers on Europeanization, No. 7, Budapest: Hungarian Centre for Democracy Studies Foundation; Dimitrova (2002).
35. Hooghe and Marks (2001: 102).
36. Gyula Horváth (1998) 'Regional and Cohesion Policy in Hungary', Discussion Paper 23, Pécs: Centre for Regional Studies of the Hungarian Academy of Sciences, 63–4.
37. European Commission (2001), *Proposal for a Regulation of the European Parliament and the Council on the Establishment of a Common Classification of Territorial Units for Statistics (NUTS)*, 14 February 2001, 2: http://europa.eu.int/eur-lex/en/com/pdf/2001/en_501PC0083.pdf.
38. European Commission (ed.) (2001), *Regular Report on Slovenia's Progress toward Accession*, Luxembourg: Office for Official Publications of the European Communities: http://europa.eu.int/comm/enlargement/report2001/si_en.pdf.
39. Jan Hoich and Kristina Larisova (1999) 'Reform der öffentlichen Verwaltung und Bildung der regionalen Selbstverwaltung in der Tschechischen

Republik im Kontext des EU-Beitritts', in Eric von Breska and Martin Brusis (eds), *Central and Eastern Europe on the Way to the European Union: Reforms of Regional Administration in Bulgaria, the Czech Republic, Estonia, Hungary, Poland and Slovakia*, Munich: Centre for Applied Policy Research.

40. European Commission (2001), *Proposal on the Establishment of a Common Classification of NUTS*, European Council Regulation (2003) No. 1059/2003 of 26 May 2003: http://europa.eu.int/eur-lex/en/dat/2003/l_154/l_15420030621en00010041.pdf.
41. European Commission (ed.) (1997) *Opinion on Hungary*, 90.
42. European Commission (ed.) (1997) *Opinion on Poland*, 88.
43. European Commission (ed.) (1997) *Agenda 2000 – Commission Opinion on Slovakia's Application for Membership of the European Union*, Doc. 97/20, Luxembourg: Office for Official Publications of the European Communities, 100.
44. European Commission (ed.) (1997) *Opinion on the Czech Republic*, 83.
45. European Commission (ed.) (1997) *Opinion on the Czech Republic*, 83.
46. Authors' interview, Polish Mission to the European Union, 28 March 2001.
47. Authors' interview, Hungarian Mission to the European Union, 15 December 2000.
48. European Commission (ed.) (1998a) *Regular Report from the Commission on Hungary's Progress towards Accession*, Luxembourg: Office for Official Publications of the European Communities, 33.
49. Authors' interview, Romanian Mission to the European Union, 13 December 2000.
50. European Commission (ed.) (1998a) *Regular Report from the Commission on Romania's Progress towards Accession*, Luxembourg: Office for Official Publications of the European Communities, 38.
51. European Commission (ed.) (2000) *PHARE Annual Report 1998*, Luxembourg: Office for Official Publications of the European Communities, 63.
52. Authors' interview, Estonian Mission to the European Union, 13 December 2000.
53. Author's interview with a senior official in the Slovenia team, DG Enlargement, European Commission, 15 December 2000.
54. Author's interview with a senior official in the Poland team, DG Enlargement, European Commission, 15 December 2000.
55. Authors' interview with senior officials in the Romania team, DG Enlargement, European Commission, 12 December 2000.
56. Authors' interview with a senior official in PHARE, DG Enlargement, European Commission, 12 December 2000.
57. Authors' interview with a senior official in ISPA, DG Regio, 14 December 2000.
58. Authors' interview with a senior official in DG Regio, 29 March 2001. Since the fall of the Orban government in 2002, police and the public prosecutor have initiated several investigations involving corruption in the handling of public contracts under Orban. The Regular Report on Hungary of 2002 noted that corruption continues to be a problem in Hungary.
59. Authors' interview with senior researchers in Forward Planning Unit, Office of the President, 12 December 2000.
60. Author's interview with a senior official, Polish Mission to the EU, 28 March 2001; Authors' interview with a senior official in DG Regio, 29 March 2001.
61. Authors' interview with a senior official in DG Regio, 29 March 2001.

62. European Commission (ed.) (2002) *Regular Report on Hungary's Progress toward Accession*, Luxembourg: Office for Official Publications of the European Communities, 100; European Commission (ed.) (2002) *Regular Report on Poland's Progress toward Accession*, Luxembourg: Office for Official Publications of the European Communities, 105–6.
63. Authors' interview with a senior official in DG Regio, 29 March 2001.

4. Monitoring conditionality and compliance

1. The six countries were Cyprus, Czech Republic, Estonia, Hungary, Poland, Slovenia.
2. See http://europa.eu.int/comm/enlargement/pas/europe_agr.htm.
3. Ibid. for the links to the individual Europe Agreements.
4. For the Accession Partnerships see the link for each candidate country: http://europa.eu.int/comm/enlargement/candidate.htm.
5. See, for example, Romania's Accession Partnership 1999, 11: http://europa.eu.int/comm/enlargement/report2001/apro_en. pdf.
6. See European Council (2002), *The Revised Accession Partnerships, 28 January 2002*, Council Decisions, Official Journal L44 of 14 February 2002, Luxembourg: Office for Official Publications of the European Communities.
7. European Commission (ed.) (1997) *Opinion on Hungary*, 90.
8. European Commission (ed.) (1997) *Opinion on Poland*, 88.
9. European Commission (ed.) (1997) *Opinion on Czech Republic*, 83.
10. European Commission (ed.) (1997) *Agenda 2000 – Commission Opinion on Bulgaria's Application for Membership of the European Union*, Doc. 97/11, Luxembourg: Office for Official Publications of the European Communities, 92–3.
11. European Commission (ed.) (1997) *Opinion on Estonia*, 88.
12. European Commission (ed.) (1997) *Opinion on Czech Republic*, 84; European Commission (ed.) (1997) *Opinion on Estonia*, 116.
13. European Commission (ed.) (1997) *Opinion on Bulgaria*, 93.
14. European Commission (ed.) (1997) *Opinion on Czech Republic*, 84
15. European Commission (ed.) (1997) *Opinion on Slovakia*, 100.
16. Ibid.
17. European Commission (ed.) (1998) *Regular Report on Lithuania's Progress toward Accession*, Luxembourg: Office for Official Publications of the European Communities, 32.
18. European Commission (ed.) (1998) *Regular Report on Bulgaria's Progress towards Accession*, Luxembourg: Office for Official Publications of the European Communities, 34.
19. European Commission (ed.) (1998) *Regular Report on Slovenia's Progress towards Accession*, Luxembourg, Office for Official Publications of the European Communities, 34.
20. European Commission (ed.) (1998) *Regular Report on Slovakia's Progress towards Accession*, Luxembourg, Office for Official Publications of the European Communities, 33.
21. European Commission (ed.) (1998) *Regular Report on Hungary*, 33; European Commission (ed.) (1998) *Regular Report on Romania*, 38.

22. European Commission (ed.) (1998) *Regular Report on the Czech Republic's Progress towards Accession*, Luxembourg, Office for Official Publications of the European Communities, 30; European Commission (ed.) (1998) *Regular Report on Romania*, 38, 49.
23. European Commission (ed.) (1998) *Regular Report on Poland's Progress towards Accession*, Luxembourg: Office for Official Publications of the European Communities, 33, 34, 43.
24. European Commission (ed.) (1998) *Regular Report on Hungary*, 33.
25. European Commission (ed.) (1998) *Regular Report on Hungary*, 44.
26. European Commission (ed.) (1998) *Regular Report on Latvia's Progress toward Accession*, Luxembourg: Office for Official Publications of the European Communities, 36.
27. European Commission (ed.) (1999) *Regular Report on Bulgaria's Progress toward Accession*, Luxembourg: Office for Official Publications of the European Communities, 46–7.
28. European Commission (ed.) (1999) *Regular Report on Latvia's Progress toward Accession*, Luxembourg: Office for Official Publications of the European Communities, 46; European Commission (ed.) (1999) *Regular Report on Lithuania's Progress toward Accession*, Luxembourg: Office for Official Publications of the European Communities, 45–6.
29. European Commission (ed.) (1999) *Regular Report on the Czech Republic's Progress toward Accession*, Luxembourg: Office for Official Publications of the European Communities, 48.
30. European Commission (ed.) (1999) *Regular Report on Poland's Progress toward Accession*, Luxembourg: Office for Official Publications of the European Communities, 12.
31. European Commission (ed.) (1999) *Regular Report on Poland*, 47, 48.
32. European Commission (ed.) (1999) *Regular Report on Romania's Progress toward Accession*, Luxembourg: Office for Official Publications of the European Communities, 51–2; European Commission (ed.) (1999) *Regular Report on Slovenia's Progress toward Accession*, Luxembourg: Office for Official Publications of the European Communities, 48.
33. European Commission (ed.) (1999) *Regular Report on Slovenia*, 48.
34. European Commission (ed.) (1999) *Regular Report on Romania*, 51–2.
35. European Commission (ed.) (1999) *Regular Report on Hungary's Progress toward Accession*, Luxembourg: Office for Official Publications of the European Communities, 46, 70–1.
36. European Commission (ed.) (1999) *Regular Report on Slovakia's Progress toward Accession*, Luxembourg: Office for Official Publications of the European Communities, 48.
37. European Commission (ed.) (1999) *Regular Report on Slovakia*, 47, 66.
38. European Commission (ed.) (2000) *Regular Report on Latvia's Progress toward Accession*, Luxembourg: Office for Official Publications of the European Communities, 104; European Commission (ed.) (2000) *Regular Report on Lithuania's Progress toward Accession*, Luxembourg: Office for Official Publications of the European Communities, 104; European Commission (ed.) (2000), *Regular Report on Slovakia's Progress toward Accession*, Luxembourg: Office for Official Publications of the European Communities, 86–7.

39. European Commission (ed.) (2000) *Regular Report on the Czech Republic's Progress toward Accession*, Luxembourg: Office for Official Publications of the European Communities, 81.
40. European Commission (ed.) (2000) *Regular Report on the Czech Republic*, 80, 111.
41. European Commission (ed.) (2000) *Regular Report on the Czech Republic*, 82, 112.
42. European Commission (ed.) (2000) *Regular Report on Hungary's Progress toward Accession*, Luxembourg: Office for Official Publications of the European Communities, 62–3.
43. European Commission (ed.) (2000) *Regular Report on Poland's Progress toward Accession*, Luxembourg: Office for Official Publications of the European Communities, 67–8.
44. European Commission (ed.) (2000) *Regular Report on Slovakia*, 63–4.
45. European Commission (ed.) (2000) *Regular Report on Slovakia*, 64–5.
46. European Commission (ed.) (2000) *Regular Report on Slovenia's Progress toward Accession*, Luxembourg: Office for Official Publications of the European Communities, 63–4.
47. European Commission (ed.) (2000) *Regular Report on Estonia's Progress toward Accession*, Luxembourg: Office for Official Publications of the European Communities, 68; European Commission (ed.) (2000) *Regular Report on Latvia*, 75.
48. European Commission (ed.) (2000) *Regular Report on Latvia*, 75.
49. European Commission (ed.) (2000) *Regular Report on Lithuania*, 76.
50. European Commission (ed.) (2000) *Regular Report on Bulgaria's Progress toward Accession*, Luxembourg: Office for Official Publications of the European Communities, 69–70.
51. European Commission (ed.) (2000) *Regular Report on Romania's Progress toward Accession*, Luxembourg: Office for Official Publications of the European Communities, 13.
52. European Commission (ed.) (2000) *Regular Report on Romania*, 69–70.
53. European Commission (ed.) (2001) *Regular Report on Hungary's Progress toward Accession*, Luxembourg: Office for Official Publications of the European Communities, 100.
54. European Commission (ed.) (2001) *Regular Report on Hungary*, 72–3.
55. European Commission (ed.) (2001) *Regular Report on Hungary*, 74.
56. European Commission (ed.) (2001) *Regular Report on Hungary*, 75.
57. European Commission (ed.) (2001) *Regular Report on the Czech Republic's Progress toward Accession*, Luxembourg: Office for Official Publications of the European Communities, 82.
58. European Commission (ed.) (2001) *Regular Report on Poland's Progress toward Accession*, Luxembourg: Office for Official Publications of the European Communities, 79.
59. European Commission (ed.) (2001) *Regular Report on Poland*, 78–80.
60. European Commission (ed.) (2001) *Regular Report on Poland*, 13.
61. European Commission (ed.) (2001) *Regular Report on Poland*, 14.
62. See Martin Brusis (2003) 'Regionalization in the Czech and Slovak Republics: Comparing the Influences of the European Union', in Michael Keating and James Hughes (eds), *The Regional Challenge in Central and Eastern Europe: Territorial Restructuring and European Integration*, Paris: P.I.E. –Peter Lang, 89–106.

63. European Commission (ed.) (2001) *Regular Report on Slovakia's Progress toward Accession*, Luxembourg: Office for Official Publications of the European Communities, 74.
64. European Commission (ed.) (2001) *Regular Report on Slovakia*, 72–3.
65. European Commission (ed.) (2001) *Regular Report on Slovakia*, 71.
66. European Commission (ed.) (2001) *Regular Report on Slovenia*, 71, 92.
67. European Commission (ed.) (2001) *Regular Report on Slovenia*, 72.
68. European Commission (ed.) (2001) *Regular Report on Estonia's Progress toward Accession*, Luxembourg: Office for Official Publications of the European Communities, 71; European Commission (ed.) (2001) *Regular Report on Lithuania's Progress toward Accession*, Luxembourg: Office for Official Publications of the European Communities, 82–3.
69. European Commission (ed.) (2001) *Regular Report on Estonia*, 71; European Commission (ed.) (2001) *Regular Report on Lithuania*, 82.
70. European Commission (ed.) (2001) *Regular Report on Latvia's Progress toward Accession*, Luxembourg: Office for Official Publications of the European Communities, 84.
71. European Commission (ed.) (2001) *Regular Report on Latvia*, 85–6.
72. European Commission (ed.) (2001) *Regular Report on Latvia*, 113.
73. European Commission (ed.) (2001) *Regular Report on Romania's Progress toward Accession*, Luxembourg: Office for Official Publications of the European Communities, 79.
74. European Commission (ed.) (2001) *Regular Report on Romania*, 80.
75. European Commission (ed.) (2001) *Regular Report on Bulgaria's Progress toward Accession*, Luxembourg: Office for Official Publications of the European Communities, 74–5.
76. European Commission (ed.) (2002) *Regular Report on Hungary*, 100.
77. European Commission (ed.) (2002) *Regular Report on Hungary*, 144.
78. European Commission (ed.) (2002) *Regular Report on Hungary*, 103, 129.
79. European Commission (ed.) (2002) *Regular Report on Poland*, 103–4.
80. European Commission (ed.) (2002) *Regular Report on Poland*, 106.
81. European Commission (ed.) (2002) *Regular Report on the Czech Republic's Progress toward Accession*, Luxembourg: Office for Official Publications of the European Communities, 101–2.
82. European Commission (ed.) (2002) *Regular Report on Czech Republic*, 103.
83. European Commission (ed.) (2002) *Regular Report on Slovakia's Progress toward Accession*, Luxembourg: Office for Official Publications of the European Communities, 98–9.
84. European Commission (ed.) (2002) *Regular Report on Slovakia*, 129.
85. European Commission (ed.) (2002) *Regular Report on Slovakia*, 137.
86. European Commission (ed.) (2002) *Regular Report on Latvia's Progress toward Accession*, Luxembourg: Office for Official Publications of the European Communities, 101–2.
87. European Commission (ed.) (2002) *Regular Report on Latvia*, 103–4.
88. European Commission (ed.) (2002) *Regular Report on Estonia's Progress toward Accession*, Luxembourg: Office for Official Publications of the European Communities, 92, 94, 119.
89. European Commission (ed.) (2002) *Regular Report on Estonia*, 133.
90. European Commission (ed.) (2002) *Regular Report on Estonia*, 101–4.

91. European Commission (ed.) (2002) *Regular Report on Slovenia's Progress toward Accession*, Luxembourg: Office for Official Publications of the European Communities, 91–3.
92. European Commission (ed.) (2002) *Regular Report on Bulgaria's Progress toward Accession*, Luxembourg: Office for Official Publications of the European Communities, 99–101.
93. European Commission (ed.) (2002) *Regular Report on Bulgaria*, 138.
94. European Commission (ed.) (2002) *Regular Report on Romania's Progress toward Accession*, Luxembourg: Office for Official Publications of the European Communities, 102–3.
95. European Council (2003) *Presidency Conclusions*, Thessaloniki European Council, 20 June 2003, Luxembourg: Office for Official Publications of the European Communities, 10: http://europa.eu.int/european_council/conclusions/index_en.htm.
96. Authors' interview with a Commission official from the Horizontal Co-Ordination Unit, 13 January 2004.
97. European Commission (ed.) (2003) *Communication to the European Parliament and the Council 'On the Implementation of Commitments Undertaken by the Acceding Countries in the Context of Accession Negotiations On Chapter 21 – Regional Policy and Coordination of Structural Instruments'*, COM (2003) 433 final, 16 July 2003: http://europa.eu.int/comm/regional_policy/sources/docoffic/official/communic/pdf/chap21/com_chapter21_en.pdf.
98. Ibid., 3–6.
99. This introductory paragraph is identical in all Comprehensive Monitoring Reports (CMRs). See, for example, European Commission (ed.) (2003) *Comprehensive Monitoring Report on the Czech Republic's Preparations for Membership*, Luxembourg: Office for Official Publications of the European Communities, 39.
100. European Commission (ed.) (2003) *Comprehensive Monitoring Report on the Czech Republic*, 40.
101. For example, the links between Chapter 21 and Chapter 28 (financial control) are clearer; and Chapter 13 (social policy and employment) now addresses minority issues more explicitly under 'non-discrimination'.
102. The CMR on Slovenia is the only one that does not provide this additional information about local and regional governance. European Commission (ed.) (2003) *Comprehensive Monitoring Report on Slovenia's Preparations for Membership*, Luxembourg: Office for Official Publications of the European Communities.
103. European Commission (ed.) (2003) *Comprehensive Monitoring Report on the Czech Republic*, 51.
104. European Commission (ed.) (2003) *Comprehensive Monitoring Report on Hungary's Preparations for Membership*, Luxembourg: Office for Official Publications of the European Communities, 12.
105. European Commission (ed.) (2003) *Comprehensive Monitoring Report on Poland's Preparations for Membership*, Luxembourg: Office for Official Publications of the European Communities, 14.
106. European Commission (ed.) (2003) *Comprehensive Monitoring Report on Slovenia*, 11.

107. European Commission (ed.) (2003) *Comprehensive Monitoring Report on Estonia's Preparations for Membership*, Luxembourg: Office for Official Publications of the European Communities, 12; European Commission (ed.) (2003) *Comprehensive Monitoring Report on Latvia's Preparations for Membership*, Luxembourg: Office for Official Publications of the European Communities, 12; European Commission (ed.) (2003) *Comprehensive Monitoring Report on Lithuania's Preparations for Membership*, Luxembourg: Office for Official Publications of the European Communities, 11.
108. European Commission (ed.) (2003) *Regular Report on Bulgaria's Progress toward Accession*, Luxembourg: Office for Official Publications of the European Communities, 91–3.
109. European Commission (ed.) (2003) *Regular Report on Romania's Progress toward Accession*, Luxembourg: Office for Official Publications of the European Communities, 94–5.
110. See European Commission (ed.) (2003) 'Strategy Paper and Report of the European Commission on the Progress towards Accession by Bulgaria, Romania and Turkey', Luxembourg: Office for Official Publications of the European Union: http://europa.eu.int/comm/enlargement/report_2003/pdf/strategy_paper2003_full_en.pdf.
111. Ibid., 3, 11.
112. Ibid., 9–11.

5. Transition, enlargement and regionalization: a comparison of Hungary and Poland

1. Poland has consistently been ranked first, and Hungary second or third, in the Freedom House 'Nations in Transit' democratization rankings between 1997–2003: http://www.freedomhouse.org/research/nattransit.htm. Hungary is ranked first and Poland fourth in the EBRD's average transition performance score for 2003 out of all the post-communist transition states: http://www.ebrd.org/pubs/tr/03/tr03.pdf.
2. Kenneth Davey (1995) 'Local Government in Hungary', in Andrew Coulson (ed.), *Local Government in Eastern Europe*, Cheltenham: Edward Elgar, 57–75.
3. Jozsef Hegedus (1999) 'Hungarian Local Government', in Emil Kirchner (ed.) *Decentralization and Transition in the Visegrad: Poland, Hungary, the Czech Republic and Slovakia*, Basingstoke: Macmillan, 133.
4. See Brigid Fowler (2002) 'Hungary: Patterns of Political Conflict over Territorial-Administrative Reform', *Regional and Federal Studies*, 12 (2), 15–40; Helmut Wollmann and Tomila Lankina (2003) 'Local Government in Poland and Hungary: from Post-Communist Reform towards EU Accession', in Harald Baldersheim, Michal Illner and Helmut Wollmann (eds), *Local Democracy in Post-Communist Europe*, Opladen: Leske & Budrich, 94.
5. Tibor Navracsics (1996) 'Public Sector Reform in Hungary: Changes in Intergovernmental Relations (1990–1995)', in Attila Agh and Gabriella Ilonszki (eds), *Parliaments and Organized Interests: the Second Steps*, Budapest, Hungarian Centre for Democracy Studies, 305.
6. See Gabor Bende Szabo (1999) 'The Intermediate Administrative Level in Hungary', in Eric von Breska and Martin Brusis (eds), *Central and Eastern*

Europe on the Way to the European Union, Munich: Centre for Applied Policy, Geschwister-Scholl-Institute for Political Science, University of Munich.

7. Peter Heil (2000) 'PHARE in Hungary: the Anatomy of a Pre-Accession Aid Programme, 1990–1999' unpublished PhD thesis, Budapest, 43.
8. Gyula Horváth (1998) 'Transition and Regionalism in East Central Europe', Occasional Paper no. 7, Tubingen: Europaisches Zentrum fur Foderalismus-Forschung, 20.
9. Brigid Fowler (2001) 'Debating Sub-State Reform on Hungary's "Road to Europe"', One Europe or Several? Working Paper 21/01, Brighton: University of Sussex, 11–14.
10. Fowler (2001: 24); Bende Szabo (1999: 16); Navracsics (1996: 289–93).
11. Bende-Szabo (1999: 6–7); Ilona Palne Kovács (2001) 'Regional Development and Governance in Hungary', Discussion Paper no. 35, Pécs: Centre for Regional Studies, 13–15.
12. Authors' interview with elite member in Pécs.
13. See Brigid Fowler (2002).
14. Bende-Szabo (1999: 5).
15. Authors' interview with head of a PAO (1999).
16. See Palne Kovács (2001: 25–36); Fowler (2001: 32); Horváth (1996: 28).
17. Fowler (2001: 34–6).
18. European Commission (ed.) (1997) *Opinion on Hungary*, 90.
19. Author's interview with official in the Hungarian Mission to the EU, Brussels, 15 December 2000.
20. Palne Kovács (2001: 29).
21. A. Cziczovszki (2000), 'The Regional Problem in the Transition to Europe: the Case of Hungary', Paper presented at the BASEES Annual Conference, Cambridge.
22. Fowler (2001).
23. European Commission (ed.) (1999) *Regular Report on Hungary*, 46: http://europa.eu.int/comm/enlargement/candidate.htm.
24. Bende Szabo (1999: 7).
25. European Commission (ed.) (2000) *Regular Report on Hungary*, 62–3; European Commission, *Regular Report on Hungary*, 75.
26. Fowler (2001: 41–2).
27. The reform was mentioned but without comment in the CMR. European Commission (ed.) (2003) *Comprehensive Monitoring Report on Hungary*, 12.
28. Wollmann and Lankina (2003: 101).
29. Frank-Dieter Grimm, 'Das Städtesystem Polens in Vergangenheit, Gegenwart und Zukunsft. Zur Einführung', in Isolde Brade and Frank-Dieter Grimm (eds), *Städtesysteme und Regionalentwicklungen in Mittel- und Osteuropa. Russland, Ukraine, Polen*, Leipzig: Institut für Länderkunde Leipzig (Beiträge zur Regionalen Geographie), 136–47 (141–5).
30. Wiktor Glowacki (2002) 'Regionalization in Poland', in Gerard Marcou (ed.), *Regionalization for Development and Accession to the EU: a Comparative Perspective*, LGI Studios, Budapest: Open Society Institute, 110–11.
31. James Hughes, Gwendolyn Sasse, Claire Gordon and Tatiana Majcherkiewicz (2004) 'Silesia and the Politics of Regionalisation in Poland', in Tomasz Zarycki and George Kolankiewicz (eds), *Regional Issues in Polish Politics*, London: UCL Press, 83–111. See also Luiza Bialasiewicz (2002)

'Upper Silesia: Rebirth of a Regional Identity in Poland', *Regional and Federal Studies*, 12 (2), 111–32.

32. Jacek Zaucha (1999) 'Regional and Local Development in Poland', in Emil Kirchner (ed.), *Decentralisation and Transition in the Visegrad, Poland, Hungary, the Czech Republic and Slovakia*, Basingstoke: Macmillan, 75.
33. Wollmann and Lankina (2003: 103); Jadwiga Emilewicz and Artur Wolek (2002) *Reformers and Politicians: the Power Play for the 1998 Reform of Public Administration in Poland, as seen by its Main Players*, Warsaw: Elipsa, 109.
34. Harald Baldersheim and Pawel Swaniewicz (2003) 'The Institutional Performance of Polish Regions in an Enlarged EU. How much Potential? How Path Dependent?', in Michael Keating and James Hughes (eds), *The Regional Challenge in Central and Eastern Europe*, Paris: P.I.E.-Peter Lang, 121–46; Michal Illner (1992) 'Municipalities and Industrial Paternalism in a Real Socialist Society', in P. Dostal et al. (eds), *Changing Territorial Administration in Czechoslovakia*, Amsterdam: University of Amsterdam, Charles University and Czechoslovak Academy of Sciences, 15.
35. See Jerzy Regulski (1999) 'Building Democracy in Poland, the State Reform of 1998', Discussion Paper no. 9, Budapest: the Local Government and Public Services Reform Initiative, Open Society: http://lgi.osi.hu/news/2001/20010202.htm.
36. Glowacki (2002: 111).
37. Aleks Szczerbiak (1999) 'The Impact of the October 1998 Local Elections on the Emerging Polish Party System', *Journal of Communist Studies and Transition Politics*, 15 (3), 86.
38. Glowacki (2002: 110–11).
39. Piotr Korcelli, 'Die Städte Polens im Wandel – ihre demographischen und ökonomischen Determinanten', in Isolde Brade and Frank-Dieter Grimm (eds), *Städtesysteme und Regionalentwicklungen in Mittel- und Osteuropa. Russland, Ukraine, Polen*, Leipzig: Institut für Länderkunde Leipzig (Beiträge zur Regionalen Geographie), 148–66 (164).
40. For details, including the debates in the Sejm, see Patricia Wyszogrodzka-Sipher (2000) 'The National and International Influences on the Reform of Polish Government Structures', paper for the workshop 'Europe, Nation, Region: Redefining the State in Central and Eastern Europe', London, Royal Institute of International Affairs.
41. Interviewee in Katowice (2001).
42. Grzegorz Gorzelak and Bohdan Jalowiecki (2001) 'Analiza wdrazania i skutków reformy terytorialnej organizacji kraju, Raport koncowy' [An analysis on the introduction and results of the territorial reform of state, the final report], Warszawa, Europejski Insytut Rozwoju Regionalnego i Lokalnego, Insytut Spraw Publicznych.
43. Interviewee in Katowice (2001).
44. European Commission (ed.) (1998) *Regular Report on Poland*; European Commission (ed.) (2000) *Regular Report on Poland*; Aleko Djildov and Vasil Marinov (1999) *Regional Policy in the Process of Integration into the European Union: a Comparative Analysis of Selected Countries*, New York: EWI.
45. Tomasz Zarycki (2003) 'The Regional Dimension of the Polish Political Scene', in Tomasz Zarycki and George Kolankiewicz (eds), *Regional Issues in Polish Politics*, London: School of Slavonic and East European Studies, University College London, 239–60.

46. Zyta Gilowska, Jozef Płoskonka, Stanislaw Prutis, Miroslaw Stec and Elzbieta Wysocka (1999) 'The Systemic Model of the Voivodship in a Democratic Unitary State', Discussion paper no. 7, Budapest: Local Government and Public Service Reform Initiative, Open Society: http://lgi.osi.hu/news/2001/20010202.htm.
47. Tatiana Majcherkiewicz (2001) 'An Elite in Transition: an Analysis of the Higher Administration of the Region of Upper Silesia, Poland 1990–1997', PhD thesis, London School of Economics and Political Science, Department of Sociology.
48. Authors' interview with a senior official, Polish Mission to the EU, Brussels, 28 March 2001.
49. Andrzej Kowalczyk (2000) 'Local Government in Poland', in Tamas Horvath (ed.) *Decentralization: Experiments and Reform*, Budapest: LGI Publications, 226.
50. Authors' interview with senior official in DG Regional Policy, European Commission, Brussels, 28 March 2001.
51. James Hughes, Gwendolyn Sasse and Claire Gordon (2004) 'Conditionality and Compliance in the EU's Eastern Enlargement: Regional Policy and the Reform of Sub-National Governance', *Journal of Common Market Studies*, 42 (3), September.
52. European Commission (ed.) (2001) *Regular Report on Poland*, 79.
53. European Commission (ed.) (2002) *Regular Report on Hungary*, 102–4; European Commission (ed.) (2002) *Regular Report on Poland*, 105–6.

6. Elites and the normative capacity for Europeanization

1. See Jeffrey Checkel (2001) 'International Institutions and Socialisation in Europe: Introduction and Framework', *ARENA Working Papers*, WP 01/11.
2. There is an extensive literature on the issues relating to the 'democratic deficit'. For recent studies see Jeffrey Anderson (ed.) (1999) *Regional Integration and Democracy: Expanding on the European Experience*, Lanham, MD: Rowman & Littlefield; Christopher Lord (1998) *Democracy in the European Union*, Sheffield: Sheffield Academic Press; Svein Andersen and Kjell Eliassen (eds) (1996) *The EU: How Democratic Is It?*, London: Sage.
3. See, for example, Anna Grzymała-Busse and Abby Innes (2003) 'Great Expectations: the EU and Domestic Political Competition in East Central Europe', *East European Politics and Societies*, 17 (1), 64–73.
4. Poland introduced a so-called 'Little Constitution' adopted in 1992, and only adopted a final version in 1997.
5. See Peter Mair (1997) 'What is Different about Post-Communist Party Systems?', in Peter Mair (ed.) *Party System Change. Approaches and Interpretations*, Oxford: Clarendon Press, 175–98; Abby Innes (2002) 'Party Competition in Postcommunist Europe: the Great Electoral Lottery', *Comparative Politics*, 35 (1), 85–104.
6. European Commission (ed.) (2001) *White Paper on European Governance*, Com (2001) 428, Luxembourg: Office for Official Publications of the European Communities, 12.
7. European Convention (2003), *Draft Treaty Establishing a Constitution for Europe*, 18 July 2003, Luxembourg: Office for Official Publications of the European Communities, articles 9 (1 and 3), and protocol on the applica-

tion of the principles of subsidiarity and proportionality: http://european-convention.eu.int/docs/Treaty/cv00850.en03.pdf.

8. For elite theory see Samuel J. Eldersfeld, Lars Stromberg and Wim Derksen (1995) *Local Elites in Western Democracies: a Comparative Analysis of Urban Political Leaders in the U.S., Sweden, and the Netherlands*, Boulder, CO: Westview; Manuel Castells (2000) *The Rise of the Network Society*, Oxford: Blackwell; Robert Putnam (1993) *Making Democracy Work: Civic Traditions in Modern Italy*, Princeton, NJ: Princeton University Press. For a study of sub-national elites in post-communist transition see James Hughes and Peter John (2001), 'Local Elites and Transition in Russia', *British Journal of Political Science*, 31 (4), 673–92.
9. For an empirical proof of this hypothesis, based on research into the attitudes of Czech civil servants, see Petr Drulák, Jirí Cesal and Stanislav Hampl (2003) 'Interactions and Identities of Czech Civil Servants on their Way to the EU', *Journal of European Public Policy*, 10 (4), 637–54.
10. Ordered probit models were used to analyse the elites' attitudes to democracy, the market, and the EU more generally. The analysis grouped the independent variables into theoretical categories of the sociological (age, education, parental occupation), previous regime socialization (membership of party and apparatchiki), role in the elite (for example, administration, private sector), level of national identification, extent of international networks and association memberships. The data analysis shows that sociological factors and elite position predict attitudes to democracy and the market. It was found that attitudes to transition were also predicted by the elite members' international networks and contacts. These results on elite attitudes to transition are being analysed in separate work by James Hughes and Peter John.
11. Authors' interviews in Pécs.
12. In Maribor, 17 per cent of respondents knew of the waste-water plant that was being built in the city though in fact the financing of this project was arranged by the EBRD and the EU funded only the construction of a water collector outside the plant.
13. See Janine Wedel (1998) *Collision and Collusion: the Strange Case of Western Aid to Eastern Europe, 1989–1998*, New York: St Martin's Press.
14. There is anecdotal evidence of contacts between Finnish and Estonian farmers which might stoke the already growing levels of Euroscepticism in Estonia. Furthermore four days prior to Poland's parliamentary elections in September 2001 a demonstration led by the prominent British farmer Sir Julian Rose was held in Warsaw highlighting the threat to Polish farming posed by EU membership: http://EUobserver.com/index.phtml?selected_topic=15&action=view&article_id=3499.
15. The interviewees were offered the following options: Economic Cohesion, Partnership for Peace, Subsidiarity, Europe of Nation States, Free Trade, Common Agricultural Policy, Europe of the Regions, Monetary Union, a Federal Europe, Common Foreign and Security Policy, Common European Home and Structural and Cohesion Funds.
16. While terms like 'subsidiarity' might be more familiar among the elites in current member states, they might not necessarily exhibit greater knowledge about their detailed meaning, thereby highlighting an EU-wide communication gap.

17. 'Trends in EU, Czech, Hungarian and Polish Public Opinion on Enlargement: Implications for EU Institutions and Industry', Central European Opinion Research Group Foundation, Joint Omnibus Survey, September 2000.
18. For a discussion see Joseph Weiler (1999) *The Constitution of Europe*, Cambridge: Cambridge University Press. For a focus on the 'demos' issue see Lars-Erik Cederman (2000) 'Nationalism and Bounded Integration: What it Would Take to Construct a European Demos', EUI Working Papers RSC No. 2000/34.
19. Yasemin Soysal (2002) 'Locating Europe', *European Societies*, 4 (3), 265–84.
20. For critical analyses of the EU's role in the development of a 'European' identity see Chris Shore (2000) *Building Europe: the Cultural Politics of European Integration*. London: Routledge; Bo Stråth (2002) 'A European Identity: to the Historical Limits of a Concept', *European Journal of Social Theory*, 5 (4), 387–401.
21. The turnouts in all the referenda on EU accession were: Czech Republic: 55.2 per cent, Estonia: 64.02 per cent, Hungary: 45.62 per cent, Latvia: 72.5 per cent, Lithuania: 63.37 per cent, Poland: 58.85 per cent, Slovakia: 52.15 per cent, Slovenia: 60.29 per cent.

Bibliography

European Union documents

European Commission (ed.) (1997) *Agenda 2000 – Vol. 1 For a Stronger and Wider Union*, COM/97/2000 final, Luxembourg: Office for Official Publications of the European Communities

European Commission (ed.) (1997) *Agenda 2000 – Commission Opinion on the Czech Republic's Application for Membership of the European Union*, Doc. 97/17, Luxembourg: Office for Official Publications of the European Communities.

European Commission (ed.) (1997) *Agenda 2000 – Commission Opinion on Bulgaria's Application for Membership of the European Union*, Doc. 97/17, Luxembourg: Office for Official Publications of the European Communities.

European Commission (ed.) (1997) *Agenda 2000 – Commission Opinion on Estonia's Application for Membership of the European Union*, Doc. 97/12, Luxembourg: Office for Official Publications of the European Communities.

European Commission (ed.) (1997) *Agenda 2000 – Commission Opinion on Hungary's Application for Membership of the European Union*, Doc. 97/13, Luxembourg: Office for Official Publications of the European Communities.

European Commission (ed.) (1997) *Agenda 2000 – Commission Opinion on Poland's Application for Membership of the European Union*, Doc. 97/16, Luxembourg: Office for Official Publications of the European Communities.

European Commission (ed.) (1997) *Agenda 2000 – Commission Opinion on Slovenia's Application for Membership of the European Union*, Doc. 97/19, Luxembourg: Office for Official Publications of the European Communities.

European Commission (ed.) (1997) *Agenda 2000 – Commission Opinion on Slovakia's Application for Membership of the European Union*, Doc. 97/20, Luxembourg: Office for Official Publications of the European Communities.

European Commission (ed.) (1998) *Regular Report on Bulgaria's Progress toward Accession*, Luxembourg: Office for Official Publications of the European Communities.

European Commission (ed.) (1998) *Regular Report on the Czech Republic's Progress toward Accession*, Luxembourg: Office for Official Publications of the European Communities.

European Commission (ed.) (1998) *Regular Report on Hungary's Progress toward Accession*, Luxembourg: Office for Official Publications of the European Communities:http://europa.eu.int/comm/enlargement/report_11_98/pdf/en/hungary_en.pdf.

European Commission (ed.) (1998) *Regular Report on Latvia's Progress toward Accession*, Luxembourg: Office for Official Publications of the European Communities.

European Commission (ed.) (1998) *Regular Report on Lithuania's Progress toward Accession*, Luxembourg: Office for Official Publications of the European Communities.

European Commission (ed.) (1998) *Regular Report on Poland's Progress toward Accession*, Luxembourg: Office for Official Publications of the European Communities.

European Commission (ed.) (1998) *Regular Report on Romania's Progress toward Accession*, Luxembourg: Office for Official Publications of the European Communities:http://europa.eu.int/comm/enlargement/report_11_98/pdf/en/romania_en.pdf.

European Commission (ed.) (1998) *Regular Report on Slovakia's Progress toward Accession*, Luxembourg: Office for Official Publications of the European Communities.

European Commission (ed.) (1998) *Regular Report on Slovenia's Progress toward Accession*, Luxembourg: Office for Official Publications of the European Communities.

European Commission (ed.) (1999) *Regular Report on Bulgaria's Progress toward Accession*, Luxembourg: Office for Official Publications of the European Communities.

European Commission (ed.) (1999) *Regular Report on the Czech Republic's Progress toward Accession*, Luxembourg: Office for Official Publications of the European Communities.

European Commission (ed.) (1999) *Regular Report on Hungary's Progress toward Accession*, Luxembourg: Office for Official Publications of the European Communities.

European Commission (ed.) (1999) *Regular Report on Latvia's Progress toward Accession*, Luxembourg: Office for Official Publications of the European Communities.

European Commission (ed.) (1999) *Regular Report on Lithuania's Progress toward Accession*, Luxembourg: Office for Official Publications of the European Communities.

European Commission (ed.) (1999) *Regular Report on Poland's Progress toward Accession*, Luxembourg: Office for Official Publications of the European Communities.

European Commission (ed.) (1999) *Regular Report on Romania's Progress toward Accession*, Luxembourg: Office for Official Publications of the European Communities.

European Commission (ed.) (1999) *Regular Report on Slovenia's Progress toward Accession*, Luxembourg: Office for Official Publications of the European Communities.

European Commission (ed.) (1999) *Regular Report on Slovakia's Progress toward Accession*, Luxembourg: Office for Official Publications of the European Communities.

European Commission (ed.) (2000) *Enlargement Strategy Paper: Report on Progress towards Accession by each of the Candidate Countries*, Luxembourg: Office for Official Publications of the European Communities.

European Commission (ed.) (2000) *PHARE 2000 Review, Strengthening Preparations for Membership*, COM (2000) 3103/2, Luxembourg: Office for Official Publications of the European Communities.

European Commission (ed.) (2000) *PHARE Annual Report 1998*, Luxembourg: Office for Official Publications of the European Communities.

European Commission (ed.) (2000) *PHARE Programme Annual Report 2000*, Luxembourg: Office for Official Publications of the European Communities.

European Commission (ed.) (2000) *Regular Report on Bulgaria's Progress toward Accession*, Luxembourg: Office for Official Publications of the European Communities.

European Commission (ed.) (2000) *Regular Report on the Czech Republic's Progress toward Accession*, Luxembourg: Office for Official Publications of the European Communities.

European Commission (ed.) (2000) *Regular Report on Estonia's Progress toward Accession*, Luxembourg: Office for Official Publications of the European Communities.

European Commission (ed.) (2000) *Regular Report on Hungary's Progress toward Accession*, Luxembourg: Office for Official Publications of the European Communities.

European Commission (ed.) (2000) *Regular Report on Latvia's Progress toward Accession*, Luxembourg: Office for Official Publications of the European Communities.

European Commission (ed.) (2000) *Regular Report on Lithuania's Progress toward Accession*, Luxembourg: Office for Official Publications of the European Communities.

European Commission (ed.) (2000) *Regular Report on Poland's Progress toward Accession*, Luxembourg: Office for Official Publications of the European Communities.

European Commission (ed.) (2000) *Regular Report on Romania's Progress toward Accession*, Luxembourg: Office for Official Publications of the European Communities.

European Commission (ed.) (2000), *Regular Report on Slovakia's Progress toward Accession*, Luxembourg: Office for Official Publications of the European Communities.

European Commission (ed.) (2000) *Regular Report on Slovenia's Progress toward Accession*, Luxembourg: Office for Official Publications of the European Communities.

European Commission (ed.) (2001) *Enlargement of the European Union: an Historic Opportunity*, Luxembourg: Offices for Official Publications of the European Communities.

European Commission (ed.) (2001) *Proposal for a Regulation of the European Parliament and the Council on the Establishment of a Common Classification of Territorial Units for Statistics (NUTS)*, 14 February 2001:http://europa.eu.int/eur-lex/en/com/pdf/2001/en_501PC0083.pdf.

European Commission (ed.) (2001) *Regular Report on Bulgaria's Progress toward Accession*, Luxembourg: Office for Official Publications of the European Communities.

European Commission (ed.) (2001) *Regular Report on the Czech Republic's Progress toward Accession*, Luxembourg: Office for Official Publications of the European Communities.

European Commission (ed.) (2001) *Regular Report on Estonia's Progress toward Accession*, Luxembourg: Office for Official Publications of the European Communities.

European Commission (ed.) (2001) *Regular Report on Hungary's Progress toward Accession*, Luxembourg: Office for Official Publications of the European Communities.

European Commission (ed.) (2001) *Regular Report on Latvia's Progress toward Accession*, Luxembourg: Office for Official Publications of the European Communities.

European Commission (ed.) (2001) *Regular Report on Lithuania's Progress toward Accession*, Luxembourg: Office for Official Publications of the European Communities.

European Commission (ed.) (2001) *Regular Report on Poland's Progress toward Accession*, Luxembourg: Office for Official Publications of the European Communities.

European Commission (ed.) (2001) *Regular Report on Romania's Progress toward Accession*, Luxembourg: Office for Official Publications of the European Communities.

European Commission (ed.) (2001) *Regular Report on Slovakia's Progress toward Accession*, Luxembourg: Office for Official Publications of the European Communities.

European Commission (ed.) (2001) *Regular Report on Slovenia's Progress toward Accession*, Luxembourg: Office for Official Publications of the European Communities: http://europa.eu.int/comm/enlargement/report2001/si_en.pdf.

European Commission (ed.) (2001) *White Paper on European Governance*, Com (2001) 428, Luxembourg: Office for Official Publications of the European Communities.

European Commission (ed.) (2002) *Directorate General Enlargement, Enlargement of the European Union, Guide to the Negotiations, Chapter by Chapter*, April 2002, Luxembourg: Office for Official Publications of the European Communities

European Commission (ed.) (2002) *Regular Report on Bulgaria's Progress toward Accession*, Luxembourg: Office for Official Publications of the European Communities.

European Commission (ed.) (2002) *Regular Report on the Czech Republic's Progress toward Accession*, Luxembourg: Office for Official Publications of the European Communities.

European Commission (ed.) (2002) *Regular Report on Estonia's Progress toward Accession*, Luxembourg: Office for Official Publications of the European Communities.

European Commission (ed.) (2002) *Regular Report on Hungary's Progress toward Accession*, Luxembourg: Office for Official Publications of the European Communities: http://europa.eu.int/comm/enlargement/report2002/hu_en.pdf.

European Commission (ed.) (2002) *Regular Report on Latvia's Progress toward Accession*, Luxembourg: Office for Official Publications of the European Communities.

European Commission (ed.) (2002) *Regular Report on Poland's Progress toward Accession*, Luxembourg: Office for Official Publications of the European Communities: http://europa.eu.int/comm/enlargement/report2002/pl_en.pdf.

European Commission (ed.) (2002) *Regular Report on Romania's Progress toward Accession*, Luxembourg: Office for Official Publications of the European Communities.

European Commission (ed.) (2002) *Regular Report on Slovakia's Progress toward Accession*, Luxembourg: Office for Official Publications of the European Communities.

European Commission (ed.) (2002) *Regular Report on Slovenia's Progress toward Accession*, Luxembourg: Office for Official Publications of the European Communities.

European Commission (ed.) (2003) *Communication to the European Parliament and the Council*, 'On the Implementation of Commitments Undertaken by the Acceding Countries in the Context of Accession Negotiations On Chapter 21 – Regional Policy and Coordination of Structural Instruments', COM (2003) 433 final, 16 July 2003; see http://europa.eu.int/comm/regional_policy/sources/docoffic/official/communic/pdf/chap21/com_chapter21_en.pdf.

European Commission (ed.) (2003) *Comprehensive Monitoring Report on the Czech Republic's Preparations for Membership*, Luxembourg: Office for Official Publications of the European Communities.

European Commission (ed.) (2003) *Comprehensive Monitoring Report on Estonia's Preparations for Membership*, Luxembourg: Office for Official Publications of the European Communities.

European Commission (ed.) (2003) *Comprehensive Monitoring Report on Latvia's Preparations for Membership*, Luxembourg: Office for Official Publications of the European Communities.

European Commission (ed.) (2003) *Comprehensive Monitoring Report on Lithuania's Preparations for Membership*, Luxembourg: Office for Official Publications of the European Communities.

European Commission (ed.) (2003) *Comprehensive Monitoring Report on Hungary's Preparations for Membership*, Luxembourg: Office for Official Publications of the European Communities.

European Commission (ed.) (2003) *Comprehensive Monitoring Report on Poland's Preparations for Membership*, Luxembourg: Office for Official Publications of the European Communities.

European Commission (ed.) (2003) *Comprehensive Monitoring Report on Slovenia's Preparations for Membership*, Luxembourg: Office for Official Publications of the European Communities.

European Commission (ed.) (2003) *Regular Report on Bulgaria's Progress toward Accession*, Luxembourg: Office for Official Publications of the European Communities.

European Commission (ed.) (2003) *Regular Report on Romania's Progress toward Accession*, Luxembourg: Office for Official Publications of the European Communities.

European Commission (ed.) (2003) *Strategy Paper and Report of the European Commission on the Progress towards Accession by Bulgaria, Romania and Turkey*, Luxembourg: Office for Official Publications of the European Communities: http://europa.eu.int/comm/enlargement/report_2003/pdf/strategy_paper 2003_full_en.pdf.

European Convention (2003) *Draft Treaty Establishing a Constitution for Europe*, 18 July 2003, Luxembourg: Office for Official Publications of the European Communities: http://european-convention. eu.int/docs/ Treaty/cv00850. en03. pdf.

European Council (1991) *Presidency Conclusions*, Luxembourg European Council, 28–29 June 1991, Luxembourg: Office for Official Publications of the European Communities: http:// www.europarl.eu.int/summits/ luxembourg/ lu2_en.pdf.

European Council (1993) *Presidency Conclusions*, Copenhagen European Council, 21–22 June 1993, Luxembourg: Office for Official Publications of the European Communities: http://www.europarl.eu.int/enlargement_new/euro peancouncil/pdf/cop_en.pdf; http://www.europarl.eu.int/enlargement_new/ europeancouncil/pdf/cop_fr.pdf.

European Council (1994) *Presidency Conclusions*, Essen European Council, 9–10 December 1994, Luxembourg: Office for Official Publications of the European Communities: http://europa.eu.int/european_council/conclusions/index_en. htm.

European Council (1995) *Presidency Conclusions*, Madrid European Council, 15–16 December 1995, Luxembourg: Office for Official Publications of the European Communities: http://europa.eu.int/european_council/conclusions/ index_en.htm.

European Council (1997) *Presidency Conclusions*, Luxembourg European Council, 12–13 December 1997, Luxembourg: Office for Official Publications of the European Communities: http://europa.eu.int/european_council/conclusions/ index_en.htm.

European Council (2002) *Presidency Conclusions*, Copenhagen European Council 12 and 13 December 2002, Luxembourg: Office for Official Publications of the European Communities: http://europa.eu.int/european_council/conclusions/ index_en.htm.

European Council (2003) *Presidency Conclusions*, Thessaloniki European Council, 20 June 2003, Luxembourg: Office for Official Publications of the European Communities. http:// europa.eu.int/ european_ council /conclusions/ index_ en.htm.

European Council (2002) *The Revised Accession Partnerships*, 28 January 2002, Council Decisions, Official Journal L44 of 14 February 2002, Luxembourg: Office for Official Publications of the European Communities.

European Council Regulation (1999) No. 1260/1999 of 21 June 1999 laying down general provisions on the Structural Funds, Official Journal L161, Luxembourg: Office for Official Publications of the European Union, 0001–0042.

European Council Regulation (2003) No. 1059/2003 of 26 May 2003, Luxembourg: Office for Official Publications of the European Communities: http://europa .eu.int/eur-lex/en/dat/2003/l_154/l_15420030621en00010041.pdf.

European Council Resolution (1991) *Resolution on Human Rights, Democracy and Development*, 28 November 1991, Luxembourg: Office for Official Publications of the European Union: http://europa.eu.int/comm/external_relations/human _rights/do c/cr28_11_91_en.htm.

European Union (1992) *Treaty of European Union*, 7 February 1992, Luxembourg: Office for Official Publications of the European Communities: http:// europa.eu.int /abc/obj/treaties/en/entoc01.htm.

European Union (1997) *Treaty of Amsterdam Amending the Treaty of European Union, the Treaties Establishing the European Communities and Related Acts*, Official Journal C 340, 10 November 1997, Luxembourg: Office for Official

Publications of the European Communities: http://europa.eu.int/eur-lex/en/search/treaties_other.html.

European Union Committee of the Regions (2001) *Opinion of the Committee of the Regions* on 'Supporting the development of institutional structures at local and regional level in the applicant countries', Luxembourg, 14 November 2001.

European Union Committee of the Regions (1999) *Resolution of the Committee of the Regions* on 'The ongoing EU enlargement process', Luxembourg, 24 November 1999.

Books, articles and other materials

Agh, Attila (2002) 'The Reform of State Administration in Hungary: the Capacity of Core Ministries to Manage Europeanisation', Budapest Papers on Europeanisation, No. 7, Budapest: Hungarian Centre for Democracy Studies Foundation.

Andersen, Svein and Eliassen, Kjell (eds) (1996) *The EU: How Democratic Is It?*, London: Sage.

Anderson, Jeffrey (ed.) (1999) *Regional Integration and Democracy: Expanding on the European Experience*, Lanham, MD: Rowman & Littlefield.

Avery, Graham (forthcoming 2004) 'The Enlargement Negotiations', in Fraser Cameron (ed.), *The Future of Europe: Enlargement and Integration*, London: Routledge.

Bache, Ian (1998) *The Politics of European Union Regional Policy. Multi-Level Governance or Flexible Gatekeeping?* Sheffield: Sheffield Academic Press.

Bachtler, John, Wishlade, Fiona and Yuill, Douglas (2001) 'Regional Policy in Europe after Enlargement', Regional and Industrial Policy Research Paper no. 44, European Policies Research Centre, University of Strathclyde, 1–39: http://www.eprc.strath.ac.uk/eprc/PDF_files/R44SubRosa.pdf.

Baga, Enikoe (2004) 'Romania's Western Connection: Timisoara and Timis County', in Melanie Tatur (ed.), *The Making of Regions in Post-Socialist Europe: the Impact of Culture, Economic Structure, and Institutions*, vol. II, Opladen: Leske+Budrich, 17–106.

Baldersheim, Harald, Illner, Michal and Wollmann, Hellmut (eds) (2003) *Local Democracy in Post-Communist Europe*, Opladen: Leske+Budrich.

Baldersheim, Harald and Swaniewicz, Pawel (2003) 'The Institutional Performance of Polish Regions in an Enlarged EU. How much Potential? How Path Dependent?', in Michael Keating and James Hughes (eds), *The Regional Challenge in Central and Eastern Europe*, Paris: P.I.E.-Peter Lang, 121–46.

Bende Szabo, Gabor (1999) 'The Intermediate Administrative Level in Hungary' in Eric von Breska and Martin Brusis (eds), *Central and Eastern Europe on the Way to the European Union: Reforms of Regional Administration in Bulgaria, the Czech Republic, Estonia, Hungary, Poland and Slovakia*, Munich: Centre for Applied Policy, Geschwister-Scholl-Institute for Political Science, University of Munich.

Bennett, Richard J. (ed.) (1993) *Local Government in the New Europe*, London: Belhaven Press.

Bennett, Richard J. (1997) *Local Government in Post-Socialist Cities*, Budapest: Open Society Institute.

Bernat, Tivadar (ed.) (1985) *An Economic Geography of Hungary*, Budapest: Akademiai Kiado.

Bialasiewicz, Luiza (2002) 'Upper Silesia: Rebirth of a Regional Identity in Poland', *Regional and Federal Studies*, 12 (2), 111–32.

Bitušiková, Alexandra (2002), 'Slovakia: an Anthropological Perspective on Identity and Regional Reform', *Regional and Federal Studies*, 12 (2), 41–64.

Börzel, Tanja A. and Risse, Thomas (2000) 'When Europe Hits Home: Europeanization and Domestic Change', *European Integration On-line Papers* (EioP), 4 (15), 1–13: http://eiop.or.at/eiop/texte/2000–015a.htm.

Breuss, Fritz (2001) 'Macroeconomic Effects of Enlargement for Old and New Members', WIFO Working Paper 143, March, Vienna, 1–22.

Brusis, Martin (1999) 'Recreating the Regional Level in Central and Eastern Europe: Lessons from Administrative Reform in Six Countries', in Eric von Breska and Martin Brusis (eds), *Central and Eastern Europe on the Way to the European Union: Reforms of Regional Administration in Bulgaria, the Czech Republic, Estonia, Hungary, Poland and Slovakia*, Munich: Centre for Applied Policy, Geschwister-Scholl-Institute for Political Science, University of Munich.

Brusis, Martin (2003) 'Regionalisation in the Czech and Slovak Republics: Comparing the Influences of the European Union', in Michael Keating and James Hughes (eds), *The Regional Challenge in Central and Eastern Europe: Territorial Restructuring and European Integration*, Paris: P.I.E.-Peter Lang, 89–106.

Burnell, Peter (1994) 'Good Government and Democratization: a Sideways Look at Aid and Political Conditionality', *Democratization*, 1 (3), 485–503.

Campbell, Adrian (1995) 'Local Government in Romania', in Andrew Coulson (ed.), *Local Government in Eastern Europe*, Aldershot: Edward Elgar, 76–101.

Caramani, Daniele (2003) 'State Administration and Regional Construction in Central Europe: a Comparative-Historical Perspective', in Michael Keating and James Hughes (eds), *The Regional Challenge in Central and Eastern Europe: Territorial Restructuring and European Integration*, Paris: P.I.E.-Peter Lang, 21–50.

Carothers, Thomas (1999) *Aiding Democracy Abroad: the Learning Curve*, Washington, DC: Carnegie Endowment for International Peace.

Castells, Manuel (2000) *The Rise of the Network Society*, Oxford: Blackwell.

Cederman, Lars-Erik (2000) 'Nationalism and Bounded Integration: What it Would Take to Construct a European Demos', EUI Working Papers RSC No. 2000/34.

Checkel, Jeffrey (2001) 'International Institutions and Socialisation in Europe: Introduction and Framework', ARENA Working Papers, WP 01/11.

Chomsky, Noam (1994) *World Orders Old and New*, New York: Columbia University Press.

Crampton, Richard J. (1994) *Eastern Europe in the Twentieth Century and After*, London: Routledge.

Crawford, Beverly and Lijphart, Arend (1995) 'Explaining Political and Economic Change in Post-Communist Eastern Europe: Old Legacies, New Institutions, Hegemonic Norms and International Pressures', *Comparative Political Studies*, 28 (2), 171–99.

Crawford, Gordon (2001) *Foreign Aid and Political Reform: a Comparative Analysis of Democracy Assistance and Political Conditionality*, Basingstoke: Palgrave.

Crawford, Gordon (2003) 'Promoting Democracy from Without – Learning from Within (Part I)', *Democratization*, 10 (1), 77–98.

Crawford, Gordon (2003) 'Promoting Democracy from Without – Learning from Within (Part II)', *Democratization*, 10 (2), 1–20.

Cziczovszki, Andrea (2000) 'The Regional Problem in the Transition to Europe: the Case of Hungary', Paper presented at the BASEES Annual Conference, Cambridge.

Davey, Kenneth (1995) 'Local Government in Hungary', in Andrew Coulson (ed.), *Local Government in Eastern Europe*, Cheltenham: Edward Elgar, 57–75.

Davey, Kenneth (2002) 'Decentralization in CEE Countries: Obstacles and Opportunities', in Gábor Péteri (ed.), *Mastering Decentralization and Public Administration Reforms in Central and Eastern Europe*, Budapest: OSI/LGI, 33–42.

Dimitrova, Antoaneta (2002) 'Enlargement, Institution-Building and the EU's Administrative Capacity Requirement', *West European Politics*, 25 (4), 171–90.

Djildov, Aleko and Marinov, Vasil (1999) *Regional Policy in the Process of Integration into the European Union: a Comparative Analysis of Selected Countries*, New York: EWI.

Drulák, Petr, Cesal, Jirí and Hampl, Stanislav (2003) 'Interactions and Identities of Czech Civil Servants on their Way to the EU', *Journal of European Public Policy*, 10 (4), 637–54.

Elander, Ingemar and Gustafsson, Mattias (1993) 'The Re-Emergence of Local Self-Government in Central Europe: Some Notes on the First Experience', *European Journal of Political Research*, 23 (3), 295–322.

Eldersfeld, Samuel J., Stromberg, Lars and Derksen, Wim (1995) *Local Elites in Western Democracies: a Comparative Analysis of Urban Political Leaders in the U.S., Sweden, and the Netherlands*, Boulder, CO: Westview.

Emilewicz, Jadwiga and Wolek, Artur (2002) *Reformers and Politicians: the Power Play for the 1998 Reform of Public Administration in Poland, as Seen by its Main Players*, Warsaw: Elipsa.

Featherstone, Kevin (2003) 'Introduction: In the Name of Europe', in Claudio Radaelli and Kevin Featherstone (eds), *The Politics of Europeanization*, Oxford: Oxford University Press, 3–26.

Fowler, Brigid (2001) 'Debating Sub-State Reform on Hungary's "Road to Europe"', One Europe or Several? Working Paper 21/01, Brighton: University of Sussex.

Fowler, Brigid (2002) 'Hungary: Patterns of Political Conflict over Territorial-Administrative Reform', *Regional and Federal Studies*, 12 (2), 15–40.

Galligan, Denis J. and Smilov, Daniel M. (1999) *Administrative Law in Central and Eastern Europe*, Budapest: CEU Press.

Gerner, Kristan (1999) 'Regions in Central Europe under Communism: a Palimpsest', in Sven Tagil (ed.), *Regions in Central Europe: the Legacy of History*, London: Hurst & Company.

Gilowska, Zyta, Ploskonka, Jozef, Prutis, Stanislaw, Stec, Miroslaw and Wysocka, Elzbieta (1997) 'The Systemic Model of the Voivodship in a Democratic Unitary State', Discussion paper no. 7, Budapest: Local Government and Public Service Reform Initiative, Open Society.

Glowacki, Wiktor (2002) 'Regionalization in Poland', in Gerard Marcou (ed.), *Regionalization for Development and Accession to the EU: a Comparative Perspective*, LGI Studies, Budapest: Open Society Institute.

Goetz, Klaus H. (2000) 'European Integration and National Executives: a Cause in Search of an Effect?', *West European Politics*, 23 (4), 211–31.

Goldsmith, Michael J.F. and Klausen, Klaus K. (eds) (1997) *European Integration and Local Government*, Cheltenham: Edward Elgar.

Gorzelak, Grzegorz (1998) 'Regional and Local Potential for Transformation in Poland', Regional and Local Studies Series no. 14, Warsaw: European Institute for Regional and Local Development.

Gorzelak, Grzegorz and Jalowiecki, Bohdan (2001) 'Analiza wdrazania i skutków reformy terytorialnej organizacji kraju, Raport koncowy' [An analysis on the introduction and results of the territorial reform of state, The final report] Warszawa, Europejski Insytut Rozwoju Regionalnego i Lokalnego, Insytut Spraw Publicznych.

Grabbe, Heather (2001) 'How does Europeanisation Affect CEE Governance? Conditionality, Diffusion and Diversity', *Journal of European Public Policy*, 8 (6), 1013–31.

Grabbe, Heather (2002) 'European Union Conditionality and the *Acquis* Communautaire', *International Political Science Review*, 23 (3), 249–68.

Grabbe, Heather and Hughes, Kirsty (1997) 'Redefining the European Union: Eastward Enlargement', RIIA Briefing paper 36, London: Royal Institute for International Affairs.

Grimm, Frank-Dieter (1998), 'Das Städtesystem Polens in Vergangenheit, Gegenwart und Zukunsft. Zur Einführung', in Isolde Brade und Frank-Dieter Grimm (eds), *Städtesysteme und Regionalentwicklungen in Mittel- und Osteuropa. Russland, Ukraine, Polen*, Leipzig: Institut für Länderkunde Leipzig (Beiträge zur Regionalen Geographie), 136–47.

Grzymała-Busse, Anna and Innes, Abby (2003) 'Great Expectations: the EU and Domestic Political Competition in East Central Europe', *East European Politics and Societies*, 17 (1), 64–73.

Hegedus, Jozsef (1999) 'Hungarian Local Government', in Emil Kirchner (ed.), *Decentralization and Transition in the Visegrad: Poland, Hungary, the Czech Republic and Slovakia*, Basingstoke: Macmillan, 132–58.

Heil, Peter (2000) 'PHARE in Hungary: the Anatomy of a Pre-accession Aid Programme, 1990–1999', Unpublished PhD thesis, Budapest.

Henderson, Karen (1999) (ed.) *Back to Europe: Central and Eastern Europe and the European Union*, London: UCL Press.

Hesse, Joachim Jens (1998) 'Rebuilding the State: Administrative Reform in Central and Eastern Europe', in Joachim Jens Hesse (ed.), *Preparing Public Administrations for the European Administrative Space*, Sigma Paper no. 23, Paris: OECD.

Hewett, Ed (1988) *Reforming the Soviet Economy: Equality vs. Efficiency*, Washington, DC: Brookings Institution.

Higley, John and Burton, Michael (1989) 'The Elite Variable in Democratic Transitions and Breakdowns', *American Sociological Review*, 54, 17–32.

Hoich, Jan and Larisova, Kristina (1999) 'Reform der öffentlichen Verwaltung und Bildung der regionalen Selbstverwaltung in der Tschechischen Republik im Kontext des EU-Beitritts', in Eric von Breska and Martin Brusis (eds), *Central and Eastern Europe on the Way to the European Union: Reforms of Regional Administration in Bulgaria, the Czech Republic, Estonia, Hungary, Poland and Slovakia*, Munich: Centre for Applied Policy Research.

Hooghe, Lisbeth (1995) 'Subnational Mobilisation in the European Union', *West European Politics*, 18 (3), 175–98.

Hooghe, Lisbeth and Marks, Gary (2001) *Multi-level Governance and European Integration*, New York: Rowman & Littlefield.

Horváth, Gyula (1996) 'Transition and Regionalism in East Central Europe', Occasional Paper no. 7, Tubingen: Europaisches Zentrum fur Foderalismus-Forschung.

Horváth, Gyula (1998) 'Regional and Cohesion Policy in Hungary', Discussion Paper 23, Pécs: Centre for Regional Studies of the Hungarian Academy of Sciences.

Horváth, Tamas (ed.) (2000) *Decentralization, Experiments and Reform*, Budapest: LGI Books.

Hughes, James and John, Peter (2001) 'Local Elites and Transition in Russia', *British Journal of Political Science*, 31 (4), 673–92.

Hughes, James and Sasse, Gwendolyn (2003) 'Monitoring the Monitors: EU Enlargement Conditionality and Minority Protection in the CEECs', *Journal of Ethnopolitics and Minority Issues in Europe*, 1, 1–28.

Hughes, James, Sasse, Gwendolyn and Gordon, Claire (2001) 'The Regional Deficit in Eastward Enlargement of the European Union: Top Down Policies and Bottom Up Reactions', ESRC 'One Europe or Several?' Working Paper 29/01, Brighton: Sussex University.

Hughes, James, Sasse, Gwendolyn and Gordon, Claire (2002) 'Saying "Maybe" to the "Return to Europe": Elites and the Political Space for Euroscepticism in Central and Eastern Europe', *European Union Politics*, 3 (3), 327–55.

Hughes, James, Sasse, Gwendolyn and Gordon, Claire (2003) 'EU Enlargement, Europeanisation and the Dynamics of Regionalisation in the CEECs', in Michael Keating and James Hughes (eds), *The Regional Challenge in Central and Eastern Europe: Territorial Restructuring and European Integration*, Paris: P.I.E.-Peter Lang, 69–88.

Hughes, James, Sasse, Gwendolyn and Gordon, Claire (2004) 'Conditionality and Compliance in the EU's Eastward Enlargement: Regional Policy and the Reform of Sub-National Governance', *Journal of Common Market Studies*, 42 (3), September.

Hughes, James, Sasse, Gwendolyn, Gordon, Claire and Majcherkiewicz, Tatiana (2004) 'Silesia and the Politics of Regionalisation in Poland', in Tomasz Zarycki and George Kolankiewicz (eds), *Regional Issues in Polish Politics*, London: School of Slavonic and East European Studies, University College London, 83–111.

Illner, Michal (1992) 'Municipalities and Industrial Paternalism in a Real Socialist Society', in Pavel Dostal, Michal Illner, Jan Kara and Max Barlow (eds), *Changing Territorial Administration in Czechoslovakia: International Viewpoints*, Amsterdam: University of Amsterdam, Charles University and Czechoslovak Academy of Sciences, 39–47.

Illner, Michal (1997) *The Territorial Dimension of Public Administration Reforms in East-Central Europe*, Prague: Institute of Sociology, Academy of Sciences of the Czech Republic.

Illner, Michal (1998) 'Territorial Decentralization: an Obstacle to Democratic Reform in Central and Eastern Europe', in Jonathan D. Kimball (ed.), *The Transfer of Power: Decentralization in Central and Eastern Europe*, Budapest: Local Government and Public Service Reform Initiative, 7–43.

Illner, Michal (2002) *Multilevel Government in Three East Central European Candidate Countries and its Reforms after 1989*, San Domenico di Fiesole, Italy: European University Institute, Robert Schuman Centre.

Innes, Abby (2001) *Czechoslovakia: the Short Goodbye*, New Haven: Yale University Press.

Innes, Abby (2002) 'Party Competition in Postcommunist Europe: the Great Electoral Lottery', *Comparative Politics*, 35 (1), 85–104.

Jacoby, Wade (2004) *The Enlargement of the European Union and NATO: Ordering from the Menu in Central Europe*, Cambridge: Cambridge University Press.

Jeffery, Charlie (2000) 'Sub-National Mobilization and European Integration: Does it Make Any Difference?', *Journal of Common Market Studies*, 38 (1), 1–23.

Johnston, Alastair I. (2001) 'Treating International Institutions as Social Environments', *International Studies Quarterly*, 45, 487–515.

Keating, Michael (1993) *The Politics of Modern Europe*, Aldershot: Edward Elgar.

Keating, Michael (1998) 'The New Regionalism', in Michael Keating, *The New Regionalism in Western Europe: Territorial Restructuring and Political Change*, Cheltenham: Edward Elgar, 72–111.

Keating, Michael and Hooghe, Lisbeth (1996) 'By-Passing the Nation-State? Regions and the EU Policy Process', in Jeremy John Richardson (ed.), *European Union, Power and Policy-Making*, London: Routledge, 216–29.

Keating, Michael and Hughes, James (2003) (eds), *The Regional Challenge in Central and Eastern Europe*, Paris: P.I.E.-Peter Lang.

Killick, John (1997) *The United States and the European Reconstruction, 1945–1960*, Edinburgh: Keele University Press.

Killick, Tony (1998) *Aid and the Political Economy of Policy Change*, London: Routledge.

Kirchner, Emil M. (1999) (ed.) *Decentralisation and Transition in the Visegrad: Poland, Hungary, The Czech Republic and Slovakia*, Basingstoke: Macmillan and New York: St Martin's Press.

Kirschbaum, Stanislav (2003) 'Czechoslovakia: the Creation, Federalisation and Dissolution of a Nation-State', in John Coakley (ed.), *The Territorial Management of Ethnic Conflict*, London, Frank Cass, 2nd edition, 229–63.

Knill, Christoph and Lehmkuhl, Dirk (1999) 'How Europe Matters. Different Mechanisms of Europeanization', *European Integration On-line Papers* (EioP), 3 (7), 1–11: http://eiop.or.at/eiop/texte/1999-007a.htm.

Kohler-Koch, Beate (2002) 'European Networks and Ideas: Changing National Policies?' *European Integration On-line Papers* 6 (6): http://eiop.or.at/eiop/texte/2002–006a.htm.

Kohler-Koch, Beate and Eising, Rainer (eds) (1999) *The Transformation of Governance in the European Union*, London: Routledge.

Kok, Wim (2003) 'Enlarging the European Union: Achievement and Challenges', Report of Wim Kok to the European Commission, RSCAS, European University Institute, 26.

Korcelli Piotr (1998), 'Die Städte Polens im Wandel – ihre demographischen und ökonomischen Determinanten', in Isolde Brade und Frank-Dieter Grimm (eds), *Städtesysteme und Regionalentwicklungen in Mittel- und Osteuropa. Russland, Ukraine, Polen*, Leipzig: Institut für Länderkunde Leipzig (Beiträge zur Regionalen Geographie), 148–66.

Kornai, Janos (1992) *The Socialist System: the Political Economy of Communism*, Oxford: Clarendon Press.

Kovrig, Bennett (1979) *Communism in Hungary: from Kun to Kádár*, Stanford, CA: Hoover Institution.

Kowalczyk, Andrzej (2000) 'Local Government in Poland', in Tamas Horvath (ed.), *Decentralization: Experiments and Reform*, Budapest: LGI Publications, 217–54.

Lacina, Karel and Vajdova, Zdena (2000) 'Local Government in the Czech Republic', in Tamas Horvath (ed.), *Decentralization: Experiments and Reform*, Budapest: LGI Publications, 255–96.

Ladrech, Robert (1994) 'Europeanization of Domestic Politics and Institutions: the Case of France', *Journal of Common Market Studies*, 32 (1), 69–88.

Lewis, Paul (1989), *Political Authority and Party Secretaries in Poland, 1975–1986*, Cambridge: Cambridge University Press.

Lewis, Paul (1994) *Central Europe since 1945*, London: Longman.

Lieven, Anatol (1993) *The Baltic Revolution: Latvia, Lithuania, Estonia and the Path to Independence*, New Haven: Yale University Press.

Lipset, Seymour Martin (1959) 'Some Social Requisites of Democracy', *American Political Science Review*, 53, 69–105.

Linz, Juan J. and Stepan, Alfred (1996) *Problems of Democratic Transition and Consolidation: Southern Europe, South America and Post-Communist Europe*, Washington, DC: Johns Hopkins University Press.

Mäeltsemees, Sulev (2000) 'Local Government in Estonia', in Tamas Horvath (ed.), *Decentralization, Experiments and Reform*, Budapest: LGI Books, 61–114.

Mair, Peter (1997) 'What is Different about Post-Communist Party Systems?', in Peter Mair (ed.), *Party System Change. Approaches and Interpretations*, Oxford: Clarendon Press, 175–98.

Majcherkiewicz, Tatiana (2001) 'An Elite in Transition an Analysis of the Higher Administration of the Region of Upper Silesia, Poland 1990–1997', PhD thesis, London School of Economics and Political Science, Department of Sociology.

Maurel, Marie-Claude (1989) 'Administrative Reforms in Eastern Europe: an Overview', in Richard Bennett (ed.), *Territory and Administration in Europe*, London: Pinter, 111–23.

Mayhew, Alan (1998) *Recreating Europe: the European Union's Policy towards Central and Eastern Europe*, Cambridge: Cambridge University Press.

Milward, Alan (2000) *The European Rescue of the Nation State*, London: Routledge, 2nd edition.

Moravsik, Andrew and Vachudova, Milada (2003) 'National Interests, State Power and EU Enlargement', *East European Politics and Societies*, 17 (1), 42–57.

Navracsics, Tibor (1996) 'Public Sector Reform in Hungary: Changes in Intergovernmental Relations (1990–1995)', in Attila Agh and Gabriella Ilonszki (eds), *Parliaments and Organized Interests: the Second Steps*, Budapest: Hungarian Centre for Democracy Studies.

Nello, Susan S. (2001) 'The Impact of External Economic Factors: the Role of the IMF', in Jan Zielonka and Alex Pravda (eds), *Democratic Consolidation in Eastern Europe*, Volume 2, Oxford: Oxford University Press, 76–111.

Nello, Susan S. and Smith, Karen (1998) *The European Union and Central and Eastern Europe: the Implications of Enlargement in Stages*, Aldershot: Ashgate.

Novotny, Vit (1998) 'Regional Government in the Czech Republic: the Process of its Creation in the Constitutional Context', Paper presented at Annual Conference of the PSA on Communist and Post-Communist Politics.

O'Donnell, Guillermo and Schmitter, Philippe (1986) *Transitions from Authoritarian Rule. Tentative Conclusions about Uncertain Democracies*, Baltimore: Johns Hopkins University Press.

Olsen, Johan P. (2001) 'The Many Faces of Europeanization', ARENA Working Papers, WP01/2: http://www.arena.uio.no/publications/wp02_2.htm.

Page, Ed (1995) 'Patterns and Diversity in European State Development', in Jack Hayward and Ed Page (eds), *Governing the New Europe*, London: Sage, 9–43.

Pálné Kovács, Ilona (2001) 'Regional Development and Governance in Hungary', Discussion Paper no. 35, Pécs: Centre for Regional Studies.

Pálné Kovács, Ilona (1999) 'Regional Development and Local Government in Hungary', in Zoltan Hajdú (ed.), *Regional Processes and Spatial Structures in Hungary in the 1990s*, Pécs: Centre for Regional Studies, 53–76.

Paraskevopoulos, Christos J. (2001) *Interpreting Convergence in the European Union. Patterns of Collective Action, Social Learning and Europeanization*, Basingstoke: Palgrave, xxi.

Perger, Eva (1989) 'An Overview of East European Developments', in Richard Bennett (ed.), *Territory and Administration in Europe*, London: Pinter, 93–110.

Piekalwicz, Jaroslaw (1980) 'Polish Local Politics in Flux', in Daniel Nelson (ed.), *Local Politics in Communist Countries*, Lexington: The University Press of Kentucky.

Przeworksi, Adam (1991) *Democracy and the Market: Political and Economic Reforms in Eastern Europe and Latin America*, Cambridge: Cambridge University Press.

Putnam, Robert (1993) *Making Democracy Work: Civic Traditions in Modern Italy*, Princeton, NJ: Princeton University Press.

Radaelli, Claudio, M. (2000) 'Whither Europeanization: Concept Stretching and Substantive Change', *European Integration On-line Papers* (EioP) 4 (8), 1–27: http://eiop.or.at/eiop/texte/2000-008a.htm.

Radaelli, Claudio and Featherstone, Kevin (eds) (2003) *The Politics of Europeanization*, Oxford: Oxford University Press.

Reddaway, Peter and Glinski, Dmitri (2001) *The Tragedy of Russia's Reforms: Market Bolshevism against Democracy*, Washington: United States Institute of Peace.

Regulska, Joanna (1997) 'Decentralization or (Re)centralization: Struggle for Political Power in Poland', *Environment and Planning C: Government and Policy*, 15 (2), 187–208.

Regulski, Jerzy (1993) 'Rebuilding Local Government in Poland', in Richard J. Bennett (ed.), *Local Government in the New Europe*, London: Belhaven Press, 197–207.

Regulski, Jerzy (1999) 'Building Democracy in Poland, the State Reform of 1998', Discussion papers no. 9, Budapest: the Local Government and Public Services Reform Initiative, Open Society: http://lgi.osi.hu/news/2001/20010202.htm.

Rustow, Dankwart (1970) 'Transitions to Democracy: towards a Dynamic Model', *Comparative Politics*, 2 (3), 337–63.

Sasse, Gwendolyn, Hughes, James and Gordon, Claire (2002) 'The Ambivalence of Conditionality: Europeanization and Regionalization in Central Eastern Europe', ECPR Joint Sessions, Workshop 4: Enlargement and European Governance, Turin.

Schimmelfennig, Frank (2001) 'The Community Trap: Liberal Norms, Rhetorical Action, and the Eastern Enlargement of the European Union', *International Organization*, 55 (1), 47–80.

Schimmelfennig, Frank, Egert, Stefan and Knobel, Heiko (2001) 'Costs, Commitment and Compliance: the Impact of EU Democratic Conditionality on Latvia, Slovakia and Turkey', *Journal of Common Market Studies*, 41 (3), 495–518.

Schimmelfennig, Frank and Sedelmeier, Ulrich (2003) 'The Europeanization of Eastern Europe: Evaluating the Conditionality Model', Paper presented at the EUI Workshop 'The Europeanization of Eastern Europe: Evaluating the Conditionality Model', Florence.

Schmitter, Philippe E. (1996) 'The Influence of the International Context upon the Choice of National Institutions and Policies', in Lawrence Whitehead (ed.), *The International Dimensions of Democratization*, Oxford: Oxford University Press, 26–54.

Schöpflin, George (1993) *Politics in Eastern Europe 1945–1992*, Oxford: Blackwell.

Setnikar-Canka, Stanka, Vlaj, Stane and Klun, Maja (2000) 'Local Government in Slovenia', in Tamas Horvath (ed.), *Decentralization, Experiments and Reform*, Budapest: LGI Books, 385–421.

Shore, Chris (2000) *Building Europe: the Cultural Politics of European Integration*, London: Routledge.

Skalnik-Leff, Carol (1988) *National Conflict in Czechoslovakia, the Making and Remaking of a Nation-State, 1918–1987*, Princeton, NJ: Princeton University Press.

Smith, David J. (2002) 'Narva Region within the Estonian Republic: from Autonomism to Accommodation?', *Regional and Federal Studies*, 12 (2), 89–110.

Smith, Graham (1994) *The Baltic States: the National Self-Determination of Estonia, Latvia and Lithuania*, London: Macmillan.

Smith, Karen E. (1998) *The Making of EU Foreign Policy: the Case of Eastern Europe*, New York: St Martin's Press.

Smith, Karen E. (2001a) 'Western Actors and the Promotion of Democracy', in Jan Zielonka and Alex Pravda (eds), *Democratic Consolidation in Eastern Europe*, vol. 2, *International and Transnational Factors*, Oxford: Oxford University Press, 31–57.

Smith, Karen E. (2001b) 'The EU, Human Rights and Relations with Third Countries: "Foreign Policy" with an Ethical Dimension?', in Karen E. Smith and Margot Light (eds), *Ethics and Foreign Policy*, New York: Cambridge University Press, 185–204.

Smith, Karen (2003) 'The Evolution and Application of EU Membership Conditionality', in Marise Cremona (ed.), *The Enlargement of the European Union*, Florence: European University Institute, 105–39.

Sorenson, Georg (1993) *Democracy and Democratization: Dilemmas in World Politics*, Boulder, CO: Westview Press.

Soysal, Yasemin (2002) 'Locating Europe', *European Societies*, 4 (3), 265–84.

Stark, David (1992) 'Path Dependence and Privatization Strategies in East Central Europe', *East European Politics and Societies*, 6 (1), 17–51.

Stiglitz, Joseph (2002) 'Who Lost Russia?', in *Globalization and its Discontents*, Harmondsworth: Penguin.

Stokke, Olav (1995) *Aid and Political Conditionality*, London: Frank Cass.

Stone, Randall (2002) *Lending Credibility: the International Monetary Fund and the Post-Communist Transition*, Princeton, NJ: Princeton University Press.

Stråth, Bo (2002) 'A European Identity: to the Historical Limits of a Concept', *European Journal of Social Theory*, 5 (4), 387–401.

Surazska, W., Bucek, J., Malikova, L. and Danek, P. (1996) 'Towards Regional Government in Central Europe: Territorial Restructuring of Postcommunist Regimes', *Environment and Planning C: Government and Policy*, 15, 437–62.

Szczerbiak, Aleks (1999) 'The Impact of the October 1998 Local Elections on the Emerging Polish Party System', *Journal of Communist Studies and Transition Politics*, 15 (3), 80–100.

Tagil, Sven (ed.) (1999) *Regions in Central Europe: the Legacy of History*, London: Hurst & Company.

Tang, Helen (ed.) (2000) *Winners and Losers of EU Integration: Policy Issues for Central and Eastern Europe*, Washington, DC: World Bank.

Trapans, Jan Arveds (1991) *Toward Independence: the Baltic Popular Movements*, Boulder, CO: Westview.

Verheijen, A.J.G. (2002) 'Removing Obstacles to Effective Decentralization: Reflecting on the Role of the Central State', in Gábor Péteri (ed.), *Mastering Decentralization and Public Administration Reforms in Central and Eastern Europe*, Budapest: OSI/LGI, 45–54.

Vintar, Mirko (1999) 'Re-engineering Administrative Districts in Slovenia', Discussion Paper No. 11, Local Government and Public Service Reform Initiative, Budapest: LGI Publications.

Wallace, Helen and Sedelmeier, Ulrich (2000) 'Eastern Enlargement', in Helen Wallace and William Wallace (eds), *Policy-Making in the European Union*, Oxford: Oxford University Press, 4th edition, 427–60.

Waller, Michael (1981) *Democratic Centralism: an Historical Commentary*, Manchester: Manchester University Press.

Walton, John and Seddon, David (1994) *Free Markets and Food Riots: the Politics of Global Adjustment*, Oxford: Blackwell.

Wedel, Janine (1998) *Collision and Collusion: the Strange Case of Western Aid to Eastern Europe, 1989–1998*, New York: St Martin's Press.

Weiler, Joseph (1999) *The Constitution of Europe*, Cambridge: Cambridge University Press.

Wollmann, Helmut (1997) 'Institution Building and Decentralization in Formerly Socialist Countries: the Cases of Poland, Hungary and East Germany', *Environment and Planning C: Government and Policy*, 15, 463–80.

Wollmann, Helmut and Lankina, Tomila (2003) 'Local Government in Poland and Hungary: from Post-Communist Reform towards EU Accession', in Harald Baldersheim, Michal Illner and Helmut Wollmann (eds), *Local Democracy in Post-Communist Europe*, Opladen: Leske+Budrich, 91–122.

Wright, Glen (2002) 'Assessment of Progress towards Local Democratic Systems', in Gábor Soós, Gábor Tóka and Glen Wright (eds), *State of Local Democracy in Central Europe*, Budapest: Local Government and Public Reform Initiative, 373–408.

Wyszogrodzka-Sipher, Patricia (2000) 'The National and International Influences on the Reform of Polish Government Structures', Paper for the workshop 'Europe, Nation, Region: Redefining the State in Central and Eastern Europe', London, Royal Institute of International Affairs.

Zarycki, Tomasz (2003) 'The Regional Dimension of the Polish Political Scene' in Tomasz Zarycki and George Kolankiewicz (eds), *Regional Issues in Polish Politics*, London: School of Slavonic and East European Studies, University College London, 239–60.

Zaucha, Jacek (1999) 'Regional and Local Development in Poland', in Emil Kirchner (ed.), *Decentralisation and Transition in the Visegrad, Poland, Hungary, the Czech Republic and Slovakia*, Basingstoke: Macmillan, 53–79.

Zielonka, Jan (2001) 'Conclusions: Foreign Made Democracy', in Jan Zielonka and Alex Pravda (eds), *Democratic Consolidation in Eastern Europe*, Volume 2, Oxford: Oxford University Press.

Statistical Appendix

A1 Distribution of elites interviewed by position

	Frequency	Percentage
Administration and politics	128	44.6
Administration and other position	56	19.5
Business/private sector	53	18.5
Professional/education/media	48	16.7
Missing	2	0.7
Total	287	100.0

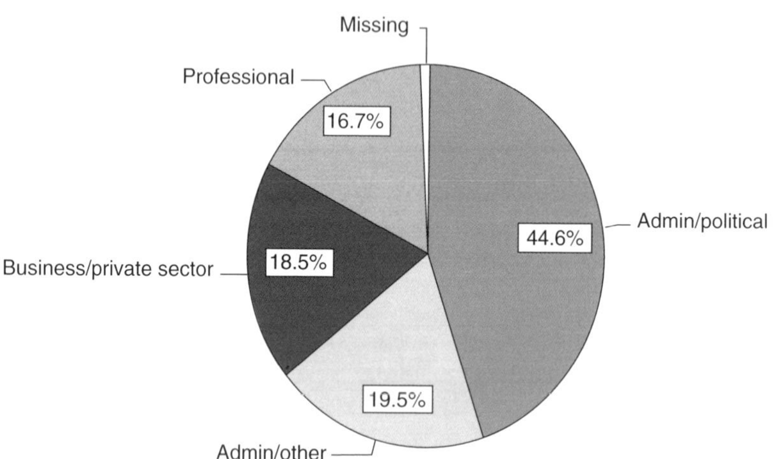

A2 Distribution of elites interviewed by position and city/country

		City				
		Maribor	Pécs	Tartu	Katowice	Total
Administration and politics	Count	34	27	23	44	128
	% within city	47.2	36.5	34.8	60.3	
	% of total	11.9	9.5	8.1	15.4	44.9
Administration and other position	Count	18	10	23	5	56
	% within city	25.0	13.5	34.8	6.8	
	% of total	6.3	3.5	8.1	1.8	19.6
Business/ private sector	Count	10	22	11	10	53
	% within city	13.9	29.7	16.7	13.7	
	% of total	3.5	7.7	3.9	3.5	18.6
Professional/ education/ media	Count	10	15	9	14	48
	% within city	13.9	20.3	13.6	19.2	
	% of total	3.5	5.3	3.2	4.9	16.8
Total	Count	72	74	66	73	285
	% within city	100.0	100.0	100.0	100.0	
	% of total	25.3	26.0	23.2	25.6	100.0

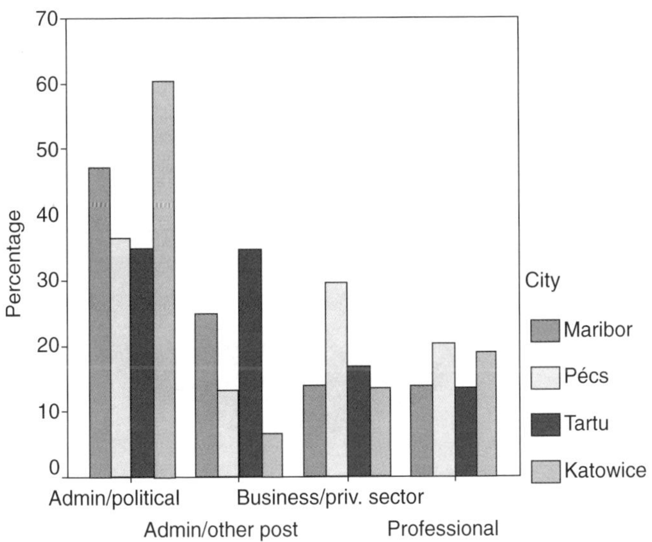

A3 Distribution of elites interviewed by age

	Frequency	Percentage
> 30	11	3.8
30–39	48	16.7
40–49	108	37.6
50–59	92	32.1
60–69	20	7.0
70>	7	2.4
Total	286	99.7
Missing	1	0.3
Total	287	100.0

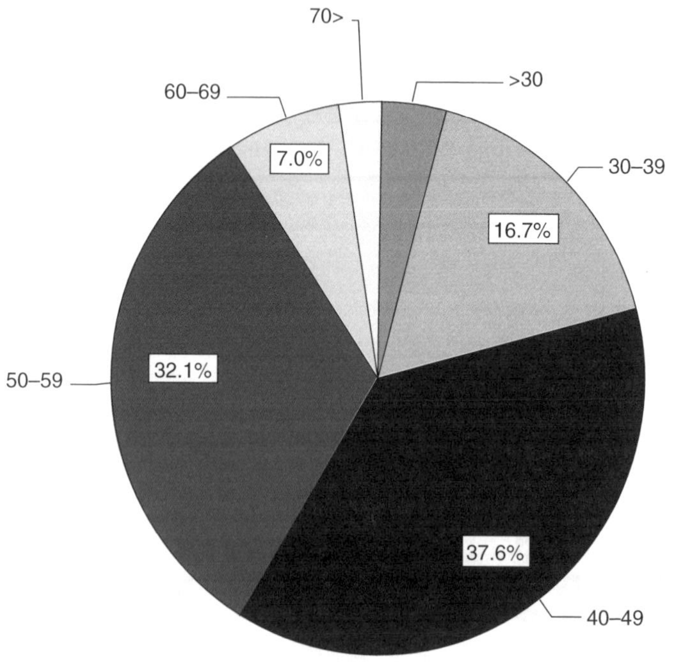

A4 Distribution of elites interviewed by education

	Frequency	Percentage
No further education	5	1.7
First degree	36	12.5
Postgraduate diploma	97	33.8
Candidate/doctorate	59	20.6
Other	46	16.0
Professional qualification	5	1.7
Total	248	86.4
Missing	39	13.6
Total	287	100.0

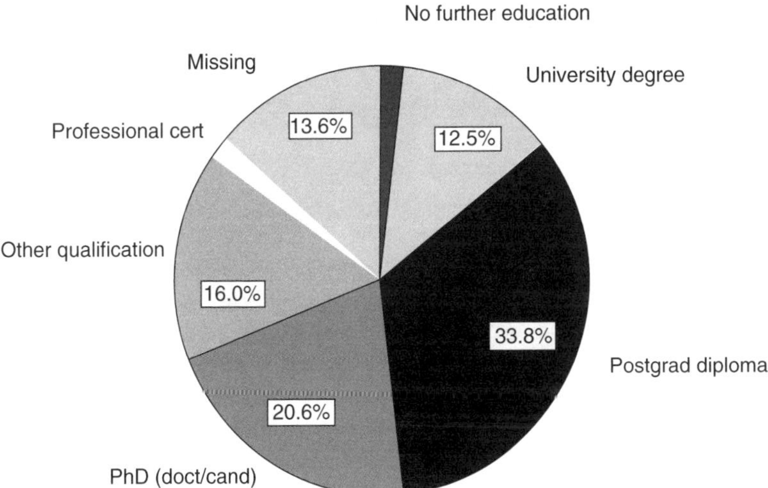

A5 Distribution of elites interviewed by sex

	Frequency	Percentage
Male	239	83.3
Female	48	16.7
Total	287	100.0

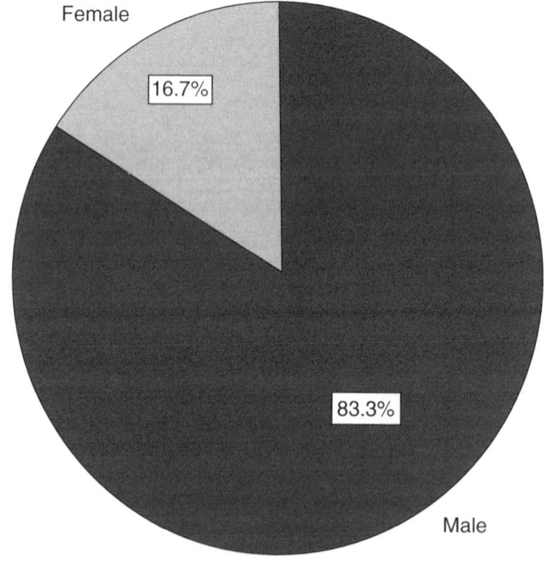

A6 Cross-tabulations

Opinion of the European Union/Travel abroad in last six months cross-tabulation

Opinion of the European Union		Travel abroad in last six months Yes	No	Total
Positive	Count	142	79	221
	% within Opinion of the European Union	64.3	35.7	100.0
	% within Travel abroad in last six months	81.1	71.8	77.5
	% of total	49.8	27.7	77.5
Negative	Count	3	6	9
	% within Opinion of the European Union	33.3	66.7	100.0
	% within Travel abroad in last six months	1.7	5.5	3.2
	% of total	1.1	2.1	3.2
Neutral	Count	30	25	55
	% within Opinion of the European Union	54.5	45.5	100.0
	% within Travel abroad in last six months	17.1	22.7	19.3
	% of total	10.5	8.8	19.3
Total	Count	175	110	285
	% within Opinion of the European Union	61.4	38.6	100.0
	% within Travel abroad in last six months	100.0	100.0	100.0
	% of total	61.4	38.6	100.0

Chi-square tests

	Value	df	Asymp. Sig. (2-sided)
Pearson chi-square	4.841[a]	2	.089
Likelihood ratio	4.730	2	.094
Linear-by-linear association	2.378	1	.123
No. of valid cases	285		

Note: [a] 1 cell (16.7%) has expected count less than 5. The minimum expected count is 3.47.

Age of respondent/Opinion of the European Union cross-tabulation

Age of respondent		**Opinion of the European Union**			
		Positive	**Negative**	**Neutral**	**Total**
< 30	Count	7	2	2	11
	% within Age of respondent	63.6	18.2	18.2	100.0
	% within Opinion of the European Union	3.2	22.2	3.6	3.9
	% of total	2.5	0.7	0.7	3.9
30–39	Count	32	1	15	48
	% within Age of respondent	66.7	2.1	31.3	100.0
	% within Opinion of the European Union	14.5	11.1	27.3	16.9
	% of total	11.3	0.4	5.3	16.9
40–49	Count	85	3	19	107
	% within Age of respondent	79.4	2.8	17.8	100.0
	% within Opinion of the European Union	38.6	33.3	34.5	37.7
	% of total	29.9	1.1	6.7	37.7
50–59	Count	76	2	13	91
	% within Age of respondent	83.5	2.2	14.3	100.0
	% within Opinion of the European Union	34.5	22.2	23.6	32.0
	% of total	26.8	0.7	4.6	32.0
60–69	Count	16		4	20
	% within Age of respondent	80.0		20.0	100.0
	% within Opinion of the European Union	7.3		7.3	7.0
	% of total	5.6		1.4	7.0
70>	Count	4	1	2	7
	% within Age of respondent	57.1	14.3	28.6	100.0
	% within Opinion of the European Union	1.8	11.1	3.6	2.5
	% of total	1.4	0.4	0.7	2.5
Total	Count	220	9	55	284
	% within Age of respondent	77.5	3.2	19.4	100.0
	% within Opinion of the European Union	100.0	100.0	100.0	100.0
	% of total	77.5	3.2	19.4	100.0

Chi-square tests

	Value	df	Asymp. Sig. (2-sided)
Pearson chi-square	18.724[a]	10	.044
Likelihood ratio	13.618	10	.191
Linear-by-linear association	1.761	1	.184
No. of Valid Cases	284		

Note: [a] 9 cells (50.0%) have expected count less than 5. The minimum expected count is .22.

Visitors from abroad in last six months/Opinion of the European Union cross-tabulation

Visitors from abroad in last six months		Opinion of the European Union			
		Positive	Negative	Neutral	Total
None	Count	85	6	27	118
	% within Visitors from abroad in last six months	72.0	5.1	22.9	100.0
	% within Opinion of the European Union	38.5	66.7	49.1	41.4
	% of total	29.8	2.1	9.5	41.4
1–3	Count	64	2	17	83
	% within Visitors from abroad in last six months	77.1	2.4	20.5	100.0
	% within Opinion of the European Union	29.0	22.2	30.9	29.1
	% of total	22.5	0.7	6.0	29.1
More than 3	Count	72	1	11	84
	% within Visitors from abroad in last six months	85.7	1.2	13.1	100.0
	% within Opinion of the European Union	32.6	11.1	20.0	29.5
	% of total	25.3	0.4	3.9	29.5
Total	Count	221	9	55	285
	% within Visitors from abroad in last six months	77.5	3.2	19.3	100.0
	% within Opinion of the European Union	100.0	100.0	100.0	100.0
	% of total	77.5	3.2	19.3	100.0

Chi-square tests

	Value	df	Asymp. Sig. (2-sided)
Pearson chi-square	6.271[a]	4	.180
Likelihood ratio	6.547	4	.162
Linear-by-linear association	4.161	1	.041
No. of valid cases	285		

Note: [a] 3 cells (33.3%) have expected count less than 5. The minimum expected count is 2.62.

Involvement in EU-funded projects/Opinion of the European Union cross-tabulation

Involvement in EU-funded projects		Opinion of the European Union			
		Positive	Negative	Neutral	Total
Yes	Count	126	5	26	157
	% within Involvement in EU-funded projects	80.3	3.2	16.6	100.0
	% within Opinion of the European Union	57.3	55.6	47.3	55.3
	% of total	44.4	1.8	9.2	55.3
No	Count	94	4	29	127
	% within Involvement in EU-funded projects	74.0	3.1	22.8	100.0
	% within Opinion of the European Union	42.7	44.4	52.7	44.7
	% of total	33.1	1.4	10.2	44.7
Total	Count	220	9	55	284
	% within Involvement in EU-funded projects	77.5	3.2	19.4	100.0
	% within Opinion of the European Union	100.0	100.0	100.0	100.0
	% of total	77.5	3.2	19.4	100.0

Chi-square tests

	Value	df	Asymp. Sig. (2-sided)
Pearson chi-square	1.780[a]	2	.411
Likelihood ratio	1.771	2	.412
Linear-by-linear association	1.737	1	.188
No. of valid cases	284		

Note: [a] 2 cells (33.3%) have expected count less than 5. The minimum expected count is 4.02.

Index